D1412256

LABOR ECONOMICS

CHOICE IN LABOR MARKETS

McGraw-Hill Book Company

*New York   St. Louis   San Francisco   Auckland   Bogotá   Düsseldorf
Johannesburg   London   Madrid   Mexico   Montreal   New Delhi   Panama
Paris   São Paulo   Singapore   Sydney   Tokyo   Toronto*

LABOR ECONOMICS

CHOICE IN LABOR MARKETS

DON BELLANTE
MARK JACKSON

Associate Professors of Economics
Auburn University

Library of Congress Cataloging in Publication Data

Bellante, Don.
    Labor economics.

    Includes bibliographies and indexes.
    1. Labor economics.   I.   Jackson, Mark, date
joint author.   II.   Title.
HD4901.B44   331   78-12054
ISBN 0-07-004397-3

LABOR ECONOMICS
Choice in Labor Markets

1234567890 DODO 7832109

This book was set in Helvetica Light by Black Dot, Inc. (ECU).
The editors were Bonnie E. Lieberman, George S. Thomas,
and J. W. Maisel;
the designer was Anne Canevari Green;
the production supervisor was Leroy A. Young.
The part-opening drawings were done by Doug Jamieson,
and all other drawings were done by J & R Services, Inc.
R. R. Donnelley & Sons Company was printer and binder.

CONTENTS

PART I
LABOR DEMAND AND LABOR SUPPLY

PART III
WAGE AND EMPLOYMENT DIFFERENCES
ATTRIBUTABLE TO IMPERFECTIONS IN COMPETITION

PREFACE

This book is a textbook in labor economics. We intend it for use in undergraduate courses where students have had a good course in the principles of economics. We assume no additional background. Our approach is to build an analytic background in Part I and to use this background to analyze in Parts II, III, and IV what we believe to be significant topics in labor economics. Part I is central to the book. In fact, each chapter beyond Part I is introduced as an extension or refinement of some aspect of Part I. From a simple model presented there, the student is able to proceed—gradually—to a much fuller understanding of labor markets. We feel confident that our approach will afford the student a better understanding of the labor market than can be obtained from the more typical nonsystematic approaches that characterize most labor economics texts.

What distinguishes this text from the many others that are available? First of all, the book consistently uses a choice-theoretic or neoclassical approach throughout. Whether the topic is collective bargaining, discrimination, or the economics of education, the issues are developed within this framework. This procedure enables us to purge ad hoc reasoning from the text. While it is uncommon for labor textbooks to take this approach, it has two distinct advantages. First, the nature of current research in economics has changed, and this textbook reflects it. Professors whose training in labor economics has been obtained in the past two decades should feel more comfortable with this text than with the type of text which extensively treats labor law, trade union history, and collective bargaining structure. While we do treat unions and collective bargaining as important topics, we emphasize the analysis of their economic impact rather than their form or structure. Further, our approach enables us to treat topics that are not normally encountered in a labor text—topics such as the economic analysis of fertility and its effect on labor supply, and the differences between public and private employee pay levels.

The use of standard economic analysis should not only make professors more comfortable with the book but should also make it easier for students to see the connection between labor economics and other postprinciples economics courses that they may take. For example, the discussion of inflation and unemployment in Chapter 16 can easily be related to what the student is exposed to in courses in macroeconomics and money and banking. Likewise, Chapter 17 contains a discussion of the interactions of monetary policy and collective bargaining. For another example, Chapter 14 contains a discussion of the optimal division of the labor resource between public and private production. Such a discussion can easily be tied to treatments of public goods provided in courses in public finance. A final example involves the treatment of regional wage differences. Labor texts will generally ignore the fact that trade in goods acts as a pressure toward equalizing wages across regions, although texts in regional economics or in international trade will not ignore it. We treat labor mobility, capital mobility, and trade as creating equalizing pressures. These examples illustrate that labor economics is applied microeconomics, that it is indeed part of the mainstream of economics, and that the labor market is part of the general economic system. Too often students of labor economics have gotten the impression that labor economics is a separate branch of economics and that the labor market operates in isolation from other markets.

In writing this book we have had to make choices. We have tried to produce a text which can be covered in its entirety in a one-semester or one-quarter course. Consequently, not every useful topic is covered. However, we believe that we have chosen the most central topics—in any event a broader range of analytical topics than is presented in most texts. We emphasize what *is* known about the operation of labor markets, not what is *not* known. In recent years students and the general public have been given the impression, fostered by journalists and even a few economists, that economists simply do not understand how the economy works. The alleged "inability" of economists to explain simultaneous inflation and unemployment is usually cited. This text will not further the belief that economists are a confused lot.

With regard to evidence, we have decided to use extensively what is available in the literature to support the theoretical analysis of the text, particularly in Parts II, III, and IV. However, we do not attempt to evaluate critically the empirical literature. Such a critique is very much beside the point in an undergraduate course. Further, such critical comparisons frequently hinge upon measurement and econometric problems, and students' backgrounds in statistics are seldom advanced enough to permit such comparisons.

At the end of each chapter we provide suggestions for further reading. These readings are limited to those which we believe can be read by a student whose analytic background is no more extensive than that obtained from our text. For instance, the student is sometimes referred to an intermediate price theory text. Additional readings of a more advanced nature are suggested in the instructor's manual that is available with this text. The questions at the end of each chapter are not intended to see if the student can repeat the contents of the chapter: most are intended to see if the student can push the analysis of the chapter a step or two further than the text does. However, the questions are not so challenging that students will wonder about what connection the questions have with the analysis of the chapter. The legends that appear with each graph contain much more information about the graphs than is customarily provided. This feature is intended to facilitate review by the student who has already thoroughly read the text material.

The work of many individuals has gone into the production of this text. Economics editors Stephen Dietrich and Bonnie Lieberman of McGraw-Hill deserve much of the credit, as do all the staff members of McGraw-Hill who have contributed to the final result in one fashion or another. We particularly appreciate the helpful suggestions of Wendy Gramm of Texas A&M University, Bruce Herrick of UCLA, and John Pencavel of Stanford University. All three read the entire manuscript and contributed significantly to the final product. We also appreciate the efforts of our colleagues at Auburn University who have generously assisted us on specific topics: Robert Ekelund and Robert Hebert on the historical background of wage theory, James Long on the economics of discrimination, Steve Morrell on the economics of the public sector, Ethel Jones on the supply of labor and labor force participation, and James Dunlevy on the migration of labor. We are also most grateful for the assistance of Sharon Smith of the Federal Reserve Bank of New York, whose work forms the framework for much of our chapter on public-private wage differences. Because we did not take all the suggestions offered us, none of these economists should be held responsible for any errors which may have slipped past us.

Finally, many thanks are due to Gene Stanaland, who has worked with us to schedule our classes so that we might have the blocks of time necessary to complete this book, as well as to Auburn University for providing us with released time from our various duties.

Don Bellante
Mark Jackson

LABOR ECONOMICS

CHOICE IN LABOR MARKETS

INTRODUCTION
TO LABOR ECONOMICS

Economics is the social science which studies the causes and consequences of choices that humans make. Labor economics is all about how the choices people make affect wages and employment in labor markets. Thus, as the title of our book indicates, we will be studying human choices and their consequences in labor markets.

How do people choose whether or not to supply any labor services? If they choose to be in the labor force, how do they choose how many hours to work where the decision could involve taking a second job? How do firms choose how much labor to employ? How do firms choose whether to use more hours or more employees? How do union officials choose their bargaining strategy? How do government officials choose the level of government employment?

What are the consequences of choices that people make? If employers choose to discriminate against females as potential employees, what are the consequences for female wages? For male wages? If more married women choose to enter the labor force, what are the consequences for teenage unemployment rates? For the incomes of nursery school owners?

No one can sort out the answers to questions such as these without some help. The facts and relationships of the world do not arrange themselves in a spontaneous way so that they can be immediately understood: they do not simply fall into place. They can, however, be put into place.

It is our intention to present in this book a system of explanation known as neoclassical economics, and to use this framework for thinking in order to understand as best we can human choices and their consequences in labor markets.

1.1
THE NEOCLASSICAL ECONOMIC MODEL

Economics begins from a model of purposive behavior by individuals. Individuals are assumed to have their own unique tastes, preferences, wants, and desires which they attempt to satisfy. Humans live in a world characterized by scarcity: they confront an environment which is external to themselves and which contains constraints which interfere with their want satisfaction. Because of these constraints, no individual is able to achieve all of his or her wants and desires: to achieve more of one objective means the sacrifice of others. Thus individuals are forced to choose. Economics explains how people make the best choices, given their tastes and preferences and the costs which they face. More importantly, economics outlines how humans will change their behavior as costs and/or tastes and preferences change.

1.1a
The individual

Only individuals can choose: only individuals have values and desires. In this sense the neoclassical model is individualistic. Even in the area of collective decision making—the area of public choice—the focus of analysis is on the individual. Although one often hears that "the administration has decided" or that "Congress has decided," economics views these collective decisions as the outcome of a process in which individuals choose.

Neoclassical economics, then, examines the choices that individuals make in their roles as consumers or as producers. We present in the balance of this chapter the characteristics of the neoclassical model with reference to the individual as consumer. Our choice could as easily have been the individual as producer. As we will see later, the nature of the choice problem that confronts both consumers and producers is identical.

1.1b
Self-improvement: Utility maximization in a world without scarcity

Economics assumes that each individual with his or her own tastes, preferences, wants, and desires attempts to satisfy them by the consumption of goods. *Utility* is the want-satisfying power of goods. By "goods" economists do not mean simply material goods. Many—perhaps most—goods are not material goods at all. Security is a good; leisure is a good; love is a good. It is from the consumption of goods that utility is received. Further, utility is subjective.[1] You receive utility from riding horses; your roommate doesn't. Your roommate receives utility from skiing; you don't. Your mother receives utility from dancing; your father doesn't. The differences across individuals in their tastes and preferences are enormous. Economics does not attempt to explain how these tastes and preferences, these wants and desires, are formed or how they change over time: this is the province of psychology. Economics takes the pattern of tastes and preferences across individuals as given.

However, given the individual's tastes and preferences, economists do make two assumptions about the individual: (1) he or she prefers more goods to fewer goods; (2) he or she experiences *diminishing marginal utility* as more of any one good is consumed. Let us look more closely at these two elements of the neoclassical model.

Suppose, as if by magic, someone offered to give you free as many goods as you would like to have. Again, by goods we mean anything from which you receive utility. Would you choose fewer goods than you are currently consuming, or more? Economics assumes that individuals would choose more goods, not fewer.

The assumption of diminishing marginal utility states that as the individual, given individual tastes and preferences, consumes more of any one good, total utility increases, but at a declining rate. That is to say, marginal utility—the *change* in total utility associated with the *change* in the consumption of the good—declines. This assumption is a recognition that individual preferences are ordered, and that consequently the first units of a good go to satisfy higher-valued wants than do subsequent units.

Try to imagine a world where it would be possible for all individuals to have as much income, time, power, commodities, love, knowledge, and all other goods as their tastes and preferences dictated. Individuals in such a world would consume the quantity of each good for which marginal utility was zero. This idea is illustrated in Fig. 1.1. Let us suppose that, given the individual's tastes and preferences, he or she receives utility from listening to music. As the consumption of music increases, *total utility* increases, but at a declining rate; marginal utility declines. The individual consumes $0Q$ music, that quantity for which total utility is at a maximum and for which marginal utility is zero. Further, he or she consumes all goods until the marginal utility of each is zero.

That this is clearly not the type of world we live in or ever expect to

---

[1] In the early development of economics it was customarily assumed that individuals maximized wealth—in particular, material wealth. Utility enters the analysis of human behavior as the cornerstone of the subjective theory of value in the last quarter of the nineteenth century. See Israel M. Kirzner, *The Economic Point of View,* Van Nostrand, Princeton, N.J., 1960.

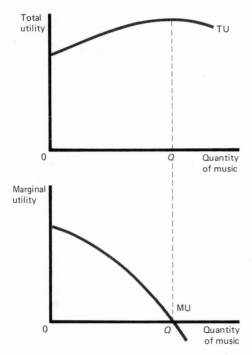

Figure 1.1. The relations between total utility, marginal utility, and the consumption of music. Increases in the quantities consumed of music increase total utility until the quantity OQ is reached. Marginal utility is equal to zero when total utility is at a maximum.

live in may be lamentable; it is true nonetheless. Individuals do not consume as much of all goods as they would like to. Individual wants do exceed the means to satisfy them, and this is the economist's concept of scarcity. Scarcity does not refer to a high-priced commodity or to a good for which there is a shortage. Scarcity is a universal condition, and the idea of being able to go "beyond scarcity" is meaningless to economists.

1.1c
Scarcity, thus choice and costs

Because of scarcity individuals must choose, and in choosing one alternative they must necessarily sacrifice others. That is, they must incur costs. The concept of costs, then, is the concept of lost alternatives. The highest-valued alternative which must be given up to have a good is the cost of the good. To continue our example of the individual and the consumption of music, for the individual to consume more music, he or she must necessarily give up other goods. Presumably, the least-valued alternatives will be given up first. However, as the individual continues to consume more music, he or she is forced to sacrifice higher-valued alternatives. Thus, the marginal cost curve—the curve that indicates how total costs *change* as the consumption of music *changes*—has a positive slope. We have illustrated in Fig. 1.2 a

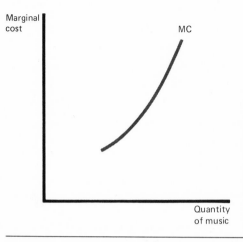

Marginal cost

MC

Quantity of music

Figure 1.2. The marginal costs of consuming music. As an individual consumes music, the least-valued alternatives are sacrificed first, but further consumption requires a sacrifice of higher-valued alternatives. Thus, the marginal costs of consuming music increase as the consumption of music increases.

marginal cost curve. It represents the marginal costs of listening to music. The individual may at first be required to sacrifice relatively low-valued alternatives to consume more music—perhaps watching TV and writing letters. As more time is devoted to the consumption of music, however, higher-valued alternatives will have to be sacrificed. There are, then, costs associated with consuming any good, and marginal cost is the measure of the highest-valued alternative that must be given up to have the additional quantity of the good.

1.1d
Self-improvement: Utility maximization given costs
Because of costs, individuals will not be able to consume all the goods they would like to have. The decision to consume more of one good is now the simultaneous decision to consume less of some other good. On what grounds do individuals choose the best combination of goods, and on what grounds do they adjust quantities of the various goods they consume? In short, how do individuals maximize total utility in a world of costs?

Total utility is maximized in a world of costs when the individual consumes that quantity of each good for which the marginal utility just equals the marginal cost. Only then will the change in total utility from consuming the last amount of the good just be equal to the highest-valued alternative which must be given up to have the good. For the consumption of music, this is the quantity $0Q'$ in Fig. 1.3. It is worth noting that individuals are worse off in a world with scarcity than they would be in a world without scarcity, worse off because they consume less of all goods and thus achieve lower levels of total utility. Recall that the best quantity of music in a world of no scarcity was $0Q$. Because of costs, the best quantity is now $0Q'$, a smaller amount of the good.

Why is it marginal utility and marginal cost that the individual

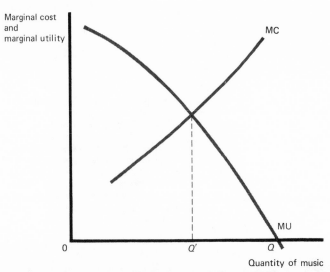

Figure 1.3. The best quantity of music to consume. Given the marginal utility and marginal costs of consuming music, $0Q'$ is the best quantity of music to consume. For the last unit consumed, the addition to total utility from consuming the last unit of the good is just equal to the addition to total costs from doing so.

considers relevant and not some other measure such as average or total utility and costs? The reason is that purposeful behavior is always future-oriented. Choices made today affect future outcomes; they cannot alter the past. In economics bygones are forever bygones. The marginal analysis which neoclassical economics incorporates is an explicit recognition of this. It focuses our attention on expected *future* utility and expected *future* costs. We say expected marginal utility and expected marginal costs because the future outcomes of choices made today are never known with certainty and never can be known with certainty. Nonetheless, individuals do act; they form expectations about the probable outcome of choices made today. This is necessarily an imperfect process, and no doubt the expectations that people do form are influenced by their past experiences.

1.1e
The predictive content of neoclassical economics
It stands to reason that if quantity $0Q'$ is best given the individual's tastes and preferences and given the costs which he or she confronts, then some other quantity will become best as these circumstances change. In Fig. 1.4 we illustrate a decline in the schedule of marginal costs of music. The marginal cost *of each quantity* of music is now less than it was. As a result of this change, $0Q'$ is no longer the best quantity of music, because now for that quantity, marginal utility (which has not

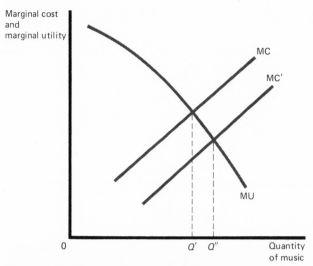

Figure 1.4. Changes in marginal costs and changes in individual behavior. A fall in the schedule of marginal costs from MC to MC′ results in the individual increasing the consumption of this good by the amount Q′Q″.

changed) is greater than marginal cost (which has changed). The individual can now reach a higher level of total utility by increasing the consumption of music. The new best quantity is $0Q''$, again the quantity for which marginal utility just equals the (lower) marginal cost.

In this example the individual is seen to change his or her behavior because costs have changed. Similarly, an adjustment would be made as a consequence of a change in tastes and preferences. Economic analysis can predict the changes in the consumption of a good such as music as a result of a change in tastes and preferences even though, as we noted earlier, economists do not know how tastes and preferences are formed or why they change. The existing pattern of tastes and preferences is assumed to be given, and although it surely changes (in an unknown fashion), such changes in tastes and preferences are always assumed to be swamped by changes in costs.

The neoclassical model does not assume that individuals face unlimited alternatives. Individuals do choose from among the alternatives available to them that combination of goods that makes them best off as far as they are concerned. Because of circumstances either real or imagined, an individual's alternatives may be very limited. By contrast, an individual may face the widest conceivable array of alternatives. But even if the individual faces a very narrow range of alternatives, the nature of neoclassical economics is still choice-theoretic. The difference is now that choices are made within a much narrower range of alternatives. Never does the neoclassical model assume that outcomes are imposed on individuals. The model is always volitional, never deterministic.[2] As we shall see later in the text, an individual's well-being is always enhanced by a wider array of alternatives.

Having outlined the nature of the choice process, let us examine now some characteristics of economics as a social science.

1.2
ECONOMICS AS A SYSTEM OF ORGANIZED RELATIONSHIPS

The essential feature of any system is organization: any system is a body of organized relationships. It makes no difference whether such a system is an economic system, a planetary system, a waterway system, or an ecological system: all systems exhibit this fundamental characteristic of order or organization. Consider the waterway system of the Mississippi River and its tributaries. Not only are we able to say that a 10-inch rainfall in St. Louis will cause water levels to rise in New Orleans, but we are also able to specify the height and timing of the crest. Similarly, economics is able to predict the effect of an increase in the demand for automobiles on the employment of auto workers, the effect on unemployment of a rise in the legislated minimum wage, the effect on hours worked by married women of a rise in their husbands' incomes, and a multitude of other cause-and-effect relationships. Such statements are possible, though, only if we approach economics as a system of organized relationships. The systems view in economics parallels identical views in physics, chemistry, biology, and other sciences. Indeed, all contemporary science has become the "science of organized complexity."

With the systems view in mind, it becomes immediately obvious that changes which affect one part of the economic system have an immediate effect there, but delayed effects throughout the remainder of the system. The initial effects may be the most powerful, the delayed effects becoming diluted as they spread through the system. On the other hand, initial effects may be minor compared to the cumulative and increasingly powerful delayed effects of the change. We will differentiate often in our discussions between initial and delayed effects of changes in the economic system.

A simple economic system can be represented by the *circular flow of income* illustrated in Fig. 1.5. In this conception an economy consists of economic agents who for our present purposes can be identified respectively as members of households or of firms. Household members

---

[2]James Duesenberry has stated that the difference between economics and sociology is very simple: "Economics is all about how people make choices. Sociology is all about why they don't have any choices to make." See J. S. Duesenberry, "Comment," in *Demographic and Economic Change in Developed Countries,* Princeton University Press, Princeton, N.J., 1960, p. 233.

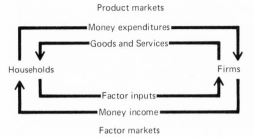

Product markets

Factor markets

Figure 1.5. A simple circular flow of income. Household members are suppliers of factor services in factor markets and demanders of goods in product markets. Firms are demanders of factor services in factor markets and suppliers of products in product markets.

are suppliers of productive services (or factors of production) such as labor services to firms. In return for supplying productive services to firms, households receive money incomes. In these transactions which take place in factor markets, households are suppliers and firms are demanders. With their money incomes, household members are able to make money expenditures on market-produced goods and services which are produced by firms. These transactions take place in product markets in which the demand and supply roles are reversed: household members are demanders of goods and services; firms are suppliers.[3]

This simple conception allows us to see immediately the broad answers to questions which any economic system must answer: What gets produced by firms? How is it produced? Who gets what is produced? In a society where (the bulk of) these decisions are not made by a central authority but by individual members of households and firms, what gets produced by firms is what firms expect households to buy with their money incomes. Producers, of course, make strenuous efforts to influence the spending patterns of households. For example, producers attempt through advertising to convince households that their product is better in some important respects than the products of competing producers. Another role of advertising is to provide households with information about the existence of new goods and services.

The money expenditures that households make on the output of the firm are the total revenue to the firm. For a firm to remain viable in the long run, the total revenues received from the sale of output must be sufficient to cover the total costs of producing the output, where total costs of production include all explicit payments to factors of production as well as all implicit costs such as the entrepreneur's opportunity costs. Firms are forced to be constantly alert to the possibilities of producing output at lower costs, particularly when economic circumstances do not permit them to raise product selling price.

Who gets the goods and services that the economic system pro-

---

[3]In this simple presentation we have abstracted from household production. We analyze this topic in some detail in our chapters on labor supply.

duces, and in what quantities? Those individuals who, because of transactions in factor markets, earn the largest incomes receive the largest quantities of market-produced goods and services. In the absence of charity and various governmental programs to shift income from one group in society to another, the quantities of market-produced goods and services that households purchase would depend simply and solely on the income earned from supplying factors of production.

The conception of the circular flow of income gives us an overview of the elements of an economic system and points out the dual roles of households and firms as both suppliers and demanders. Our interest in labor economics is in households as suppliers of labor services, firms as demanders of labor services, and the resulting patterns of wages, employment, and income.

1.3

LABOR ECONOMICS AS A SUBSYSTEM OF THE ECONOMIC SYSTEM

Labor economics is also a system of organized relationships, but it is a subsystem of the larger economic system. In terms of Fig. 1.5, labor economics focuses on the behavior of individuals in their roles as suppliers of labor services and as demanders of labor services.

In the market for labor, demand and supply jointly determine the number of people who will be employed and the wages they will receive. In this respect the market for labor is like the market for a good such as wheat. In both markets the choices of buyers and sellers are reflected in the terms of exchange in the market. But the market for labor is unlike the market for wheat in many important respects. Indeed, it is the differences between the labor market and the product market that are most interesting to labor economists. If there were no special characteristics of the labor market, there would be no rationale for the existence of separate courses in labor economics. A chapter or two in an economic principles text would provide sufficient background for the analysis of the labor market.

The labor market, however, has more dimensions than the market for wheat. For instance, one bushel of wheat is largely indistinguishable from any other bushel of wheat, whereas the labor market is characterized by an infinite variety of kinds and qualities of workers. Instead of a single labor market, we have many interrelated labor markets. Further, the supplier of wheat neither knows nor cares about how or where his or her wheat is used, once it is sold. The individual who sells his or her work effort, on the other hand, considers a package of working conditions (location and environment of the work place, job security, opportunities for advancement, and so forth) before deciding to accept employment. This fact alone presents complexities which so radically differentiate the labor market from other markets that the casual observer is unable to recognize that the labor market is in fact a market. The failure of many individuals to recognize the implications for labor of the laws of demand and supply has resulted since time immemorial in policies which have consequences unforeseen by their proponents.

To take into account simultaneously all the factors that make labor markets more complex than product markets would be impossible as well as pointless. The logic of the labor market can be most readily comprehended if we first construct a model that abstracts from the special characteristics of this market and concentrates on the common characteristics of markets. In short, we should first examine a model which concentrates upon those characteristics that the market for wheat and the market for labor have in common. Upon such a foundation of theory, it is possible to add building blocks one at a time, the building blocks being the individual complexities of the labor market. Taken one at a time, these complexities can be examined for their effect on the overall operation of the market without reducing our understanding of the logic of the price system as it applies to the labor market. The foundational model is constructed by initially making assumptions which all would agree are unrealistic, but which greatly simplify the analysis. One at a time, the assumptions can be relaxed.

The value of this approach to economic analysis can be understood with an analogy to the physical sciences. Suppose we want to examine the separate effect of wind resistance on the speed of decline of a falling object, perhaps because we want to explain why a feather dropped from a 10-story building takes longer to reach the ground than a lead ball of equal weight. Before we can gauge the importance of wind resistance, we must first know how fast the feather and ball would drop in the absence of wind resistance. We accomplish this by first assuming (unrealistically, of course) that feathers and lead balls drop in a vacuum. The knowledge that in a vacuum both feathers and lead balls decline at the same rate enables us to proceed to disentangle the effect of wind resistance from the separate effect of gravity.

Similarly, if we want to examine the effect of racial discrimination in labor markets on the earnings of blacks, it is necessary to know what blacks would earn if there were no discrimination in labor markets. To achieve this theoretical basis of comparison, we must first construct a model in which employers are assumed to be totally indifferent as to whether their employees are black or nonblack. We can then relax the assumption of employer indifference and analyze the result of such a relaxation. The purpose of economic theory, after all, is to make the realities of a complex world understandable. The objective of the theory we present in this text is to make the labor market understandable.

In Chap. 2 we use the neoclassical model to examine the choices that individuals make as producers. We develop a microeconomic model of the firm and see that a downward-sloping demand curve for labor is a major conclusion of the neoclassical model for labor market analysis.

QUESTIONS AND EXERCISES
1. Per capita income in the United States has never been higher than it is today. Thus, the United States has overcome scarcity. Comment.
2. Assume you receive utility from playing tennis. (*a*) What are the costs of doing so? (*b*) Outline how the costs of playing tennis could fall. What adjustments would you then make in the consumption of this good? Why? Is this changed behavior a result of changes in tastes and preferences?
3. What is meant by the phrase: "The economic model is always volitional, never deterministic"?
4. What other courses are you taking in which you are exposed to a system of organized relationships? What are the organizing principles involved in each?
5. Explain the organizing principles in economics.

REFERENCES FOR FURTHER READING
An eminently readable and lucid introduction to the method of scientific inquiry is Sir Peter B. Medawar, *Induction and Intuition in Scientific Thought,* American Philosophical Society, Philadelphia, 1969. Students who find Medawar's remarks provocative may wish to read Karl R. Popper, *The Logic of Scientific Discovery,* Basic Books, New York, 1959; and Ervin Laszlo, *The Systems View of the World,* George Braziller, New York, 1972.

Discussions of the method and purpose of economics are found in Frank H. Knight, *On the History and Method of Economics,* The University of Chicago Press, Chicago and London, 1956; Lionel Robbins, *An Essay on the Nature and Significance of Economic Science,* 2d ed., St. Martin's Press, New York, 1962; George J. Stigler, *Essays in the History of Economics,* The University of Chicago Press, Chicago and London, 1965; Ludwig von Mises, *Human Action,* Yale University Press, New Haven, 1949; F. A. von Hayek, *The Counter-revolution of Science,* Free Press, Glencoe, Ill. 1952; and L. Robbins, *The Theory of Economic Policy in English Classical Political Economy,* Macmillan, London, 1965, lectures 1 and 6.

PART I

PART 1

LABOR DEMAND
AND LABOR SUPPLY

In a macroeconomics course the economy is described as being composed of four broadly defined markets: the commodities market, the bond market, the money market, and the labor market. Although we pointed out in Chap. 1 that the labor market is highly interrelated with the other markets, it is nonetheless possible to focus our attention on the labor market and examine its workings in detail. That is the task of this book. The task of Part I is to provide a foundation upon which our examination of the labor market is based. The tools of analysis are labor demand and labor supply. Whereas Chap. 2 develops the demand for labor from the perspective of the individual firm, Chap. 3 develops the concept of the market demand for labor and presents a theory of wage determination. Chapters 4 and 5 develop an analysis of the supply of labor in its many dimensions, both in the short run and in the long run. Chapter 6 combines demand and supply and examines their interaction. A careful reading of Part I should provide one with a good grasp of how the labor market would operate under simple and idealized conditions. This understanding will make more readily accessible the more complex dimensions of the labor market that we discuss in the remainder of the book.

THE DEMAND FOR LABOR IN THE SHORT RUN AND IN THE LONG RUN

The firm is the economic unit engaged in production, where production is the transformation of inputs (factors of production) into outputs. The firm's demand for inputs is a *derived demand,* derived from consumer demand for the firm's product. From hiring inputs, firms are able to produce output whose sale generates revenue to the firm. But in hiring inputs, firms also incur costs. As we noted in Chap. 1 when we presented the concept of the circular flow of income, in order for the firm to remain viable in the long run, its total revenues from the sale of output must be sufficient to cover the total costs of producing output.

The firm is headed by the entrepreneur. The entrepreneur makes choices about the employment of labor as well as other productive inputs such as capital. Further, he or she chooses as well what type of output to produce and in what quantities to produce it. In labor economics our interest is in the decisions that the entrepreneur makes with regard to the employment of labor. On what grounds does the entrepreneur choose the best quantity of labor to employ, and on what grounds does he or she make adjustments in the best quantity?

The firm's behavioral objective is assumed to be profit maximization. Because of this, the entrepreneur is vitally concerned with how the firm's total revenues can be expected to change versus how its total costs will change as a result of hiring additional inputs. Inputs that will add more to the firm's total revenues than to its total costs will always be employed by the firm, because to do so will add to the firm's profits. Conversely, inputs that will add more to the firm's total costs than to its total revenues will never knowingly be hired because the firm will incur losses as a result of such a decision.

The firm, given a sufficient amount of time, can always make whatever adjustments are necessary to alter completely the mix of inputs in production as well as make any other adjustments it deems necessary for survival, such as perhaps even producing a different output. In the following section, however, we consider the choices that are available to the entrepreneur during that period of time when the choices are not unlimited, but are constrained. This is the economist's concept of the *short run.* The short run can be defined as that period of time during which at least one input in production cannot be changed. We assume for purposes of exposition that the input that is fixed and cannot be changed is capital, the firm's plant and equipment. Further, we make two additional assumptions: (1) the firm is selling its output in purely competitive markets, and (2) it is purchasing its inputs in purely competitive markets. Thus, product selling price and the price of labor are given to the firm. The entrepreneur can choose how much to sell at the prevailing market price and how much labor to employ at the prevailing market wage rate, but cannot choose what price to charge for the output produced or what wage to pay labor. These prices are dictated by the market.

Our purpose, then, is to develop the schedule which shows the quantities of the variable input, labor, that the firm will demand at various alternative prices of labor. This demand for labor we derive in a set of circumstances called the short run, subject to the additional considerations that the entrepreneur is forced to accept both the product selling price and the wage rate as given. After we develop the firm's demand for labor in the short run, we turn our attention to the demand for labor in the long run. In the long run, the entrepreneur can vary all inputs. The theory that we present is known as the marginal productivity theory of the demand for labor in competitive markets.

2.1

THE DEMAND FOR LABOR IN THE SHORT RUN

The relations that exist between inputs of factors of production and the firm's output are production relations. Given the technology in use by the firm (where technology is the technique by which inputs are transformed into output), the larger the quantities of inputs of labor and capital employed by the firm, the greater the output produced.

2.1a
Production relations: Marginal physical product

The input-output relations of a typical firm are illustrated graphically in Fig. 2.1. Units of capital employed in the production process are shown on the vertical axis; units of labor, which we measure in worker-days, are

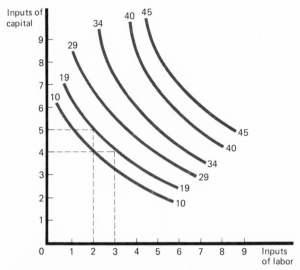

Figure 2.1. Production isoquants for coal. Any given quantity of coal can be produced with various combinations of labor and capital. For example, 19 tons of coal can be produced with 5 units of capital and 2 units of labor, or with 4 units of capital and 3 units of labor.

shown along the horizontal axis.[1] The curved lines called *isoquants* show the various combinations of labor and capital that the firm can use to produce "equal quantities" of output. For example, our typical firm, which let us suppose arbitrarily to be a coal-mining operation, can mine 19 tons of coal by employing five units of capital and two units of labor, four units of capital and three units of labor, or by all other combinations of labor and capital along the same isoquant. Labor and capital, then, are substitutes in the production process.

But labor and capital are not perfect substitutes for each other (if they were, they would be the same factor of production), but imperfect substitutes. The isoquant has its particular curvature for that reason. In general, if a firm were to successively reduce by one unit its use of one factor of production, it would have to employ successively larger amounts of the other factor of production in order to keep the quantity of output unchanged. This fact is reflected in the curvature of the isoquants which are described as being convex to the origin.

As can be seen from Fig. 2.1, the firm can increase its output from 19 tons of coal to say, 29 tons by increasing the amount of capital it employs, by increasing the amount of labor it employs, or by increasing

---

[1]The unit of measure for the labor input is arbitrary. We could have used worker-hours as the unit of measure; indeed, worker-hours is more commonly used. However, the numerical examples used in this chapter can be kept simpler with the use of worker-days.

both inputs. Given complete freedom to choose, the entrepreneur will produce any particular output with the combination of capital and labor that is the least costly. However, because of our assumption that the firm is in the short run, it is unable to alter the quantity of capital that it uses. The firm cannot in the short run increase output except by increasing its employment of labor.

The effect on output of combining increasing amounts of labor with a fixed amount of capital is demonstrated in Fig. 2.2. If the firm possesses three units of capital, we can observe the effect on total output of adding successive units of labor to the fixed quantity of capital (denoted by the straight line K^* in Fig. 2.2a). The total output when one unit of labor is used is 10. When two units of labor are used, total output rises to 19, and so forth. The total output obtained from various quantities of labor is of less significance for the demand for labor than are the *additions* to total output association with *additional* quantities of labor employed. The addition to total output (or, alternately, total product) brought about by an increase of one unit of labor is the *marginal physical product of labor.*

Table 2.1 shows, for each input of labor L, the relation between the labor input, total product TP, and marginal physical product MPP revealed in Fig. 2.2a. Table 2.1 also shows the average physical product APP of labor which is the average output per unit of labor TP/L. The derivation of MPP from the production isoquants is illustrated in Fig. 2.2b. The MPP of the first unit of labor is 10. If production is carried on with two units of labor instead of one unit, TP will be 19 instead of 10. Thus the MPP of the second unit of labor is 9. The MPP of the third unit of labor is 8, and so forth with other quantities of the labor input. The MPP of labor thus declines with each additional unit of labor, declining to zero with the eleventh unit. Beyond this quantity of labor, the addition of labor will actually reduce total product; the MPP of labor will be negative.

The entire schedule of the MPP of labor would be greater if the capital stock of the firm were greater. For example, the marginal product of the first unit of labor would be about 19 if the firm had four units of capital instead of three. Thus, the MPP of labor will normally be increased by an increase in the firm's capital.

The input-output relations in Fig. 2.2 and Table 2.1 are quite general, although the particular numbers chosen to illustrate the general principle are arbitrary. As any firm employs additional units of labor to a fixed stock of capital, output begins to increase. Output may or may not initially increase at an increasing rate, depending mainly on the unique characteristics of the firm's particular production process. More importantly, one can say with certainty that after some quantity of labor has been employed, output will begin to increase at a decreasing rate. In other words, MPP will be positive but diminishing. *Diminishing returns in production* is thus characteristic not only of this production process but of every production process in the short run. Although

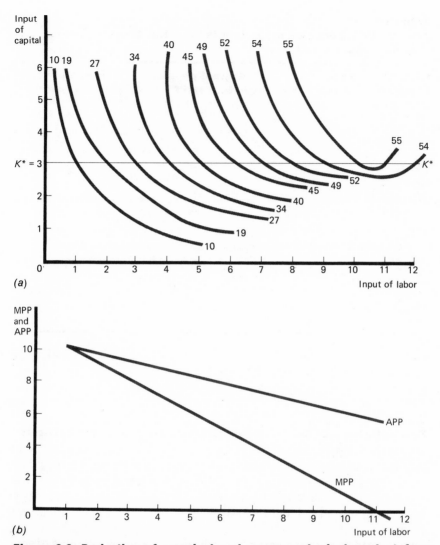

Figure 2.2. Derivation of marginal and average physical product from production isoquants. Figure 2.2a demonstrates the quantities of labor required to produce the quantities of output indicated by the various isoquants, given that the firm uses three units of capital. Figure 2.2b shows the addition to total output, MPP, associated with the addition of successive units of labor. Average physical product APP is also illustrated and is the output per unit of labor employed. MPP and APP are calculated from the information contained in Fig. 2.2a.

diminishing returns is an engineering phenomenon, it has crucial implications for economic analysis. Its main implication is that after some quantity of labor is used, the firm will be willing to employ additional inputs of labor only at lower wages; this is because after some

Table 2.1
The relation between labor inputs and the total, marginal, and average products of labor

Quantity of labor	Total product (TP)	Marginal physical product (MPP)	Average physical product (APP)
1	10	10	10
2	19	9	9.5
3	27	8	9
4	34	7	8.5
5	40	6	8
6	45	5	7.5
7	49	4	7
8	52	3	6.5
9	54	2	6
10	55	1	5.5
11	55	0	5
12	54	−1	4.5

quantity of labor is used, each additional unit brings forth less additional output. As a consequence, the short-run demand curve for labor will always have a negative slope.

2.1b
The schedule of the value of the marginal physical product
We are not yet in a position to specify the firm's demand for labor because we do not yet know the maximum price that the firm would be willing to pay for various quantities of labor. That amount depends on the revenue the firm will obtain from the sale of output produced by its labor. We have assumed that our firm sells its product in a purely competitive product market. Figure 2.3 illustrates the determination of price in the product market in which the firm sells its output. The market price of coal is determined by the interaction of the demand for coal and the supply of coal. Figure 2.3a shows the equilibrium price of coal to be $40 per ton. Because the firm is purely competitive, its actions have no effect on the market price of coal. (This is because its sales make up such a small part of total industry sales that its decisions to expand output or to go out of business do not affect the market supply of coal, and thus the price of coal.) As Fig. 2.3b shows, the demand for the firm's output can be represented by a horizontal line at the market price of $40 per ton. The firm cannot sell any output above this price; there is no reason to sell at less than this price because it can sell as much coal as it wishes to at a price of $40 per ton. The firm's revenue will increase by $40 for each ton of coal that it sells, an amount equal to product selling price.

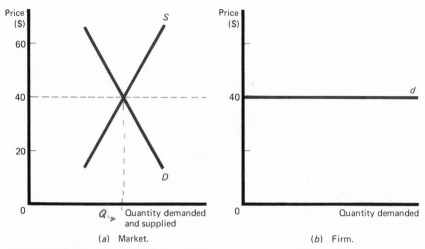

Figure 2.3. Demand curves for coal: the market and the firm. The price of coal is determined by the interaction of market demand D and supply S as in panel a. As a result, the purely competitive firm's demand curve is perfectly elastic at the market price of $40.

We can now construct a schedule that shows the amount by which the firm's *revenue* will increase as it increases its employment of labor. When the firm adds one more unit of labor, its revenue will increase by the amount of the *value of the marginal physical product* VMPP, which is the price of each unit of output *P* multiplied by the number of units of output produced by the additional unit of labor (the MPP of labor from Fig. 2.2*b*). Figure 2.4 illustrates the schedule of VMPP for our coal producer. As the figure shows, each successive input of labor yields successively less and less additional revenue to the firm. This is because of diminishing returns in production. The first unit of labor adds $400 to the firm's revenue, the second unit adds $360, and the third unit adds $320. Because the eleventh unit of labor has a zero MPP, employment of that unit would bring no additional revenue to the firm.

2.1c
VMPP is the firm's demand for labor
The VMPP schedule is the firm's demand for labor. It is the firm's demand curve because it determines the maximum price that the firm will pay for the various quantities of labor. Any firm which is assumed to maximize profits will not knowingly pay any input more than that input adds to the total revenue of the firm.

In Fig. 2.4 the horizontal line at $80 is the supply of labor to the firm. Because the firm is purely competitive in the factor market, it can hire all the labor it chooses at $80 per worker-day, a price set by the market demand for and market supply of labor. Thus, the *marginal factor cost* MFC, the amount by which total costs change as the firm hires additional

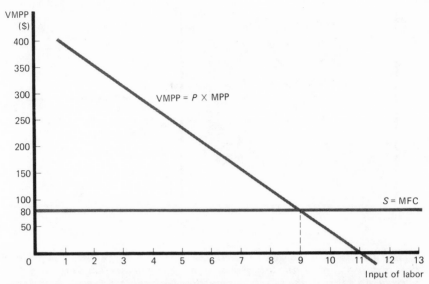

Figure 2.4. The value of marginal physical product for a purely competitive firm. The value of marginal physical product VMPP is the marginal physical product of labor MPP multiplied by the product price P at each quantity of labor employed. The VMPP schedule is the firm's demand curve for labor. If the market wage rate is $80 per worker-day, the firm faces a perfectly elastic supply curve of labor at that wage, a wage equal to the marginal factor cost to the firm. The firm would maximize profits by employing 9 worker-days of labor.

inputs of labor, is $80, an amount equal to the wage per worker-day. The quantity of labor that the firm would employ if the market wage were $80 per worker-day is 9 worker-days, the quantity for which VMPP equals MFC. If the firm were to hire 8 worker-days it would be earning less than the maximum profit possible because an additional worker-day of labor would produce revenues in excess of the $80 per day cost. If the firm were to hire 10 worker-days, it would incur a loss (and thus not earn the maximum profit possible) because all worker-days in excess of 9 cost more to hire than the revenue they produce for the firm. Thus, at a wage of $80, 9 worker-days of labor is the best quantity of labor for the firm to hire. Of course, if the wage rate were to rise to $120 per worker-day, 8 worker-days would be the best quantity; if the wage were to fall to $40, 10 worker-days would be best. Thus, the amount of labor demanded by any firm is inversely related to the wage rate.

The downward-sloping demand curve for labor is the major conclusion for labor economics of the neoclassical theory of the firm. The profit-maximizing firm can choose the best quantity of labor to employ. That quantity in pure competition is always the amount for which the VMPP of labor equals the wage. Further, the firm will adjust the quantity of labor it employs as the cost of labor changes. If the cost of labor rises, the firm reduces employment; if the cost of labor declines, the firm increases employment. Thus, because we have assumed the input of capital to be fixed in the short run, an adjustment in the quantity of labor is the only adjustment possible to the purely competitive firm in the short run.

But there are other adjustments available to the firm in other circumstances. For example, if the wage rate rises, the firm may use less labor but more capital. This is a long-run adjustment which we consider in the following section. Further, the firm may be able to raise the price of its product to offset the rise in the cost of an input. This is a possibility if the firm sells its output in imperfectly competitive markets. We delay consideration of this possibility and its effect on the employment of labor until Chap. 10, when we discuss imperfections in competition.

2.2

THE DEMAND FOR LABOR IN THE LONG RUN

The long run in the theory of the firm is the concept of the firm making full adjustment to changed economic circumstances. It is not to be thought of as any specific time, like next July; it is not a point that will be arrived at some day in the future. The distinction between the short-run and the long-run demand for labor is the distinction between (1) adjustments in the use of labor that the firm can make when it is *not* able to alter its other inputs and (2) adjustments in the use of labor that the firm can make when it *is* able to alter its other inputs. Let us examine, then, the firm's demand for labor in the long run.

2.2a
Adjustment of the firm's capital

Our production isoquant analysis demonstrated that a particular level of output can be produced by any one of a variety of different combinations of labor and capital. Figure 2.5 uses the same input-output relationships discussed in the previous section. As Fig. 2.5 shows, an output of 19 tons of coal can be produced with one unit of labor combined with four units of capital. It can also be produced with two units of labor and three units of capital. As we have established, 19 tons of coal can be produced by any of the combinations of capital and labor shown along the relevant isoquant. If the entrepreneur is free (as he or she is) in the long run to choose any combination of capital and labor, what combination will be chosen so as to maximize profits? The entrepreneur will produce that output with whatever combination of labor and capital is least costly.

The cost of 1 worker-day of labor is easily identified: it is the daily wage plus the per diem costs of any fringe benefits. In our analysis we will simplify the explanation by ignoring fringe benefits and assume that the wage rate is the only labor cost.

The cost of capital is not so readily identified. To avoid some of the

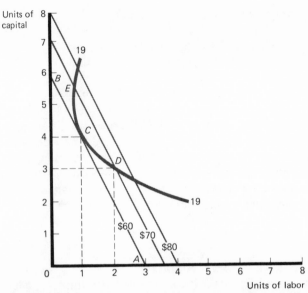

Figure 2.5. The least-cost combination of labor and capital. The firm can produce 19 tons of coal with different combinations of capital and labor, including those shown in points C, D, and E. However, the firm should choose combination C, since at $60 it is the cheapest combination with which to produce 19 tons of coal.

difficulties involved in a full presentation of the cost of capital, we will assume that the firm can rent capital equipment on a daily basis rather than buy it. The price of capital, then, will simply be the per unit daily rental fee of the capital equipment.[2] Let us say that the rental price of a unit of capital is $10 per day and the wage rate is $20 per worker-day. We could then ask how much labor and how much capital could be bought with an arbitrary expenditure of money, say $60. If the entire sum were spent on labor, it could purchase three units of labor ($60/$W = $60/$20 = 3$). If the entire sum were spent on capital, the services of six units of capital ($60/P_k = $60/$10 = 6$) could be purchased, where P_k is the daily rental price of capital. The quantities of labor and capital mentioned are given by points A and B respectively in Fig. 2.5 The straight line connecting points A and B represents the various combinations of labor and capital that can be purchased with $60. Because all the combinations represent an "equal cost" of $60, the line is called an *isocost* line. Given the values of W and P_k, it should be clear that an additional unit of labor can be purchased by renting two fewer units of capital. The amount of capital that must be given up to acquire each

---

[2]A simple but more complete discussion of the cost of capital is contained in C. W. Baird, *Macroeconomics,* Science Research, Chicago, 1973, pp. 116–121.

additional unit of labor ($\Delta K/\Delta L$) is given by the negative of the ratio of the cost of labor to the cost of capital, $W/P_k = \$20/\$10 = 2$. The slope of the isocost line, then, is $- W/P_k$. For any sum of money, there will be a relevant isocost line. Two additional isocost lines are illustrated in Fig. 2.5. The farther an isocost line lies from the origin, the more expensive are the combinations of labor and capital given by the line.

Note that the slope of each isocost line is the same, $- W/P_k$. In producing 19 tons of coal, the entrepreneur will find one combination of capital and labor to be least costly, namely, that combination given by the isocost line that is tangent to the 19-ton isoquant. The least-cost combination in Fig. 2.5 is combination C, consisting of one unit of labor and four units of capital at a total cost of $60. Clearly, 19 tons can be produced by the combinations given at each point on the isoquant (for example, points D and E), but these two combinations cost $70, so that these are not minimum-cost combinations.

We know from the previous section that the demand curve for labor is a downward-sloping curve. Our analysis of long-run choice enables us to compare now the slope of the long-run demand curve for labor with that of the short-run demand curve. Let us assume that the firm depicted in Fig. 2.6 is initially in equilibrium with respect to both the short run and the long run, and is therefore operating with the combination of labor and

Figure 2.6. Short-run and long-run adjustments to a rise in the wage rate. The firm is initially in equilibrium with K* units of capital at point A. A rise in the wage rate will pivot the isocost line inward, and the firm will reduce its employment to that indicated by point B in the short run. In the long run, even if the firm were to continue to produce I' units of output, it would produce that level with K*' units of capital and the quantity of labor given by point C.

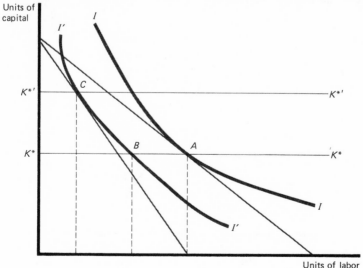

Units of labor

capital given by point A. (If the firm is in equilibrium in the short run, then labor's VMPP is equal to the wage rate.) How will the firm react to a rise in the wage rate? We know that in the short run, the firm will reduce the quantity of labor that it combines with the fixed capital stock K^*. The reduction in employment places the firm on a lower isoquant, I', at point B. In the long run, however, the firm will reduce even further its employment of labor. Even if the firm were to continue to produce the same quantity of output indicated by I', it would choose to do so with less labor and more capital than at point B. The firm would move to point C, which, given the new price of labor relative to capital, will provide the least-cost combination of capital and labor with which the firm can produce at the output level indicated by I'. The movement from point A to point B is termed the *output effect* of a change in the wage rate because it involves a reduction in the firm's level of output. The additional movement from point B to point C (which is the delayed effect of a wage increase) is called the *substitution effect* since it involves a lowering of the cost of production through the substitution of capital for labor.

2.2b
Elasticity of the demand for labor
In Fig. 2.7 we can draw a demand curve for labor that illustrates the movement from point A to B to C. The firm's short-run response to an

---

Figure 2.7. Long-run and short-run demand curves for labor. In response to a rise in the wage rate from W₁ to W₂, the firm will reduce the quantity of labor it demands as it moves from point A to point B. In the long run, it will reduce further the quantity of labor by substituting capital for labor as it moves from point B to point C.

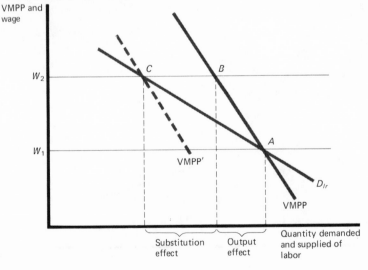

increase in the wage rate from W_1 to W_2 is to move upward along the demand curve from point A to B. As the firm makes its long-run substitution of capital for labor, however, the quantity of labor it demands is reduced further to the level indicated by point C. Thus, the quantity of labor demanded by the firm in response to the higher wage rate declines more in the long run than in the short run.

If the firm had faced a decrease in the wage rate, it would have increased its employment of labor, first by increasing the scale of operations and, in the long run, also by substituting labor for capital. Thus, the part of Fig. 2.7 that lies to the right of the initial point A shows the long-run demand curve, D_{lr}, to be above the short-run demand curve (the VMPP schedule). The initial VMPP schedule pertains to a given capital stock K^*. When the firm makes its long-run adjustment to point C, a new short-run demand curve VMPP' becomes relevant. VMPP' shows the short-run adjustment that the firm will make to any subsequent wage change, given that the capital stock of the firm is now $K^{*'}$ instead of K^*. In fact, each point on the long-run demand curve is crossed by a short-run demand curve.

Figure 2.7 and our accompanying discussion have demonstrated that the demand for labor is more elastic in the long run than in the short run. Demand elasticity is a measure of the sensitivity of quantity demanded to changes in price. More specifically, elasticity of demand is defined as the percentage change in quantity demanded divided by the percentage change in price: $\%\Delta Q/\%\Delta P$. For example, if a 1 percent increase in price leads to a 3 percent decrease in quantity demanded, then the elasticity of demand is 3.00. (The negative sign of the elasticity measure is ignored because all negatively sloped demand curves will have a negative elasticity.) The elasticity of demand for labor is the percentage change in the quantity of labor demanded divided by the percentage change in the wage rate. Hence the long-run demand curve for labor is more elastic than the short-run demand curve because any given increase in the wage rate will lead to a greater percentage decrease in the quantity demanded of labor in the long run than it will in the short run.

The elasticity of demand for labor will normally vary from one industry to another. In an early study Paul Douglas found the elasticity of demand for labor, when averaged over all industry, to be about 4.00.[3] More recent updating of Douglas's work has not signficantly altered this finding. We will develop the determinants of the elasticity of demand for labor in Chap. 6, by which point we will have developed the appropriate tools of analysis.

The primary purpose of this chapter has been to demonstrate that the quantity of labor demanded by a firm is negatively related to the wage rate at which the competitive firm can hire labor. We have seen that in the

[3] P. H. Douglas, *The Theory of Wages,* Macmillan, New York, 1934.

short run, given a particular product price, the negative relation is the result of (a) profit-maximizing behavior of firms and (b) the diminishing marginal physical productivity of labor. In the long run, the negative relation is further influenced by the price and marginal productivity of capital.

We have explained the firm's reaction to changes in the wage rate in both the short run and the long run. However, we have not provided an explanation of how that market wage rate is determined. This is the subject of the following chapter.

QUESTIONS AND EXERCISES

1. What will be the effect of an increase in the demand for coal on the demand for labor in the coal-mining industry?

2. The "substitution effect" shown in Fig. 2.7 is based on the assumption that the firm would choose to produce the same quantity of output in the long run as in the short run after a change in the wage rate. Is the firm likely to desire to produce the same quantity of output? If not, what factors will determine the desired level of output?

3. What will be the effect on a firm's employment of labor of a legal minimum wage that is higher than the market equilibrium wage?

4. Referring to Fig. 2.5, suppose there is a technological improvement such that the same level of output could be produced with less capital for any given employment of labor. How would the isoquant change?

5. What is the effect on a firm's MPP schedule of an increase in its use of capital?

REFERENCES FOR FURTHER READING

One of the best treatments of the demand for labor is in C. Ferguson and C. Maurice, *Economic Analysis,* Irwin, Homewood, Ill., 1975, chap. 11.

For a criticism of marginal productivity analysis at the level of the firm, see R. Lester, "Shortcomings of Marginal Analysis for Wage-Employment Problems," *American Economic Review,* vol. 36, March 1946, pp. 63–82. Lester's criticisms are rebutted in F. Machlup, "Marginal Analysis and Empirical Research," *American Economic Review,* vol. 36, September 1946, pp. 519–554; and in G. Stigler, "Professor Lester and the Marginalists," *American Economic Review,* vol. 37, March 1947, pp. 147–154.

For a nontechnical presentation of some evidence of the downward slope of the demand curve for labor, see L. Reynolds and P. Gregory, *Wages, Productivity, and Industrialization in Puerto Rico,* Irwin, Homewood, Ill., 1965, pp. 41–103.

WAGES AND EMPLOYMENT: THE BASIC MODEL

The marginal productivity theory that we presented in Chap. 2 is a theory of the firm's demand for labor. When one makes the appropriate assumptions, however, the marginal productivity theory can become a theory of wages and employment for the aggregate economy. That is, as a macroeconomic theory it can explain the general level of wages and the economywide volume of employment.

It is our intention in this chapter to present marginal productivity theory as a macroeconomic theory of wages and employment. The basic model we present as the foundation of modern neoclassical wage and employment theory, though greatly simplified, is essentially the model developed by John Bates Clark in *The Distribution of Wealth*.[1] During Clark's time his theory was accepted as a more or less complete theory of wages and employment rather than as a mere foundation. Over the years neoclassical economists have added to the foundation established by Clark and have met the criticisms leveled against the model, although not all have been met with equal success. Despite the criticisms, some of which remain unresolved, Clark's model in a much more enriched form remains the central core or skeleton of neoclassical wage and employment theory.

We make a number of somewhat unrealistic simplifying assumptions in the basic Clarkian model which we present here. The purpose of doing so is to eliminate *for the moment* the complexities of real world

---

[1] J. B. Clark, *The Distribution of Wealth,* Macmillan, New York, 1899.

labor markets. This enables us to gain some understanding of the fundamental forces affecting wages and employment in a simple, frictionless labor market. There is much to be gained from this procedure.

But, more importantly, this procedure points the way to a fuller understanding of actual labor markets. By identifying as we do here the assumptions necessary to eliminate the complexities of real world labor markets, we are in a position in each of our succeeding chapters to replace one at a time these simplifying assumptions with realistic assumptions. As we do so we encounter increasing complexity, but the nature of the complexity is clearly identified. Thus, as we proceed through the book, our understanding of actual labor markets is continuously increased.

3.1

THE MARKET DEMAND FOR LABOR

If the demand curve, the schedule of VMPP, shows the amount of labor the firm would choose to employ at various alternative wage rates, what then determines the market wage rate? The answer requires the definition of the market (or economywide) demand for labor. The scope of that market depends on the assumptions that we make about the nature of that market. For the purposes of this chapter only, we make the following assumptions.

1. All labor is homogeneous. This means that all workers have the same level of skill and can transfer from one job to another in the economy without incurring any training costs. Employers will regard all workers as perfect substitutes for each other.
2. All workers have perfect knowledge and mobility. Thus, for example, all workers have perfect knowledge about job opportunities throughout the economy and there is no cost of movement from one geographical location to another, either for employees or employers.
3. All jobs are assumed to be equally agreeable (or disagreeable).
4. All employers are perfectly competitive in both product markets and markets for factors of production.
5. The size of the labor force is given. Thus, the quantity of labor available for work is assumed to be given and is insensitive to the wage rate.
6. The level of aggregate demand is given.
7. All product prices and wages are perfectly flexible.

Under this set of assumptions there will be one and only one labor market in the entire economy.

The VMPP curve of the firm was described in the previous chapter as labor's marginal physical product MPP multiplied by product price P for each possible level of labor input. Because of the law of diminishing returns, MPP declined with increasing employment of labor. However, product price was taken as given, or in other words, unaffected by the quantity of labor employed by the firm. Indeed, for a single firm in a competitive industry, the increased output resulting from an increased use of labor can be sold without affecting the market price of the product. We were thus correct in defining a single firm's demand curve for labor in terms of a constant product price.

When we derive an industry's demand curve for labor, on the other hand, we must recognize that a change in employment and hence output which takes place across an entire industry does affect product price. To illustrate this point, we first derive an industry demand curve for labor as if product price were unaffected by changes in the industry's employment. We then illustrate the effect of a changing product price.

With a constant product price, the industry demand curve for labor is simply the sum of the quantities of labor demanded by each of the firms in the industry at each particular wage rate. In Fig. 3.1 we illustrate a hypothetical industry which for simplicity we assume to be made up of three firms, though we recognize that a perfectly competitive industry would be made up of many more firms. If in Fig. 3.1 we sum the quantities of labor demanded at each wage rate by the *firms* in panels *a*, *b*, and *c*, we arrive at the *industry* demand curve for labor in panel *d*. Stated otherwise, the industry demand or VMPP curve for labor is simply the sum of the VMPP schedules of the individual firms in the industry. The industry's demand curve is the value of marginal physical product for the industry as a whole.

The downward slope of the industry demand curve for labor demonstrates that the lower the wage rate, the greater will be the industry's employment of labor, *ceteris paribus,* and the greater will be the

Figure 3.1. The derivation of industry demand for labor: constant product price. The industry demand for labor is found by summing the quantities of labor demanded by each of the firms in the industry at each possible wage. The industry VMPP schedule is then the sum of the VMPP schedules of all firms in the industry.

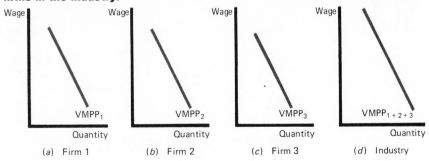

| (a) Firm 1 | (b) Firm 2 | (c) Firm 3 | (d) Industry |

industry's output. But because the demand curve for the industry's product is also a negative function of product prices, we know that any increased output can be sold only at a lower product price. We now take this price effect into account.

If the wage rate were to be lowered for all firms in an industry, all firms would wish to increase their employment of labor up to the point where the VMPP of labor in each firm is equal to the now lower wage rate. If each firm increases employment, the total supply of output of the industry increases and product price falls. Because for each firm VMPP $=P \cdot$ MPP, the lower product price will shift each firm's VMPP schedule downward. Consequently, the industry's response to a fall in the wage rate will be less than it would be if product price did not change.

Figure 3.2 illustrates this process. The curve ΣVMPP$_1$ is the sum of the VMPP schedules of the three firms in the industry at the initial product price. The initial wage rate is W_1. At this wage rate, industrywide employment of labor is N_1. Now suppose that the wage rate falls to W_2. If each firm desires to expand employment out to the profit-maximizing level, given the initial product price, the total quantity of labor demanded by the industry would be N^*. However, the necessary fall in product price would lower every firm's VMPP schedule with the result that the sum of the firms' VMPP schedules shifts downward to ΣVMPP$_2$. Consequently the quantity of labor finally demanded by the industry at W_2 is N_2.

Figure 3.2. Industry demand for labor: Variable Product Price. At each possible wage rate, a different product price will prevail. $\sum$VMPP$_1$ and $\sum$VMPP$_2$ are the sums of firm VMPP schedules at product prices P_1 and P_2 respectively. P_1 and P_2 are the product prices that prevail at wage rates W_1 and W_2 respectively. The industry demand or VMPP schedule, D, shows the quantity of labor that will be demanded by the industry at each possible wage rate.

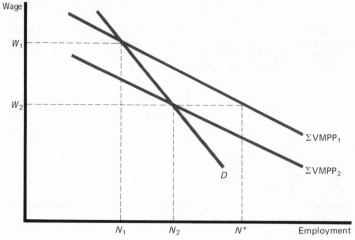

For every possible wage rate there will be a corresponding product price and ΣVMPP curve. Figure 3.2 illustrates two of them. For every wage rate there will be a quantity of labor demanded by the industry which will be determined by the point of intersection of the wage rate and the ΣVMPP curve associated with that wage rate. The locus of all such points is the industry demand curve which we label D in Fig. 3.2. The industry demand curve for labor is the value of the marginal physical product (VMPP) schedule for the industry: it indicates the market value of the additional output associated with an increased use of labor by the industry. But it is not simply the sum of the VMPP schedules of the individual firms in the industry.

Having derived the industry demand curve for labor, we can now deduce the labor demand curve for the entire labor market. Although the economy consists of many industries, let us for the moment assume it to be made up of three industries, I, II, and III. If at each possible wage rate we sum the quantities of labor demanded in the three industries, we have derived the market demand curve for labor. The derivation of the market demand curve is illustrated in Fig. 3.3. This market demand curve can be thought of as a value of marginal physical product schedule of labor for the economy as a whole.

The given supply of labor is illustrated in Fig. 3.3 by the vertical line labeled S. Combining the market demand for and supply of labor enables us to determine the equilibrium wage rate. The equilibrium wage rate will be that wage rate for which the quantity of labor demanded is equal to the quantity of labor supplied. In Fig. 3.3 it is the wage rate W_e. For each industry the quantity of labor that will be demanded at a wage of W_e can be determined from the individual industry demand curves. Recall that industry demand curves show the

Figure 3.3. Market demand and supply: determination of the market wage rate. The market demand for labor is found by adding, at each possible wage rate, the quantities of labor demanded by each of the industries in the market. The industry demand curves are D_I, D_{II}, and D_{III}. The market wage rate W_e is determined by the interaction of market demand $D_{I+II+III}$ and the market supply of labor S.

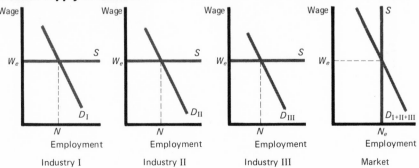

sum of the quantities of labor demanded by the firms in that industry, as we demonstrated in the discussion of Fig. 3.2. Hence, all the firms in the economy face a perfectly elastic supply of labor at the wage rate W_e. Each firm then reacts to the market-determined wage rate by employing the profit-maximizing quantities of labor.

3.2

EQUILIBRIUM IN THE LABOR MARKET

The concept of equilibrium is that of "no net tendency to change." In equilibrium all economic agents will have made full adjustments to economic circumstances as they exist and will have no net tendency to change.

In Fig. 3.4 W_e is the equilibrium wage and N_e is the volume of employment. We might ask what would happen if the market wage rate for whatever reason were above the equilibrium wage rate, say at W_1. At this wage rate the total quantity of labor demanded, N_1, would be less than the quantity supplied; some persons wishing to work would be unemployed. Workers would compete against each other for the available jobs, and such competition would force the wage downward. The reduced wage rate would induce employers to hire more labor. The wage rate would continue to fall and employment continue to increase until the excess supply of labor (unemployment) is eliminated. Equilibrium is restored when the wage rate falls to W_e and total employment expands to N_e.

Figure 3.4. Equilibrium in the labor market. The equilibrium wage rate is W_e. At a wage rate of W_1, there is an excess supply of labor. At a wage rate of W_2, there is an excess demand for labor.

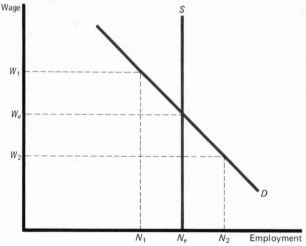

On the other hand, what would happen if the market wage rate were below the equilibrium wage rate, say at W_2? In this case the quantity of labor that the firms in the market would demand, N_2, would exceed the total quantity of labor supplied. Each employer in trying to increase his or her work force would have to offer wages higher than the existing wage so as to bid workers away from the other firms. In this manner competition among employers causes the market wage to rise, and the rising wage reduces the quantity of labor demanded by each firm. The wage rate rises until equilibrium is restored at the wage rate of W_e and employment of N_e.

3.3

IMPLICATIONS OF THE BASIC MODEL

The basic model has implications with respect to the efficient allocation of labor within the economy, wage differences in the economy, full employment, and wage levels. Let us spell them out briefly.

3.3a

Allocative efficiency

The basic model leads to the conclusion that, in equilibrium, the wage rate of labor will be equal to its aggregate VMPP. Further, because the wage rate is equal for all firms, the VMPP of labor will be equal across all firms. The equality of VMPP across all firms assures that total value of output of the economy (or gross national product) will be the maximum that can be produced given the state of technology and the supplies of labor and capital. To see why output would be at a maximum, refer to Fig. 3.3 and assume initially that all firms in each of the three industries are in equilibrium. What would happen if one worker were to leave a firm in industry I and go to work for a firm in industry II (ignoring the fact that the owner of the firm in industry II would not want to hire the person at the market wage)? The value of the marginal physical product attributable to the one worker given up by the firm in industry I would be equal to the wage rate W_e. But because of the diminishing marginal productivity of labor, adding one more worker to a firm in industry II will increase the value of that firm's total output by an amount less than W_e. If the *reduction* of the output of industry I is greater than the *increase* in the output of industry II, then total output for society must be less than before. The same will be true for any allocation of labor across firms other than the allocation depicted in Fig. 3.3.

3.3b

No wage differences

Another implication of the basic model is that there will be no geographical, industrial, or occupational wage differences. Wages could not be higher, in equilibrium, in one region of the country than in another because workers would seek out their best opportunities. With perfect knowledge and in the absence of any prior investment in the skills specific to their current jobs, workers would always migrate to the highest-paying region. Figure 3.5 illustrates the effect of labor migration on regional wages. Suppose that initial wages W_1 are higher in region A than in region B because of differences in the relative abundances of labor and capital in the two regions. The existence of the higher wage in region A will lead workers to leave region B for region A, thereby reducing the supply of labor in region B to S_{B2} and increasing the supply of labor in region A to S_{A2}. These supply shifts cause wages to rise in region B and to fall in region A. Migration will continue to erode the wage differentials until wages in both regions converge to the mutual equilibrium wage W_e.

A convergence of regional wages also could be accomplished by the movement of capital, even in the absence of labor migration. We stated previously that the VMPP of labor is greater the larger the stock of capital with which labor works. The implications of capital flows for regional wages are demonstrated in Fig. 3.6. Again we assume that the wage rate is initially higher in region A. Some entrepreneurs in region A will move their capital to region B in order to take advantage of the lower labor costs there. The increase in the stock of capital in region B will raise the demand for labor (the regional VMPP schedule) in region B, thus raising wages in that region. At the same time the reduction of the stock of capital in region A would reduce the value of labor's marginal

---

Figure 3.5. The elimination of regional wage differences by labor migration. If the original wage rate W_1 is higher in region A than in region B, the supply of labor in region A, S_{A1}, will be increased by the migration of labor from region B to region A. The supply of labor in region B is reduced from S_{B1} to S_{B2}, and equality of wages across the two regions is established at W_e.

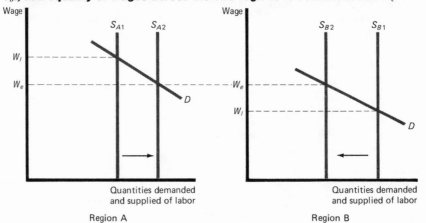

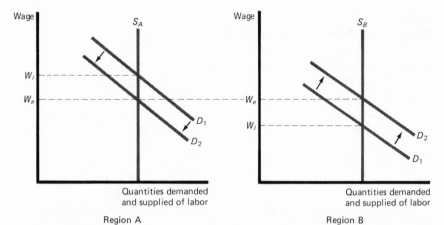

Figure 3.6. The elimination of regional wage differences by capital movement. A higher wage in region A than in region B results in a movement of capital from region A to region B. The increased capital stock in region B raises the demand for labor and consequently the wage rate. The opposite changes occur in region B.

physical product (and thus wages) in that region. Movement of either labor or capital would thus lead to a convergence of regional wage levels.

The same reasoning that led us to conclude that, given our assumptions, regional wage levels would converge can be used to explain why there would tend to be no industrial or occupational wage differences. Suppose that the two graphs, Figs. 3.5 and 3.6, represent two different industries instead of two different regions. If wages are higher in industry A than in industry B, there would be a movement of workers from B to A, thereby causing wages in A and B to move toward equality. A similar example could be illustrated for the case of occupational wage differences. In this case also, movement of workers would tend to equalize wage rates.

3.3c
Full employment
Another conclusion of the model is that competition among employers and among workers produces a wage rate which, in equilibrium, results in full employment. Looking at Fig. 3.4, we can visualize a situation where the wage rate is above the equilibrium wage of W_e. The difference between the quantities of labor demanded and supplied at the "too high" wage rate measures the amount of unemployment. As we have previously pointed out, competition among workers for the available jobs would result in a return of the wage rate to a level consistent with full employment.

3.3d
Determinants of the general level of wages

The basic model leads us instantly to a recognition of why general wage *levels* vary across economies and within the same economy at different times. Why are wage levels in the United States higher than they are in India? Why are wage levels in the United States today higher than they were in 1900? The general level of wages always depends on the economy's capital stock relative to the population. Given the population in the United States today, wage levels would be higher than they are if the capital stock were larger. Similarly, India's wage level would be higher, given its existing capital stock, if its population were less than it is. Economists have always pointed to an economy's capital stock relative to its population as the basic determinant of wage levels within the economy.

3.4

THE ASSUMPTIONS OF THE BASIC MODEL REEXAMINED: THE PLAN OF THE BOOK

The model we have presented depicts a world of equality of wages, full employment, and absolute efficiency in the allocation of the labor resource. By specifying the assumptions that must be made in order to arrive at these outcomes, we spotlight the factors that distinguish the complex world about us from the simplified world of our basic model. By relaxing in subsequent chapters the simplifying assumptions we have made to arrive at these outcomes, we proceed to develop a much richer model that explains the characteristics of real world labor markets. But we reach a fuller understanding a step at a time.

Alfred Marshall was one of the earliest critics of the marginal productivity theory of wages and employment. In essence Marshall criticized the assumption of a fixed supply of labor. The marginal productivity theory, Marshall contended, is a theory of the demand for labor. To use Marshall's analogy, it is as incorrect to view demand as determining wages as it is to view the upper blade of a pair of scissors as doing the cutting. To have a complete theory of wages we must also have a theory of the supply of labor because it is the interaction of demand and supply that determines wage levels. In Chap. 4 we relax the assumption of a fixed supply of labor in the short run. In that chapter we see that the quantity of work that an individual supplies is a choice variable. Just as producers make choices about the quantity of labor demanded given a particular wage rate, so too will individual household members make choices in response to their potential wage rate.

For any given population, there will be a relation between the wage rate and the quantity of labor supplied. In Chap. 5 we examine the long-run supply of labor, dropping the assumption of a fixed population. We will see that the size of the population is not determined entirely

outside of the economic system, but is influenced by economic variables. In Chaps. 4 and 5 the total supply of labor is derived from
individual choices of hours of work. But for some individuals the choice
will be to supply no hours of work at all to the market. Particularly in
Chap. 4 we analyze the factors influencing the decision to enter or exit
the labor force. Labor force participation will be viewed as a decision
involving the allocation of time in competing uses: market labor,
household production, schooling, and leisure. The demographic characteristics associated with those people who choose to be or not to be in
the labor force will also be examined.

Labor demand and labor supply are brought together in Chap. 6.
Once the interactive effects of demand and supply are understood, it is
possible to examine a number of dynamic considerations such as the
connection between capital growth and per capita income, and between
population growth and wage levels. We also give attention to the
interaction between product and labor markets and to the determinants
of the elasticity of demand for labor.

The conclusion in our basic model that all wages will be equal in
equilibrium depends critically on several of the assumptions that we
made. Most critical was the assumption of homogeneity of labor. Once
we relax the assumption that workers are equally skilled and that those
skills can be transferred without cost from one occupation to another, the
conclusion that wages will tend toward equality must be modified. Nor
will we expect wages to tend toward equality if we relax the assumption
that all workers have the same preferences and regard all work as
equally pleasant or unpleasant. In the world, differences in skill levels of
workers is the major factor explaining permanent differences in occupational wage rates. In Chap. 7 we examine the relationship of education,
training, and experience to wage levels. In Chap. 8 we examine the
effect of varying working conditions and tastes and preferences on
occupational wage rates.

In Chap. 9 we relax the assumptions of perfect knowledge and
costless movement of workers. As we shall see, the realization that
neither the acquisition of information nor the movement of workers is
costless leads us to predict that there will be occupational, industrial,
and regional differences in wage rates that may be transitory, not
permanent.

In Chap. 10 we relax the assumptions that employers are perfectly
competitive in their product and labor markets. This enables us to outline
the effects of monopoly and monopsony on the allocation of labor and on
the levels of wages and employment.

We have assumed in our basic model that employers regard all
workers as perfect substitutes for each other. To the extent that workers
differ in terms of their productivities, wage differences will emerge, and
these differences will have been discussed in Chap. 7. However,
employers may discriminate among workers on the basis of factors

unrelated to skill level or productivity. Common forms of discrimination are by race and sex. The effects of race and sex discrimination on wage and employment opportunities are discussed in Chap. 11.

We have implicitly assumed in our simple model that there are no impediments such as unions or government restrictions to the allocation of labor and the determination of wages. This assumption is relaxed in Chaps. 12 and 13, where we examine the effects of labor unions on wages and employment, not only in the unionized sectors of the labor market but in the nonunion sectors as well. The effect of unionization on the size of gross national product is analyzed. The impact on the labor market of minimum wage and "right-to-work" legislation is also considered.

The basic model we have presented applies to profit-maximizing firms. The rapidly advancing importance of the government as an employer requires us to broaden the coverage of our analysis so as to include the public sector. While public sector employment has long been considered to be outside the realm of neoclassical economics, the development of an area of economic analysis known as *public choice theory* has demonstrated the applicability of the analysis of utility maximization behavior to the public sector. In Chap. 14 we apply the neoclassical framework to the wage and employment decisions in the public sector.

Our model's macroeconomic conclusion of full employment depends on assumptions 1, 2, 6, and 7 above, namely, that all labor is assumed to be homogeneous, that workers have perfect knowledge and mobility, that the level of aggregate demand is given, and that all prices and wages are flexible. In Chap. 15 on unemployment we consider the various types of unemployment that are attributable to the absence of these assumed conditions in the world. The most controversial aspects of marginal productivity theory involve the theory's macroeconomic implications. We give considerable attention to developments in neoclassical theory which emphasize disequilibrium analysis. This contrasts with the Keynesian view of unemployment as an equilibrium condition.

In Chap. 16 we analyze another macroeconomic topic, the relations between wages, employment, and inflation. From these relations we are able to outline the effect of inflation on wages and on employment. We present an analysis of the Phillips relation both in the short run and in the long run.

Marginal productivity theory has throughout its history been a vehicle for the study of the distribution of income within society. In fact, the distribution of income was the main interest of J. B. Clark and probably served as major motivation in developing the theory. More recently, the question of the distribution of income has attracted the attention of more economists than it has at any time since Clark's original discussion. Chapter 17 contains a discussion of the income distribution question, again using marginal productivity analysis as the starting point of the discussion.

Finally, in Chap. 18 we recapitulate and reflect upon the main thrusts of the neoclassical analysis of the labor market.

At this point we should step back and be reminded of the general method and purpose of this book. We begin with the simple model presented in this chapter. It is based on a number of assumptions which simplify the analysis—assumptions which are not realistic. The model is useful in itself though, because it gives us an indication of how a simple, frictionless labor market would operate. The model has the same utility as the model of perfect competition does in price theory: it provides us with a basis of comparison with the real world. As we have indicated earlier, we cannot know the effects of unionization, imperfect information, discrimination, and so forth unless we know what would happen in their absence.

The model we have thus far presented has other uses besides being simply a basis of comparison with the real world, however. It is the starting point from which we begin our description of the complexities of real world labor markets. By replacing gradually each initial assumption with one that is more realistic, we are able to arrive ultimately at a detailed understanding of how the complex labor markets of our economy work. That understanding is the goal of this book.

3.5

THE MARGINAL PRODUCTIVITY THEORY IN HISTORICAL PERSPECTIVE[2]

Our objective in this section is to indicate the major schools of thought concerning wages both prior to and after the development of the marginal productivity theory in the late nineteenth century. Ideas about what wages are or ought to be can be found throughout recorded history. However, serious theorizing of a systematic nature begins with the English classical school with which we associate the names of Adam Smith, David Ricardo, and Thomas Malthus. The *wages fund doctrine* was the cornerstone of classical wage theory.

3.5a
The wages fund, the law of population, and the iron law of wages

The wages fund doctrine is most readily understood if we view it as an argument concerning an entirely agricultural economy even though the early classical economists did not view their argument as limited to such

---

[2]This somewhat brief discussion of wage theories in historical perspective can be omitted, if one chooses, without a loss in the continuity of our argument and presentation.

an economy. The wages fund for the current period consists of the entire output of the previous period less what is removed for the entrepreneur's consumption. The fund represents the total amount that is available for wages in the present period. The current wage W is the result of dividing the wages fund F by the labor force L. Thus, $W = F/L$. Any factor such as technological improvements which changes the size of F will change the wage rate in the same direction. However, a direct extension of Malthus's law of population implies that any increase in the wage rate will bring forth an increase in the population and, ultimately, in the labor force. Hence, competition for the wages fund among the members of the larger labor force would tend to lower the wage rate. In fact, any wage rate above the subsistence level would bring forth an eventual increase in the labor force; a wage rate below the subsistence level would cause the labor force to contract because of increased numbers of deaths. The classical economists (with the major exception of Smith) thus combined the wages fund doctrine and Malthus's views on population to formulate the "iron law of wages," the position that regardless of the possibility of upward movement in wages in the short run, they would return to the subsistence level in the long run. This pessimistic view of the long-run prospects of the working class is what caused economics to be labeled the "dismal science."

Among later classical economists, most notably John Stuart Mill, the wages fund doctrine fell into disrepute. In fact, the latter half of the nineteenth century was characterized by dissatisfaction with classical analysis along several fronts. Two schools of thought emerged as reactions to classical thought: the Marxist and neoclassical schools.

3.5b

Marxism

While in many areas (particularly value theory) Marxism constitutes a radical departure from classical economics, Marxist wage theory is very close to that of the earlier classical economists such as Ricardo. To Marx the wage rate under capitalism is limited in the long run to the subsistence level. There is a question as to whether Marx's definition of the subsistence wage is compatible with the classical economists' conception of subsistence. Is it a wage determined solely by physical requirements of survival (as with the classical economists) and therefore invariant over time? Or is it partly determined by the customs of society and therefore subject to change over time? That question is still debated.

More important in Marxian analysis is the role of labor in the creation of value. Marx viewed all value as attributable to labor, capital being nothing more than the stored-up productive power of past labor. Again, this labor theory of value is similar to that of the early classical economists. The treatment of capital as a distinct source of value is attributable to the neoclassical (or marginalist) school.

3.5c
The neoclassicists and the marginal revolution

The development of marginal productivity theory was part of a larger development in value theory: the so-called marginalist revolution. Whereas the classical economists had viewed cost of production as the determinant of product price, the early marginalists conceived of marginal utility, i.e., demand, as the determinant of product price. The wage of labor was conceived to be determined by the demand for labor, represented by the value of the marginal physical product of labor. It is the earlier marginalist wage theory that we have presented in the earlier part of this chapter. Later neoclassical analysis, particularly that of Alfred Marshall, viewed value as being determined by the interaction of demand (utility) and supply (cost of production). This is, of course, the standard approach of modern economics. Similarly, the wage rate was viewed as the result of the interaction of demand and supply. This neoclassical theory of wages and employment, with significant modification, continues to be the mainstream approach to the analysis of the labor market. However, the predominance of neoclassical labor theory has by no means been continuous.

3.5d
The Keynesian revolution, bargaining theories, and Institutional economics

The acceptance of the macroeconomic implications of neoclassical economics was virtually eliminated by the serious economic depression of the 1930s. An important conclusion of neoclassical theory is that the economy is in equilibrium only at full employment. Although neoclassical economists are often caricatured as having believed unemployment to be impossible, such a belief is inaccurate. Neoclassical economists of the early twentieth century were very much aware of the possibility of unemployment, but they viewed it as a *disequilibrium* phenomenon. However, the tenacity and duration of the extremely high levels of unemployment severely damaged the belief in a theory which viewed the existence of unemployment as a disequilibrium situation, and by implication, a temporary problem. The British economist John Maynard Keynes provided a theory designed to explain how an economy could be in equilibrium at less than full employment. The Keynesian view of macroeconomics quickly became the dominant view, and in modified form remains so.

The key feature in the Keynesian explanation of unemployment equilibrium is the concept of rigid, inflexible wages. In the Keynesian view wages do not respond to excess supply. In effect, the existing wage rate becomes an exogenous (or given) variable, below which all labor will be withheld from the market. The treatment of the wage rate as determined outside of the macroeconomic system opened the way for the development and acceptance of noneconomic theories of wage determination. These theories ranged from extensions of the Institution-alist school's approach to the game-theoretic approach. Both of these approaches view wage determination as a matter concerning the relative strength of unions and management. Heavy emphasis is placed on the structure of collective bargaining. In extreme form, the various bargain-ing theories treat the wage determination process as developing in isolation from market forces. In fact, the domination of the field of labor economics by Institutional economists during the 1940s and 1950s led to the isolation of labor economics from the mainstream of economic thought. The efforts of labor economists during this period seemed neither to affect nor to be affected by developments in the other areas of economics. One of the many unfortunate consequences of this isolation was the development by labor economists of views on the determination of inflation that are simply inconsistent with general equilibrium analy-sis, whether of the Keynesian or neoclassical varieties.

3.5e
The resurgence of neoclassical analysis of labor markets
Despite the dominance of the Institutionalist and bargaining theory approaches for over a quarter of a century, the neoclassical tradition in labor economics remained alive among a minority of labor economists. During the late 1950s and early 1960s the neoclassical approach began to regain its former preeminence in labor economics. The collective bargaining approach was further displaced by the development of "dual labor market" and "radical" approaches, the former being an outgrowth of the earlier Institutional approach, and the latter a modern version of Marxism. The neoclassical labor economics of the 1960s and 1970s, labeled by some as the "new labor economics," emerged in much more enriched form than the pre-Keynesian version of neoclassical econom-ics. Further, the new labor economists benefited from the influence of Institutional labor economics. Neoclassical economists extended their method into the analysis of collective bargaining, discrimination, popu-lation growth, and a number of other areas that had been ignored by pre-Keynesian neoclassical economists.

By the 1970s labor economics had clearly returned to the main-stream of economic theory. As a result, labor economists have been influenced by and have contributed to developments in other areas of economics, particularly macroeconomics. For example, the literature on the long-run and short-run tradeoffs between inflation and unemploy-ment is really the joint product of labor economics and monetary economics. At the same time, in the area of macroeconomics, the division between Keynesians and neoclassical economists has become for the most part unsubstantial. Modern macroeconomics, though di-verse and in a state of flux, is actually a combination of the Keynesian and neoclassical contributions. Few macroeconomists would today feel comfortable with either label. Hence, what is taught in modern courses in macroeconomics is no longer inconsistent with what is taught in modern labor economics courses. The collective bargaining approach continues to prosper, but its chief field of operation today (at least in an academic setting) is in departments of industrial relations and personnel management.

QUESTIONS AND EXERCISES

1. The following table presents hypothetical quantities of labor demanded for the three firms in Fig. 3.1 at several possible wage rates. Construct a labor demand schedule for the entire industry assuming that product price remains constant.

Wage	D_1	D_2	D_3
$10	2	3	5
$ 8	4	5	6
$ 6	6	7	7

2. Again assuming that product price remains constant, what would be the market wage rate if the supply of labor is perfectly inelastic at 15 workers and our hypothetical industry is the only industry in the market?

3. We concluded in Sec. 3.1 that an increase in the output of an industry results in a fall in product price which further results in a fall in each firm's VMPP schedule. What factors influence the extent to which each firm's VMPP shifts downward?

4. Referring to Fig. 3.4, what would be the effect on the equilibrium wage rate of an increase in the MPP of labor due either to an increased capital stock or to technological change? What will be the effect on the wage rate of an increase in the supply of labor?

5. If you know that the average propensity to save (the proportion of national income that is saved) is higher in Japan than in the United States, in which country would you expect the wage rate to grow more rapidly? Why?

REFERENCES FOR FURTHER READING

For a discussion of some criticisms of marginal productivity theory, see A. Cartter, *Theory of Wages and Employment,* Irwin, Homewood, III., 1959, chap. 4.

An assessment of the position of J. B. Clark in the history of economics is contained in the appendix to chap. 13 of R. B. Ekelund, Jr., and R. H. Hebert, *A History of Economic Theory and Method,* McGraw-Hill, New York, 1975.

A thorough but nontechnical treatment of Marxian economics is provided by A. Balinky, *Marx's Economics,* Heath, Lexington, Mass., 1970.

THE SUPPLY OF
LABOR IN THE SHORT RUN

In the basic model of wages and employment developed in Chap. 3, we made the simplifying assumption that the total quantity of labor supplied to the economy was given and that this total quantity was insensitive to changes in the market wage. In this and the following chapter we relax this simplifying assumption in order to establish the relation between the market wage and the quantity of labor supplied. This is the study of *labor supply.* We see that the total quantity of labor supplied by household members in an economy is indeed a function of the market wage and that changes in the total quantity of labor are related in systematic ways to changes in wages.

The total quantity of labor supplied to an economy depends on (1) the size of the population, (2) the percentage of that population that chooses to be in the labor force, and (3) the hours that labor force participants choose to supply. Further, each of these three components of the total quantity of labor supplied depends on market wages. Thus, we see immediately that labor supply is inherently a complex phenomenon. Nonetheless, we can make progress in our understanding of labor supply by making one important simplifying assumption which holds for this chapter, namely, that the size of the population is given. Thus, in this chapter we analyze how both the percentage of a *given* population that chooses to be in the labor force, as well as the hours that those labor force participants choose to supply, depend on market wages. This is the study of labor supply in the short run.

The short run always refers to that period of time during which some adjustments are not possible, where some circumstances cannot be altered. In Chap. 2, when we presented the neoclassical theory of the firm, we analyzed the firm's demand for labor during that period of time when the firm could not alter its input of capital. In this chapter we make a similar assumption: we assume a period of time during which individuals in a given population cannot alter the amount of their human capital. Thus, we assume most importantly that the skills of household members are given. Further, we rule out other adjustments, such as migration, that individuals can and do make to changes in wages. What we examine, then, is how individuals in a given population with given skills choose the best quantity of hours to supply to market activities so as to maximize total utility, as well as how individuals adjust the hours they supply as economic circumstances change.

We begin by outlining in some detail a traditional utility maximization model of individual choice in order to see that the hours supplied of labor are a function of market wages. We then turn our attention to the second dimension of labor supply examined here—the decision to enter or leave the labor force. Because the concept of the labor force has a very precise meaning in labor economics, our discussion of labor force participation is preceded by a detailed examination of this concept. We conclude our discussion of labor supply in the short run by developing a market supply of labor in which the total quantity of labor supplied to an economy is seen to be the result of both the hours choice and the participation choice by individuals.

In Chap. 5 we turn our attention to labor supply in the long run. As always, the long run is the concept of more complete adjustment. Thus, we examine there how utility-maximizing household members adjust the quantity of labor supplied over time as market wages change over time. Part of their adjustment will be an hours adjustment. But part of their adjustment will consist of changes in the labor force status of some family members. In particular, the most dramatic changes in the United States have been in the increasing labor force participation of married women, and in the decreasing labor force participation of both teenagers and older workers.

The hours adjustment and the labor force adjustment that we will discuss are from individuals in existing households of given size. But the average size of households in the United States has declined over time in response to the secular rise in market wages. Why have individuals in the United States (and in other high-income countries as well) chosen to have smaller numbers of children? In particular, how can we understand the relation between rising market wages and smaller average family size? A complete discussion of labor supply in the long run must analyze this fertility decision, because as we have seen, the total quantity of labor supplied to an economy depends on population size.

Labor supply in the long run is inherently somewhat more complex than the same relation in the short run. Accordingly, we present a more powerful analytical model to help understand those complexities. The model which we present and use in Chap. 5 is the model of the allocation of time developed by Gary S. Becker.[1] The Becker model is a neoclassical model, and in Chap. 5 we stress the similarities between that model and the traditional model which we present in the following section of this chapter. But there are important differences as well. Our decision to present and use the Becker model is primarily because it aids understanding of long-run labor supply. But its use also illustrates that the neoclassical model is not handed down unchanged through the years. While it maintains its essential organizing principles of choice and costs, it can be elaborated and extended to yield particularly fruitful insights into household decision making.

We begin our discussion of labor supply in the short run with a model of individual choice. This model will enable us to understand how utility-maximizing household members adjust the quantity of labor they supply as wages change.

4.1
A UTILITY MAXIMIZATION MODEL OF INDIVIDUAL CHOICE

In a model of individual choice, it is useful to divide the goods that a household member consumes into two mutually exclusive and exhaustive groups—market goods and nonmarket time. Because nonmarket time is treated as a good, the difference between the total time available to the individual and the amount of that total time the individual chooses to consume as nonmarket time will represent hours supplied to market activities.

The utility individuals receive from various combinations of nonmarket time and market goods can be illustrated by the use of an analytical tool known as *indifference curves.*

4.1a
Utility

Consider Fig. 4.1. In the figure, point A is a combination of two goods, $0Y$ market goods and $0X$ nonmarket time. From consuming this combination of the two goods, the individual receives some amount of total utility. If the individual consumed combination B, would total utility be greater than from consuming combination A? Yes, because combination B contains no less market goods (that amount is still $0Y$) but more of the other goods, $0X'$ nonmarket time. Because total utility depends on consumption, the individual's total utility is clearly greater. Further, the individual receives greater total utility from any combination of nonmar-

---

[1]Gary S. Becker, "A Theory of the Allocation of Time," *Economic Journal,* vol. 75, September 1965, pp. 493–517.

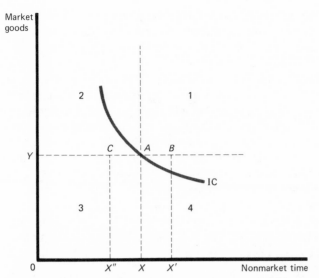

Figure 4.1. An indifference curve for an individual. An indifference curve passing through combination A will contain combinations of the two goods which lie in quadrants 2 and 4.

ket time and market goods in quadrant 1 than from combination A. This is true because each combination in quadrant 1 contains more of at least one of the goods. Most combinations, of course, contain more of both goods. Thus, any combination in quadrant 1 is preferred to combination A.

What about combination C relative to combination A? Both combinations contain the same amount of market goods, $0Y$, but combination C contains less nonmarket time, $0X''$, than does combination A. C, then, is inferior to A because the total utility associated with C is less. Further, any combination in quadrant 3 yields less total utility than does combination A, because each combination in quadrant 3 contains less of at least one good. Most combinations, of course, contain less of both goods.

This leads us, then, to a consideration of all those combinations which yield the individual the same amount of total utility. These combinations will always contain more of one good *but less of the other.* These combinations will lie in quadrants 2 and 4, and can be connected by a line called an *indifference curve.* An indifference curve, then, always has a negative slope and contains all those combinations of nonmarket time and market goods which yield the individual the same amount of total utility. It is because total utility is constant along an indifference curve that individuals are "indifferent" to the various combinations which lie on the curve. As far as the individual is concerned, the loss in total utility from consuming less of one good is exactly offset by the gain in total utility from consuming more of the other good. Thus, the slope of an indifference curve measures the rate at which the individual *is willing* to make substitutions in consumption while keeping total utility unchanged.

Individuals differ in the rate at which they are willing to substitute nonmarket time for market goods. Such differences are attributable to differences in tastes and preferences for the two goods. Some individuals may have a preference for market goods over nonmarket time, while others may have the opposite preference. We are able to illustrate such differences in tastes and preferences by varying the slope of indifference curves. Consider Fig. 4.2. The individual represented in Fig. 4.2*a* has a strong preference for nonmarket time over market goods as compared with the individual represented in Fig. 4.2*b.* We know this because of the larger amount of market goods that the first individual is willing to give up to achieve a given increase *XX'* in nonmarket time.

We can readily generalize our discussion of the total utility an

---

Figure 4.2. Differences in slopes of indifference curves reflect differences in tastes and preferences. The individual represented in panel a has a stronger preference for nonmarket time than does the individual represented in panel b. We know this because of the larger amount of market goods YY' he or she is willing to give up to attain a given increase XX' of nonmarket time.

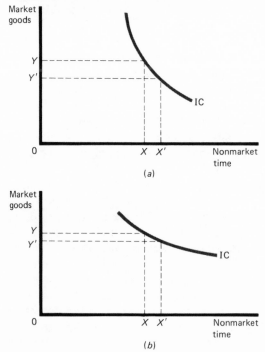

individual receives from various combinations of nonmarket time and market goods. Will there be some combinations which yield the same amount of total utility as combination B? Surely, and all such combinations will lie on a negatively sloped indifference curve which passes through combination B. Whereas the individual is indifferent to any combination along the indifference curve passing through B, any of these combinations is preferred to any combinations on the indifference curve passing through A. Why? Because the individual preferred combination B to combination A to begin with.

We have illustrated in Fig. 4.3 only three of many such indifference curves. This "family" of indifference curves represents some important characteristics of individuals. First, indifference curves are "everywhere dense." This means simply that every possible combination of the two goods will lie on some indifference curve. Second, indifference curves do not intersect. An individual will not prefer a combination on a higher indifference curve to a combination on a lower indifference curve, yet simultaneously be indifferent to a combination which lies on both. Lastly, note that each indifference curve is not a straight line, but rather is convex with respect to the origin. If an indifference curve were a straight line, what would it represent about the individual? We know from mathematics that the slope of a straight line is constant. Thus, if an indifference curve were a straight line, it would indicate that an individual could maintain a given level of total utility by substituting nonmarket time for market goods at a constant rate. But this violates the law of

---

Figure 4.3. A "family" of indifference curves for an individual. Only three of many possible indifference curves are illustrated here. Each possible combination of the two goods will lie on some indifference curve.

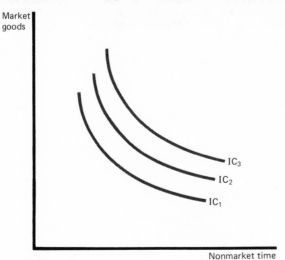

diminishing marginal utility. We explained in Chap. 1 that, given tastes and preferences, additional quantities of any good consumed yield less and less additions to total utility. Individuals will not be willing to give up constant amounts of nonmarket time to attain additional quantities of market goods, for example, when those additional amounts of market goods yield less and less marginal utility. Consequently, indifference curves will not be straight lines, but will be convex with respect to the origin. The convexity of indifference curves illustrates the fact that individuals will indeed be willing to substitute one good for another, but only at a declining rate.

What is it, then, that prevents individuals from achieving infinitely large levels of total utility? In terms of Fig. 4.3, why don't individuals choose a combination on the highest indifference curve? They surely can attain higher levels of total utility if they do. The reason is that they are constrained. Let us look, then, at the constraints facing individuals as labor suppliers.

4.1b
The constraints
What amount of nonmarket time could an individual consume if he or she spent all the available time in nonmarket activities? It depends on the time frame for analysis, 24 hours a day, 7 days a week, 52 weeks a year, or the years in a lifetime. In any event, there is the concept of some maximum amount of nonmarket time available to each individual, and this is a constraint. This is the quantity $0X$ in Fig. 4.4. What amount of

---

Figure 4.4. A budget constraint for an individual. The line XY is a budget constraint. It contains the maximum combinations that the individual can attain. The slope of the budget constraint, $\Delta Y/\Delta X$, is the wage rate, the rate that nonmarket time can be substituted for market goods.

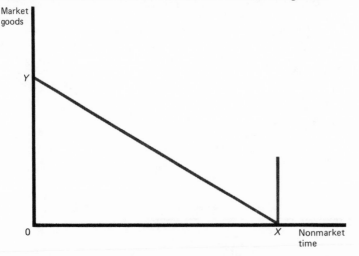

market goods could an individual consume if he or she spent all the available time in market activity? This depends on another constraint facing the individual, the market wage for an individual with his or her talents and skills. Given that wage, the maximum amount of market goods that the individual could consume if all the available time were spent in market activity is $0Y$. The straight line XY is the *budget constraint* and contains the maximum combinations of market goods and nonmarket time that the individual can attain. The slope of the budget constraint is the wage rate. It illustrates the rate at which this individual can transform nonmarket time into market goods ($4 of market goods per hour, for example). The fact that the budget constraint is a straight line illustrates that this rate is assumed to be constant.

4.1c
The best combination: Utility maximization given the constraints

Which of the combinations of nonmarket time and market goods that the individual can attain will be chosen? The best combination is that which will provide the individual with the most total utility, the combination lying on the highest attainable indifference curve. This is combination U in Fig. 4.5, the combination for which the budget constraint is tangent to ("touches") indifference curve IC2. Notice that combination T is attainable but is not chosen. Notice also that combination V is preferred to U,

---

Figure 4.5. The utility-maximizing combination of the two goods. Combination U is the utility-maximizing combination of market goods and nonmarket time. This combination contains 0Y' market goods and 0X' nonmarket time. If the individual consumes 0X' of the total nonmarket time available (0X), then X'X is the quantity of labor supplied.

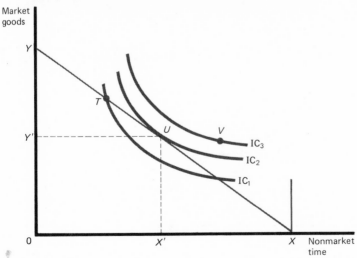

but is not attainable. Given this individual's tastes and preferences and the constraints that he or she faces, the utility-maximizing combination is U, the attainable combination for which total utility is at a maximum. This combination contains $0Y'$ market goods and $0X'$ nonmarket time. Thus, hours supplied is the quantity $X'X$.

One feature of this result bears further discussion. At U in Fig. 4.5, the slope of the budget constraint necessarily equals the slope of the indifference curve. We have already seen that the slope of the budget constraint is the rate at which hours can be transformed into market goods, i.e., the wage rate. The slope of the indifference curve is interpreted somewhat differently. As Fig. 4.6 indicates, the slope of the indifference curve between A and B is G_1G/H_1H. But combinations A and B are both on the same indifference curve. Because both combinations A and B yield the same amount of total utility, it has to be the case that the increase in the quantity of market goods multiplied by the marginal utility of those market goods is exactly offset by the decrease in hours multiplied by the marginal utility of those hours:

$$(dG)(\mathrm{MU}_G) = (dH)(\mathrm{MU}_H) \tag{4.1}$$

Rearranging, we have

$$\frac{dG}{dH} = \text{wage rate} = \frac{\mathrm{MU}_H}{\mathrm{MU}_G} \tag{4.2}$$

Figure 4.6. Interpreting the slope of an indifference curve. Because combinations A and B are on the same indifference curve, the gain in total utility from consuming more market goods (G_1G) offsets the decline in total utility from consuming less nonmarket time (H_1H) so that total utility remains unchanged.

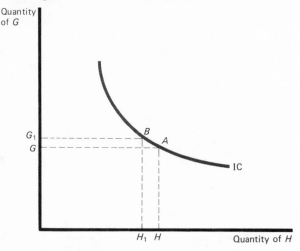

Thus, for the best combination, the wage rate is equal to the ratio of the marginal utilities of hours to market goods. In an important sense, the rate at which the individual is willing to make substitutions in consumption is equal to the rate at which he or she can.

4.1d
Changing the constraints

If combination U in Fig. 4.5 is best given the individual's tastes and preferences and the constraints he or she faces, it will not continue to be best as constraints change. Let us examine, then, changes in hours worked as the constraints change.

Changes in income: The income effect What will be the effect on hours worked of an increase in nonlabor income? This is a question that has very practical policy implications in the United States today, for we have been experimenting with various programs designed to provide individuals with income which is independent of hours worked. In Fig. 4.7 we illustrate an increase in income by shifting the budget constraint outward parallel to the original budget constraint. Notice that now, even if individuals choose all the available time, $0X$, as nonmarket time, they could still consume some market goods, the quantity XT. This is due to nonlabor income, income which is received independent of hours worked. We are able to predict that hours worked will decline, *ceteris paribus*, if nonlabor income increases. The best amount of nonmarket time increases from $0X'$ to $0X''$. Thus, hours supplied decline by $X'\,X''$.

Figure 4.7. A pure income effect. An increase in nonlabor income increases the quantity consumed of nonmarket time by X'X". Thus, hours supplied decline by the same amount.

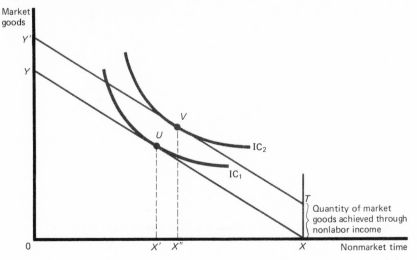

This is an illustration of a pure *income effect*. This effect states that as income increases, individuals purchase more of all "normal" goods. If nonmarket time is a normal good (and evidence suggests that it is), then individuals unambiguously choose larger quantities of it as their incomes increase.

Changes in the wage rate: The substitution (relative price) effect Another constraint that can change is the rate at which the individual can transform nonmarket time into market goods, i.e., the wage rate. Let us change this rate and examine how the individual adjusts hours supplied. We want to understand how changes in this rate *acting alone* change the individual's behavior. This means, then, that he or she is not allowed to become (for these purposes) better off as a result of the wage increase. Thus, we keep total utility the same by confining the individual to a given indifference curve. We illustrate this procedure in Fig. 4.8.

We have shown three different wage rates in Fig. 4.8. At the initial wage, the best combination is A, and X_1X represents hours supplied. As the wage successively rises, combination B, then C, becomes the best combination. Hours supplied increase from X_1X to X_2X to X_3X. The pure *substitution effect* always acts unambiguously to increase hours supplied. The logic of the argument is that as nonmarket time becomes more expensive relative to market goods, the individual always

---

Figure 4.8. A pure substitution (relative price) effect. As nonmarket time becomes more expensive relative to market goods, the individual "buys" less of it. Thus, hours supplied increase from X_1X to X_2X to X_3X.

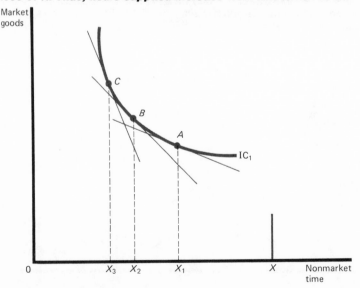

substitutes market goods for nonmarket time. Thus, hours supplied always increase.

Changes in the wage rate: A labor supply curve in the short run Changes in wages result simultaneously in changes both in relative prices and in income. We illustrate in Fig. 4.9 two increases in the wage by pivoting the constraint upward from the pivot point X. The slope of the constraint increases and the slope of the constraint is the wage rate. The individual can now transform nonmarket time into market goods at higher rates. Notice also, however, that because the individual can attain higher levels of total utility, his or her real income has also increased. At the original wage, combination A was best; as a result of the first wage increase, combination B becomes best; as the wage rises again, combination C becomes best. Each of these three different combinations is best given the different constraints. Note, however, that each of these best combinations contains different hours supplied. The curve that traces out the quantity supplied of labor at various alternative wage rates is the *labor supply curve.*

At the beginning wage in Fig. 4.9, hours supplied was X_1X, represented as $0Q_1$ in Fig. 4.10. At the higher wage, hours supplied

---

Figure 4.9. The best combinations for three different wage rates. As the wage rate rises, utility-maximizing individuals adjust the quantities consumed of nonmarket time. Thus, hours supplied change as the wage rate changes.

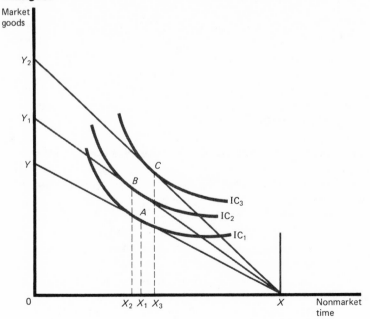

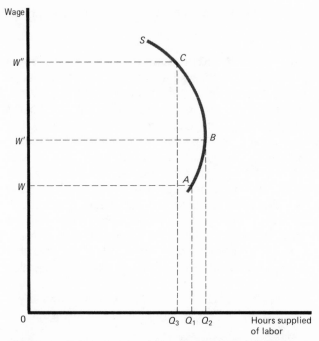

Figure 4.10. A labor supply curve. At the initial wage 0W the quantity supplied of labor is $0Q_1$ (X_1X from Fig. 4.9). At the higher wage 0W' the quantity supplied increases to $0Q_2$ (X_2X from Fig. 4.9). At wage 0W'' the quantity supplied of labor declines to $0Q_3$ (X_3X from Fig. 4.9).

increased to X_2X, represented as $0Q_2$; at the highest wage, hours supplied declined to X_3X, represented as $0Q_3$ in Fig. 4.10. In other words, this labor supply curve has a backward-bending portion: the highest wage resulted in the individual's reducing hours supplied. Thus, a negative relation between wages and hours worked is a theoretical possibility which can be understood by disentangling the income effect of the wage change from the substitution effect.

Income and substitution effects of a wage change Earlier in Fig. 4.7 we illustrated a pure income effect. We did this by shifting the constraint outward parallel to itself. In Fig. 4.11 we represent the pure income effect the same way by shifting the budget constraint parallel to itself so that it is tangent to indifference curve 2 at C. We see that as a result of the income effect, the individual would have reduced hours supplied by the amount X_1X_3. As in our earlier example, the pure income effect acted to reduce hours supplied.

But this is not the only effect. As a result of the wage increase, not only has the individual's real income increased but relative prices have changed as well. The rate at which nonmarket time can be transformed

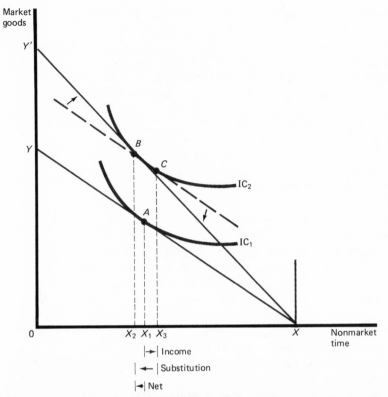

Figure 4.11. Income and substitution effects of a change in the wage rate. The substitution effect of the wage change more than offsets the income effect so that the quantity supplied of labor increases by X_2X_1 as a result of the rise in the wage.

into income is now higher; thus the price of nonmarket time has become higher. The individual makes substitutions in consumption as these relative prices change. He or she "buys" less nonmarket time as its price rises. The pure substitution effect is isolated in Fig. 4.11. The individual is at combination C as a result of the pure income effect. We now pivot the dashed line so that it reflects the new price ratio, and we achieve a new point of tangency at B. What we have done conceptually is keep real income constant (combinations C and B are on the same indifference curve) and confront the individual with higher prices of nonmarket time. As before, the individual always adjusts to the higher price of nonmarket time by buying less of it. The pure substitution effect acting alone would have increased hours supplied by the amount X_2X_3.

The *net* effect of the income and substitution effects acting jointly is to increase hours supplied by the amount X_2X_1. In this case the substitution effect (which acts to increase hours supplied) has overwhelmed the income effect (which acts to reduce hours supplied) so that, on balance, the individual increases hours supplied by X_2X_1 as a result of the wage increase. In terms of Fig. 4.10, hours supplied increased as the wage rose from $0W$ to $0W'$ because the substitution effect dominated the income effect. But a further increase in the wage to $0W''$ reduced hours supplied because of a dominant income effect. The backward-bending portion of a labor supply curve is always the result of a dominant income effect. In general, whether hours supplied increase or decrease as the wage changes is theoretically indeterminate. Either outcome is possible, depending on the relative strengths of the income and substitution effects.

4.1e
Elasticity of labor supply
In Chap. 2 we defined elasticity as the percentage change in quantity divided by the percentage change in price: $\%\Delta Q/\%\Delta P$. Elasticity of labor supply is the percentage change in the quantity supplied of labor divided by the percentage change in the price of labor, i.e., the wage rate: $\%\Delta QS/\%\Delta W$. If the percentage increase in the quantity supplied of labor is greater than (less than) the percentage increase in the wage, then supply is elastic (inelastic). Whether the coefficient of elasticity of labor supply is positive or negative, however, depends, as we have seen, on whether the substitution or income effect of the wage change is dominant.

We will have occasion in Chap. 6 to use the concept of elasticity of the supply of labor when we examine the Lewis model, for that model outlines the effect on the aggregate wage level of increases in the stock of capital and/or technological improvements when the aggregate labor supply is perfectly elastic.

4.2
LABOR FORCE PARTICIPATION
The size of the labor force L depends on the size of the *age-eligible population* P and the aggregate *labor force participation rate L/P,* the percentage of the age-eligible population that chooses to be in the labor force:

$$L = P(L/P) \tag{4.3}$$

The age-eligible population is defined as all noninstitutionalized individuals 16 years of age or older. "Noninstitutionalized" means those individuals not in prisons or mental institutions, or in other ways institutionalized. The minimum age of 16 is to some degree arbitrary. (Until 1967 the minimum age was 14 years.) However, it is the segment of the population which is 16 or more years old that is most likely to exercise a choice in its labor force status.

Because in the short run the population size is given, changes in the size of the labor force in the short run are dominated by changes in the aggregate labor force participation rate. Further, changes in the aggregate labor force participation rate are concentrated among certain groups in the age-eligible population. Numbers of workers such as some married women, students, and some of the retired enter the labor force when wages rise and job prospects in general improve, and just as readily leave the labor force when these conditions are reversed. Such individuals whose labor force participation is intermittent are known as *secondary workers.* By contrast, some individuals such as many male and female heads of households and many male and female single individuals tend to remain in the labor force either as employed or as unemployed, irrespective of wages and other market conditions. Individuals whose labor force participation does not tend to vary as wages and other market conditions change are known as *primary workers.*

In this section we develop a simple analysis of the labor force participation decision in the short run so as to understand the labor force behavior of both primary and secondary workers. But before we begin this analysis, we look carefully at the concepts of labor force, employed, and unemployed, for these concepts have very specific meanings in labor economics.

4.2a
The labor force[2]

The broadest labor force concept is the *total labor force,* defined as the total in any one week of all noninstitutionalized individuals 16 years of age or older, including the military, who are either employed or unemployed. The *civilian labor force* is defined the same way, except that it excludes the military. The civilian labor force, then, is simply the sum of its two component parts—the employed and the unemployed. Individuals who are neither employed nor unemployed are not in the labor force.

The numbers of individuals reported as employed, unemployed, or not in the labor force are estimates. These estimates are arrived at through a sample of households each month throughout the United States. Each month, as part of its Current Population Survey, the Bureau of the Census conducts a survey of approximately 47,000 households. The week of the survey is always the week of each month which includes the nineteenth day of the month. During that week each household in the sample is visited and questions are asked about the labor force activities during the previous week of each household member 16 years of age or older. Thus, the labor force information gathered pertains to the

---

[2] The most complete (and official) discussion of labor force concepts is in U.S. Department of Labor, Bureau of Labor Statistics, *BLS Handbook of Methods,* Bulletin 1910, 1976, chap. 1.

week of the month which includes the twelfth day of the month. This week is known as the "survey week." It is on the basis of the individual's *activity* during the survey week that his or her labor force status is determined. The household data are forwarded to the Bureau of Labor Statistics (BLS), where they are compiled and published.

The employed What should a person have been doing during the survey week to be classified by the BLS as employed? A person could have been doing any one of three things. First, if an individual did any work at all for pay during the survey week, he or she is employed. It makes no difference for these purposes whether the individual worked 4 hours or 40 hours; in both instances the person is employed.

A second category includes some individuals who worked during the survey week for no pay. If a person worked at least 15 hours during the survey week for no pay in a family-operated enterprise or farm, that person is classified as employed. An example of this kind of activity would be a 17-year-old female who operates the cash register at her family's business for at least 15 hours for no pay.

The third category includes those individuals who did no work during the survey week but had a job. All those persons who had a job during the survey week but were absent from it because of vacation, illness, bad weather, etc., are classified as employed.

To summarize, individuals are classified as employed if, during the survey week, they:

1. Did any work at all for pay
2. Worked at least 15 hours for no pay in a family-operated enterprise or farm
3. Did no work during the survey week but had a job from which they were temporarily absent because of vacation, illness, or bad weather

The unemployed To be classified as unemployed, a person must satisfy *all* the following criteria: He or she (1) did no work during the survey week, but (2) was available for work, and (3) had made some specific effort during the prior 4 weeks to find a job. To be available for work means that a person must be able to accept a job if it is offered. This stipulation means, for example, that college students who are looking unsuccessfully for jobs in March but who are not available for work until June are not counted as unemployed in March. Making specific efforts to find a job means that the individual must have answered want ads, visited employment services, or done any of a host of other specific activities designed to find a job.

In three limited circumstances a person may be classified as unemployed even though he or she had not made specific efforts to find a job during the prior 4 weeks. These circumstances apply if the individual (1) is waiting to be called back to a job from which he or she had been laid off, (2) is waiting to report to a new job within 30 days, or (3) is prevented from looking for a job by temporary illness.

Labor force statistics In Table 4.1 we present the labor force status of the civilian age-eligible population in September and October 1977. The labor force participation rate L/P in September was 97,868,000/156,982,000, or 62.3 percent. In October this rate rose to 62.4 percent. The unemployment rate U/L in September was 6,773,000/97,868,000, or 6.9 percent, and it rose in October to 7.0 percent. Thus, even though the number employed increased by 135,000 from September to October, the number unemployed also increased—by 99,000. This increase was due in part to an increase in the labor force participation rate. Not all the new entrants (and perhaps reentrants as well) were successful in finding employment immediately; some spent time in searching for jobs and were classified as unemployed while they did so.

We see from an examination of Table 4.1 that increases both in the number unemployed and in the unemployment rate were not due to a decline in the number of jobs. Rather, the increase in labor force participation increased the number of individuals in the labor force looking for work, and this monthly increase exceeded the number of jobs created during the same period.

Given the fact that the labor force expands and contracts because of changes in the aggregate labor force participation rate, there has been substantial discussion as to whether the unemployment rate serves as a useful cyclical indicator of labor market conditions, or whether some

Table 4.1
Labor force status of the civilian, noninstitutionalized population, 16 years of age or older, September and October 1977

Civilian age-eligible population (P)

156,982,000 (September)
157,201,000 (October)

In the labor force (L)	Not in the labor force
97,868,000 (September)	59,114,000 (September)
98,102,000 (October)	59,099,000 (October)

Employed (E)	Unemployed (U)
91,095,000 (September)	6,773,000 (September)
91,230,000 (October)	6,872,000 (October)

SOURCE: U.S. Department of Labor, Bureau of Labor Statistics, *Monthly Labor Review*, vol. 100, no. 12, December 1977, table 2, p. 82.

alternative measure (such as the ratio of the employed to the age-eligible population, E/P, for example) might mirror labor market conditions better. This is a subject we discuss later in Chap. 15 when we examine the causes and consequences of unemployment. Let us turn now to a simple model of labor force participation so as to understand better this labor supply decision by both primary and secondary workers.

4.2b
The labor force participation decision

Given an individual's tastes and preferences and the wage which he or she faces in the labor market, the best quantity of labor to supply may be zero hours. We illustrate this outcome in Fig. 4.12, where the utility-maximizing combination for this individual is T. This combination contains $0X$ nonmarket time and zero market goods. This is what economists define as a "corner solution." Because this individual chooses to use all of the available time as nonmarket time, he or she is not in the labor force. This is not an unusual occurrence, for as we can see from Table 4.1, 37.7 percent of the age-eligible population in September 1977 did not choose to be in the labor force. Those 59,114,000 individuals chose instead to spend their time in a variety of nonmarket activities.

The relation between changes in the wage rate and changes in labor force participation can be understood with the aid of Fig. 4.12. Although this individual chose not to be a labor force participant at the existing

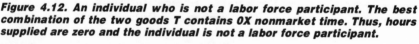

Figure 4.12. An individual who is not a labor force participant. The best combination of the two goods T contains 0X nonmarket time. Thus, hours supplied are zero and the individual is not a labor force participant.

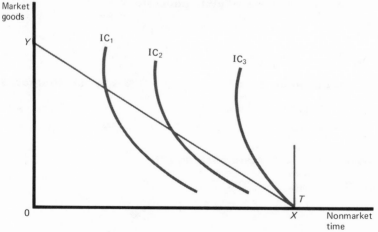

market wage, a higher market wage (not shown in Fig. 4.12) could induce him or her to enter the labor force. Given the value of individuals' activities outside the labor force, a rise in the market wage increases the cost of time spent in those nonmarket activities, and, at the margin, attracts into the labor force those individuals for whom the cost of nonmarket activities now exceeds, at the higher wage, the value they assign to those activities.

Individuals differ greatly both in the value of their activities outside the labor force and in the market wage they confront in the labor market. For example, those individuals who are usually identified as primary workers are likely to have low productivities in nonmarket production (for whatever reasons) relative to the wage they can earn in market work. Male heads of households are a good example of this combination. By contrast, many individuals who are usually identified as secondary workers are likely to have high-valued options outside of the labor force relative to the wage they can earn in market work. Many married women with children, for example, tend to have high-valued options in the home. Similarly, teenagers are likely to assign a high value to their educational activities, and older workers (65 years of age or older) to place a high value on their leisure. If secondary workers such as these choose not to participate in the labor force at existing market wage rates, such behavior can indicate simply that, as far as these individuals are concerned, their choice of zero hours of market work is a utility-maximizing choice.

If an individual chooses to enter the labor force as the market wage rises, it is the wage that he or she *expects* to receive that has influenced behavior. An expected wage can best be thought of as a wage which an individual knows (or thinks) is associated with a job, adjusted for the probability of finding a job that pays that wage. The probability of finding employment varies inversely with the unemployment rate, and economists have been successful in showing that short-run changes in labor force participation rates of secondary workers do vary with changes in the probability of finding employment.[3]

4.2c
Cyclical changes in the size of the labor force

Given that primary workers are those individuals who remain in the labor force either as employed or as unemployed irrespective of short-run

---

[3] E. Alban and M. Jackson have shown that the appropriate theoretical specification of the probability of finding employment is the ratio of the number of job vacancies V to the number unemployed U. They find the ratio V/U to be significantly related to labor force participation rates of secondary workers. See E. Alban and M. Jackson, "The Job Vacancy–Unemployment Ratio and Labor-Force Participation," *Industrial and Labor Relations Review,* vol. 29, April 1976, pp. 412–419.

changes in wages and market conditions, changes in the size of the labor force during a rise or fall in the level of economic activity are due primarily to changes in the labor force participation rates of secondary workers. Whereas the aggregate labor force participation rate has risen to about 60 percent in periods of "full employment," it has fallen below that in periods of cyclical downturn in the level of economic activity. One or two percentage points in aggregate L/P may seem modest, but note that a one percentage point change in L/P, given the size of the age-eligible population in September 1977, represents a flow of approximately 1,570,000 individuals into or out of the labor force, and this flow can affect substantially the monthly values of the unemployment rate.

In the not-too-distant past there was considerable controversy as to the net labor force movement of secondary workers over the course of the business cycle. The two competing hypotheses were the *additional worker* hypothesis and the *discouraged worker* hypothesis. The additional worker hypothesis argued that as primary workers became unemployed during a downturn in the level of economic activity, additional workers from the family would enter the labor force in hopes of finding a job so as to maintain family income. This hypothesis argued, then, that labor force participation rates of secondary workers should be directly related to the unemployment rate. The discouraged worker hypothesis argued differently. When employment declined, primary workers did remain in the labor force as unemployed. However, many secondary workers became "discouraged" about the prospects of finding a new job and left the labor force rather than remain in it as unemployed. This hypothesis argued, then, that labor force participation rates of secondary workers should be inversely related to the unemployment rate.

Many statistical studies have been undertaken to attempt to resolve this question, and the studies have reached the same conclusion: The labor force participation rate of secondary workers is inversely related to the unemployment rate. The dominance of the discouraged worker effect does not mean that no secondary workers enter the labor force when primary workers in the household lose their jobs. Some certainly do. But more secondary workers leave the labor force than enter it, so that labor force participation rates of secondary workers are negatively related to the unemployment rate.[4]

Government officials, union leaders, and some economists have expressed concern about the individuals who withdraw from the labor

---

[4]Some studies which examine the relation between unemployment rates and labor force participation rates are reviewed in J. Mincer, "Labor-Force Participation and Unemployment: A Review of Recent Evidence," in R. A. Gordon and M. S. Gordon, eds., *Prosperity and Unemployment,* Wiley, New York, 1966, pp. 73–112.

force as job prospects deteriorate. They argue that discouraged workers should be classified as "hidden unemployed," and that an estimate of the hidden unemployed be added to the official unemployment statistics. This procedure, of course, would yield larger unemployment rate estimates. Jacob Mincer has stated that this suggestion is evidence of a "myopic preoccupation with GNP."[5] By this he means that this suggestion implies that only market work yields utility to secondary workers, and that other uses of time are in some sense less preferred by these workers and, presumably, less valued by society. Mincer agrees totally that we should indeed be concerned about those individuals whose job prospects are chronically limited, but suggests that we view cyclically sensitive labor force participation by secondary workers in general as a source of strength in the economy. Many individuals do want to include some market work in their array of activities, and simply time their labor force activities to coincide with improved prospects of finding employment. Because of this timing, secondary workers constitute the important source of "labor reserves" in the economy.

4.3

THE MARKET SUPPLY CURVE OF LABOR IN THE SHORT RUN

A market supply curve of labor is an aggregate relation between market wages and hours supplied to market activities, and is derived by summing the hours supplied by all market participants at various wage rates. As such, market relations always reflect choices made by individual labor market participants.

In Fig. 4.13 we show the choices made by three representative individuals at three various wage rates, as well as the market labor supply curve which summarizes those choices.

For individual 1, the substitution effect of rising market wages dominated the income effect so that hours supplied increased from 40 to 45 to 50 hours. For individual 2 just the opposite was true. The income effect dominated the substitution effect so that hours supplied declined from 40 to 35 to 30 hours as the market wage rose. The third individual was not a labor force participant at wage W_1, but entered the labor force at wage W_2 to supply 40 hours, and increased hours supplied to 45 hours as the wage rose to W_3.

The market supply curve of labor S_m is the horizontal summation of the quantities of labor supplied by these three individuals at various alternative wage rates. As such, it reflects the choices made by utility-maximizing individuals in response to changes in the wage rate.

---

[5]Ibid.

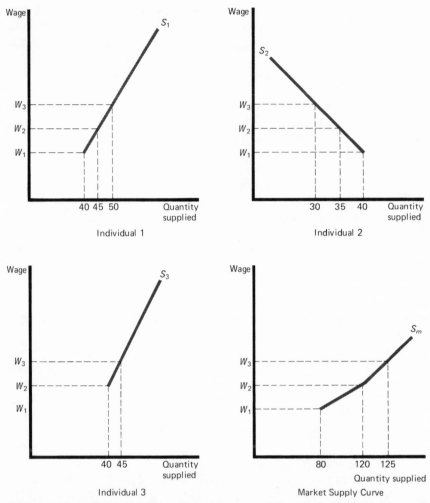

Figure 4.13. Individual labor supply curves and the market supply curve of labor in the short run. The three individuals react differently to changes in the market wage rate. The market supply curve of labor S_m summarizes the choices made by these individuals.

QUESTIONS AND EXERCISES

1. Explain how labor supply is a conclusion of a utility maximization model of individual choice.

2. Show the effect on an individual's quantity supplied of labor of (1) an increase in nonlabor income and (2) an increase in the legislated minimum wage rate. Which of these two changes do you think would result in the greater reduction of hours supplied of labor? Why?

3. Tom, Dick, and Harry did no work during the survey week. Yet Tom was classified as employed, Dick as unemployed, and Harry as not in the labor force. Explain.

4. If the unemployment rate rises, then the number of jobs in the economy has declined. Comment.

5. What groups classified by age, sex, race, and marital status would you expect to have low rates of labor force participation? High rates? Why?

6. Why does the labor force participation rate of primary workers not change as unemployment rates change?

7. Is it possible that, in the short run, the total quantity of labor supplied to the market might decline as market wages rise? Explain.

REFERENCES FOR FURTHER READING

An early analysis of the labor supply choice is in H. Gregg Lewis, "Hours of Work and Hours of Leisure," *Proceedings of the Ninth Annual Meeting of the Industrial Relations Research Association,* 1957, pp. 196–206.

Students who desire more detail concerning the concepts of employed, unemployed, and labor force should see U.S. Department of Labor, Bureau of Labor Statistics, *BLS Handbook of Methods,* Bulletin 1910, 1976, chap. 1.

A wealth of information concerning the statistical relations between labor force participation rates of groups of workers and market wages, income, and other explanatory variables is found in W. G. Bowen and T. A. Finegan, *The Economics of Labor Force Participation,* Princeton University Press, Princeton, N.J., 1969.

An entire issue of the *Journal of Human Resources* (vol. 9, Spring 1974) is devoted to the labor supply effects of the Graduated Work Incentive Experiment, more commonly known as the New Jersey–Pennsylvania negative income tax experiment. The article by A. Rees in that volume, "An Overview of the Labor-Supply Results," discusses the income and substitution effects that were expected by those working with the experiment, and also presents some important findings of the experiment.

THE SUPPLY OF
LABOR IN THE LONG RUN

In the previous chapter we outlined the adjustments that utility-maximizing individuals make in the quantity of labor they supply as the constraints of market wages and income change. Because our analysis of labor supply was in the short run, individuals were assumed to be in a given-size population and to possess given skills. We saw that adjustments individuals can make in this set of circumstances were limited to an hours adjustment among those individuals in the labor force, and to an adjustment by some individuals in their labor force participation.

In this chapter we examine labor supply in the long run. The long run is always the concept of more complete adjustment to changes in constraints. Thus, a long-run analysis of labor supply allows individuals the time necessary to adjust more completely to changes in the environment. One adjustment will be secular (or long-run) changes in labor force participation. Whereas the labor force participation rate in the aggregate has remained relatively constant at about 0.60, there have been dramatic shifts in the age and sex composition of the labor force. In particular, there have been dramatic increases in the labor force participation rates of married women, and declines in the participation rates of both older and younger workers.

Another adjustment will be in the size of the population. A long-run analysis of labor supply explores the relation between fertility and long-run changes in market wages and income. As we have stated earlier, the size of the population is one of the three determinants of the total quantity of labor supplied to an economy.

In our discussion of labor supply in the long run, we present and use G. S. Becker's model of the allocation of time. This neoclassical model is more powerful than the model we used in the previous chapter. Our decision to use the Becker model is based on its ability to yield what we view as particularly helpful insights into the labor force participation decisions and fertility decisions made by household members.

5.1
A MODEL OF THE ALLOCATION OF TIME
In the Becker model of the allocation of time, the household is viewed as a producer as well as a consumer.[1] The household produces "commodities" which, when consumed, provide the household with utility. The household is assumed (as always) to maximize utility. Households produce commodities by combining market-produced goods, the time of household members, and other inputs. The total time available to household members not only is fixed but also has alternative uses: it can be used in market activities so as to purchase market-produced goods, as well as in the production and consumption of commodities.

A utility maximization model of the allocation of time leads us to consider the best uses of household members' time, as well as enabling us to predict how household members will adjust time spent in the various activities as the price of time (the wage rate) changes.

5.1a
Utility
Household members receive utility from consuming commodities. For example, a boat ride is a commodity. The production of this commodity requires inputs of market-produced goods such as a boat, gasoline, and oil; inputs of time spent in traveling to and from the boat landing; and other inputs. The two assumptions we made in Chap. 4 with reference to "goods" hold here with reference to commodities. That is, (1) household members prefer more commodities to fewer commodities; (2) increased consumption of any commodity yields diminishing marginal utility. As before, indifference curves between commodities are convex with respect to the origin.

5.1b
The constraints
Household members face three important constraints which prevent them from consuming infinite amounts of commodities. First, the total expenditure that households can make on market-produced goods is

---

[1]G. S. Becker, "A Theory of the Allocation of Time," *Economic Journal,* vol. 75, September 1965, pp. 493–517.

limited by their money income—the sum of labor income and all other sources of income. Second, the time used to produce commodities plus the time spent in other activities such as market work, education, and leisure cannot exceed the total time available. Third, the input-output production relations are assumed to be fixed. That is, the techniques by which the household transforms inputs of market-produced goods, time, and other inputs into commodities are given.

5.1c
Utility maximization given the constraints
How does a household member maximize utility given the constraints which he or she faces? We saw in Chap. 4 that the best combination of market goods and nonmarket time was that for which the ratio of the marginal utilities of time to goods was equal to the ratio of the marginal costs of the two goods:

$$\frac{\text{MU}_H}{\text{MU}_G} = \frac{\Delta G}{\Delta H} \tag{5.1}$$

where $\Delta G/\Delta H$ is the wage rate. Our conclusion here is identical. In this model, the best combination of commodities (say, commodities i and j) is that for which the ratio of marginal utilities is equal to the ratio of the marginal costs of the two commodities:

$$\frac{\text{MU}_i}{\text{MU}_j} = \frac{\text{MC}_i}{\text{MC}_j} \tag{5.2}$$

The major new insight here is that the marginal cost of a commodity includes both a goods-cost component and a time-cost component, because commodities are produced using inputs of market-produced goods and time. That is,

$$\text{MC}_i = \text{GC}_i + \text{TC}_i \tag{5.3}$$

where GC_i and TC_i are respectively the marginal cost of the goods input and the marginal cost of the time input necessary to produce commodity i.

5.1d
Changing the constraints
Changes in nonlabor income and in wage rates have the same effects as before when we discussed labor supply in the short run. Let us examine each separately.

An increase in nonlabor income (holding the wage rate constant) increases the quantities consumed of all "normal" commodities. Because commodities are produced using inputs of market goods and time, this necessarily increases the total amount of goods and time used to produce commodities. Time at work by some household member(s) would thus decline.

An increase in the wage rate (holding real income constant) has two relative price or substitution effects. First, market goods are substituted for time in the *production* of commodities. This is true because an increase in the wage raises the price of time relative to the price of goods. Second, there is a substitution of goods-intensive commodities for time-intensive commodities in *consumption.* Both these substitutions reduce the time spent in production and consumption and tend to increase the time spent in market activities by some household members.

Increases in the wage rate, of course, change both real income and relative prices and thus generate both income and substitution effects. As before, whether changes in the quantity supplied of labor of various household members are positively or negatively related to changes in the wage rate depends on the relative strengths of the income and substitution effects.

In the following section we use this model of the allocation of time to explain the secular changes in labor force participation for important labor force subgroups.

5.2
SECULAR CHANGES IN LABOR FORCE PARTICIPATION

During this century there has been a spectacular increase in the labor force participation rates of the group identified as "married women, husband present." Glen G. Cain has observed that "the labor force participation rate of married women in the United States more than doubled from 1900 to 1940 and then doubled again from 1940 to 1960." Further, "the principal change in the composition of the labor force and the most important source of its growth has been the increased participation of married women. Between 1940 and 1960, the labor force increased by 14.4 million. The category 'married female, husband present,' accounted for slightly more than 56 percent (8.1 million) of this increase. Between 1950 and 1960 this category comprised nearly 60 percent of the labor force growth."[2] By 1970, the labor force participation rate of married females had risen to 40.5 percent.

Paralleling this rise have been secular declines in labor force participation for teenage males and for males 65 years of age and older. Participation rates for teenage males have declined by about 25 percent since the beginning of this century; participation rates for elderly males have declined by about 50 percent.

It is our purpose to examine the secular changes in labor force

---

[2]Glen G. Cain, *Married Women in the Labor Force,* The University of Chicago Press, Chicago and London, 1966.

participation for these groups within a model of the allocation of time. Our particular interest is in outlining the influence on labor force participation of market wages and income, variables which have risen secularly throughout this century.

5.2a
Married women, husband present

1. What has been the influence on the labor force participation of married women of the secularly rising wage rates of their husbands? A rise in the husband's wage, *ceteris paribus,* increases family income. It does not, however, change the value of the wife's time. The effect of an increase in family income is to increase the quantities consumed of all normal commodities. Because commodities are produced using inputs of goods and time, this necessarily reduces the amount of time devoted to market work by some household members. Thus, the secularly rising wages of husbands has been a force tending to reduce the labor force participation of married women.

2. However, paralleling the secular rise in husbands' wages have been a number of factors which exert a positive effect on the participation of married women. One important factor has been the secularly rising wage rates for each skill or educational level of married women. A rise in the wife's wage has both income and substitution effects. It raises the price of time used in household production. As a result of this, the household tends to substitute market goods for time in the production of commodities. (For example, the household may in the production of meals at home use more prepared foods.) A rise in the wife's wage also induces the household to substitute goods-intensive commodities for time-intensive commodities in consumption. Both the production and consumption substitutions that take place as a result of the increase in the wife's wage tend to reduce the time input in household production and consumption and tend to increase the time spent in market activities by the wife.

The income effect of a rise in the wife's wage, of course, tends to increase the demand for commodities and thus discourage labor force participation. Whether the substitution or income effect of a rise in the wife's wage is dominant is a statistical (not theoretical) question.

3. Not only have wages been rising secularly for given skill and educational levels of married women, but also levels of education for married women have risen, both in absolute terms and, most importantly, relative to male educational attainment. Because of this, the level of skills that they bring to the labor force has risen relative to that of men. This has resulted in a rise in wages (and the price of the wife's time) which goes beyond that mentioned above in item 2, and has acted to amplify the time spent in market activities by the wife.

4. Moreover, because educational levels and pleasantness of the job are positively correlated, the nonpecuniary returns to market work have been raised for married females, encouraging increased participation.
5. The presence of children in the household tends to discourage labor force participation by wives. Although birth rates surged upward after World War II, they have declined markedly since then. The presence of children in the home creates a demand for a type of household production known as child care. Further, child care is a time-intensive production activity. There are, nonetheless, market-produced goods and services such as child-care centers, nurseries, and maids, which some households can substitute for the wife's time in the production of child care, and such substitutions release time to market activities. On balance, though, the presence of children in the household tends to discourage labor force participation of married women.

Two other factors that have been related to rising participation of married women are the decline in the standard work week and the technological changes that have taken place in household production. The decline in the standard work week in this century has reduced the amount of time in household production (and other nonmarket uses of time) that wives must sacrifice in order to participate in the labor force. This factor has no doubt been of limited significance since the 40-hour work week was established in interstate commerce by the Fair Labor Standards Act of 1938, but it was a factor of some consequence in the earlier part of this century. Closely related to the decline in the standard work week is the increasing availability of part-time work for women. The economic argument is the same as before: The availability of part-time work reduces the amount of time in household production and other nonmarket activities that must be sacrificed to be in the labor force. (Recall from our discussion in Chap. 4 that a person is employed if he or she does any work at all during the survey week. Female part-time workers are labor force participants.)

What has been the effect of the rapid technological improvements in household production, improvements such as automatic dishwashers, washers and dryers, microwave ovens, and vacuum cleaners? These improvements have clearly made possible a substitution of market goods for time in household production. Wives have chosen to take advantage of these improvements not entirely by increasing production of household goods (or by increased leisure or added education), but at least partially through increased participation in market activities.

For the census week of 1960, Cain examined the relationships between labor force participation rates of married women living in large metropolitan areas and a number of the variables we have identified as important theoretical determinants of their participation. He estimated that, across this sample of married women, a 1 percent rise in wages of their husbands was associated with a reduction in L/P of married women of 0.68 of 1 percent. A 1 percent increase in wages of the married women in the sample was associated with a rise in L/P of 0.42 of 1 percent, documenting the dominance of the substitution effect. Nonlabor income and the presence of children were both found to be associated with reduced labor force participation.[3]

Will the secular rise in labor force participation of married women continue? To make a prediction about the likely trend of L/P for married women, one needs to know the likely trend in the variables associated with their participation. For example, we do know that the cost of children continues to rise secularly, a factor which we shall see in the following section has tended to reduce birth rates, and reduced birth rates are associated with rising participation. But birth rates are currently at a level which, if continued, yield approximately zero population growth. Will they continue to decline in the future? Similarly, legislation which has resulted in equal pay for equal work for females has raised female wages relative to those of males with comparable skills. Also, female educational levels have continued to rise. Both these factors tend to increase L/P for females. But one can argue that the impact of the legislation has already made itself felt, and that educational levels of females have now risen to approximately that of males so that these factors should be of less consequence in the future. The fact is, no one is sure of the future trend in female labor force participation, but many labor economists believe that future growth in L/P for this group will be slower than in the past.

5.2b
Males and females, 16 to 19 years of age

Paralleling the rapid rise in participation rates for married women has been the decline in labor force participation for teenagers, both male and female. How can the secular decline in L/P for these groups be explained within a model of the allocation of time? In particular, what have been the effects of rising market wages and incomes on the participation rates of these groups?

Increases both in husbands' wages and in wives' wages increase household income. Increases in household income increase the demand for normal commodities, where education of children is a normal commodity. Thus, the secular increase in incomes has been a factor reducing L/P for teenagers.

There are two major components to the costs of education. One is explicit costs, such costs as tuition, books, and other fees. These costs have declined secularly (particularly the private tuition costs of education), and this decline has tended to reduce labor force participation and

---

[3]Cain, op. cit., table 15, p. 59.

increase school attendance. The other component of costs is implicit costs, the opportunity cost of the individual's time. Education is a production (as well as consumption) activity that requires a major input of time. The effect of secularly rising wages for teenagers has been to increase the value of their time and thus to encourage market work and discourage education. But this has been offset to some degree by minimum wage legislation. Teenagers, in deciding whether to invest in schooling or seek employment, take into account not only what the market wage is for a person with their limited skills, but also the probability of obtaining such a wage. One of the many effects of minimum wage legislation has been to increase the unemployment rate of teenagers. (The annual average unemployment rate in 1975 was 8.5 percent; for the 16 to 19 group it was 19.9 percent.) We know from various studies that unemployment rates and school enrollment rates are positively related. As teenage unemployment rates have risen over time, the probability of finding a job at the higher market wages has declined and the alternative of school attendance has become relatively more attractive. Because of this institutional impediment, school enrollment rates are higher than they otherwise would be. Thus, one of the effects of minimum wage legislation has been to block employment opportunities for teenagers and cause the quantity of education demanded by these groups to be higher than it otherwise would have been. Consequently, their labor force participation rates are lower than they otherwise would have been.

5.2c
Males, 65 years of age and older

Secularly rising income and wages are both factors that are theoretically important determinants of declining participation rates for older workers. Secularly rising wages generate both income and substitution effects, and the dominant effect is not theoretically determinate. Statistical studies, however, do not show a consistently significant relation between earnings of older males and their labor force participation.

One variable which is a significant determinant of L/P for older workers, however, is nonlabor income. Studies relating L/P and nonlabor income show a consistently negative relation between these two variables.

The major sources of nonlabor income for older workers are Social Security income and income from private retirement programs. Not only have these sources of nonlabor income risen over time (for example, Social Security payments have become larger) but also the eligibility requirements have been liberalized. One feature of the Social Security program that has reinforced the trend in labor force withdrawal of older workers is the provision which stipulates that benefits be lowered if labor earnings exceed a certain amount. This provision, of course, effectively lowers the real wage (the rate at which nonmarket time can be trans-

formed into market goods) and tends to discourage labor force participation for some older workers.

5.3
THE FERTILITY DECISION AND POPULATION[4]

The choices that individuals make as to family size can be analyzed
within the same framework that we have used to analyze other choices
that individuals make. As economic goods, children yield a flow of
benefits or utility to their parents. Parents also incur a flow of costs in
having and raising children. In deciding to have a child, parents are
assumed to take into consideration the expected benefits from having a
child relative to the expected costs. It is clear that both the benefits and
costs of children have changed as market wages and incomes have
risen over time. In particular, the benefits of children have fallen and the
costs have risen. Individuals have chosen on the basis of changes in the
benefit-cost structure to reduce the desired number of children, and the
consequences of these choices have important and far-reaching implications for population growth as well as for the long-run movement of
real wages. Although it is premature to say that economics has provided
a complete and detailed theory of population, the economic approach
has made a substantial contribution to our knowledge of the determinants of population, and the potential for further contributions in this area
appears to be very promising.

5.3a
Utility and costs of children [5]

Children yield a flow of utility and productive services to their parents. In
low-income (mainly agricultural) economies children are an important
source of income for the family because of the contribution to real output
of the family farm and because of other productive services in the home.
They may also be a source of income to the parents in their old age. In
addition to these benefits which flow from the fact that children represent
investment goods to their parents ("poor man's capital," to use Schultz's

---

[4] We conclude in this section that changes in the size of the population result ultimately in
shifts in the aggregate supply curve of labor, *ceteris paribus.* With this conclusion in
mind, our discussion of fertility and population can be omitted with no loss of continuity in
the major arguments we develop in Part I.

[5] Our discussion in Sec. 5.3 is based on works by T. W. Schultz and G. S. Becker. See T. W.
Schultz, "The Value of Children: An Economic Perspective," *Journal of Political
Economy,* vol. 81, pt. II, March/April 1973, pp. S2–S13, and "The High Value of Human
Time: Population Equilibrium," *Journal of Political Economy,* vol. 82, pt. II, March/April
1974, pp. S2–S10. See also G. S. Becker, "An Economic Analysis of Fertility," in
Demographic and Economic Change in Developed Countries, Princeton University
Press, Princeton, N.J., 1960, pp. 209–231.

phrase), children also provide utility to their parents which is similar in many ways to the utility received from other types of consumption goods. In high income (mainly nonagricultural) economies the flow of producer services from children is likely to be minimal (perhaps nonexistent), even though the flow of consumer services that children yield need not differ across low- and high-income economies.

The costs of children include a money price as well as a time price. This latter price has risen dramatically because of the rise in women's wages which has occurred over time.

Using the Becker model, we can outline the effects of changes in incomes and wages on the quantity of children that families choose to have.

5.3b
The effects of changes in income and wages on the quantity of children

An increase in family income increases the demand for normal commodities in the Becker model. It would seem, then, that rising incomes are associated with increasing numbers of children. Becker and H. G. Lewis have argued, however, that because *quantity* of children and *quality* of children are substitutes, it is plausible that the income elasticity of demand with respect to quality of children is substantially larger than the income elasticity of demand with respect to quantity of children.[6] Consequently, as incomes rise, *ceteris paribus,* parents may choose a smaller number of higher-quality children.

Secular rises in women's market wages, *ceteris paribus,* have increased the price of time associated with having and raising children. There is little room for doubt that, as the price of women's time has risen, this rise has been a major factor contributing to the secular decline in birth rates.

Thus, as both income and wages have risen through time, parents appear to have chosen a smaller number of higher-quality children. This adjustment in desired family size has important implications for population growth and the movement of aggregate wages.

5.3c
Population changes and real wage changes[7]

An increase in population has the effect of shifting the aggregate supply curve of labor to the right. Within the framework of the basic model of

---

[6]G. S. Becker and H. G. Lewis, "On the Interaction between the Quantity and Quality of Children," *Journal of Political Economy,* vol. 81, pt. II, March/April 1973, pp. S279–S288.

[7]Our discussion here parallels much of what is found in T. W. Schultz, "The High Value of Human Time: Population Equilibrium."

Chap. 3, an increase in the aggregate supply of labor, *ceteris paribus,* tends to reduce the real wage.

We discussed in Sec. 3.5 the view of the classical economists with regard to the movement of real wages over time. Their formulation of the "iron law of wages" hinged, as we saw, on the direct relation between rising wages and subsequent population increases. As Schultz has noted, "It is a dismal view of human behavior that has long been an important idea in social thought."[8] The new work in fertility behavior which we have cited here in part presents an entirely new forecast of population changes and makes possible a radically different view of the future. The transition that economies make from high birth rates and high death rates (Stage I) to low birth rates and low death rates (Stage III) is known as the "demographic transition." Economies which are characterized currently by low death rates and high birth rates (Stage II) are the economies in which population is growing most rapidly at the present time. But the rate of population growth can be expected to slow in these economies in the course of economic development as individuals choose smaller families because of declining benefits and rising costs of children. Economists thus tend to dismiss as inaccurate the vision of those who extrapolate present birth rates in developing countries and arrive at horrifying estimates of population several generations into the future. Quite the opposite view tends to be supported by the available evidence. Per capita income is in general rising and not falling in developing countries, and there are appreciable gains in health and life expectancy. Further, birth rates are falling substantially in an increasing number of developing countries. Thus, the negative relation between rising wages and rates of population growth means that as increases in capital formation and technological change continue, they can be expected to lift the level of real wages indefinitely into the future.

QUESTIONS AND EXERCISES

1. Within the framework of Becker's model of the allocation of time, how would you be required to argue if you wanted to make the case that labor force participation rates of married women will continue to increase at a rate comparable to that of the recent past?

2. Within Becker's framework, what factors other than the ones we have mentioned do you think might be responsible for the secular decline in labor force participation rates of older males? Why?

3. What would the differences be in the cost of a child to (*a*) a high school graduate and (*b*) a college graduate? Would you expect there to be any differences across the population in birth rates by level of education? Why?

---

[8] Schultz, ibid., p. S4.

4. Outline as best you can both the benefits and costs of children in the United States today. What factors would you argue result in differences across the population in perceived benefits and costs?

5. If rates of population growth slow as wages and incomes rise, what upper limit do you see to the growth of real wages and income over time?

REFERENCES FOR FURTHER READING

Two interpretive articles by T. W. Schultz provide an excellent overview of current research results in fertility. See T. W. Schultz, "The Value of Children: An Economic Perspective," *Journal of Political Economy,* vol. 81, pt. II, March/April 1973, pp. S2–S13, and "The High Value of Human Time: Population Equilibrium," *Journal of Political Economy,* vol. 82, March/April 1974, pp. S2–S10. See also Marc Nerlove, "Household and Economy: Toward a New Theory of Population and Economic Growth," *Journal of Political Economy,* vol. 82, March/April 1974, pp. S200–S218.

A dissenting view of the new economic research in fertility is in Harvey Leibenstein, "An Interpretation of the Economic Theory of Fertility: Promising Path or Blind Alley?" *Journal of Economic Literature,* vol. 12, June 1974, pp. 457–479.

THE INTERACTION OF LABOR DEMAND AND LABOR SUPPLY

Having examined separately the demand for and supply of labor, we are now in a position to discuss the interaction of demand and supply. We begin by examining the process by which equilibrium is established, then proceed to a discussion of the changes in the length of the average work week. We then examine the determinants of the elasticity of the demand for labor, a concept we defined in Chap. 2 but discussed only briefly. We outline the relations among wages, prices, and productivity, and, in the final section, discuss the effects of changes in population, the capital stock, and technology on wages and employment.

6.1

LABOR MARKET EQUILIBRIUM

The market demand for labor and the market supply of labor jointly determine an equilibrium level of the wage rate and an equilibrium level of employment. If we continue with the assumption of previous chapters that labor is homogeneous, Fig. 6.1 can be used to illustrate labor market equilibrium. If D and S represent initial demand and supply schedules, the equilibrium wage rate will be W_e and the equilibrium quantity of labor employed will be N_e. Now let us assume that the demand for labor (for whatever reason) increases to D^*. At the existing wage rate W_e, the quantity of labor demanded will be N_d, which exceeds the quantity supplied at that wage rate. As pointed out in Chap. 3, the shortage of labor will induce competition among firms for the available quantity of

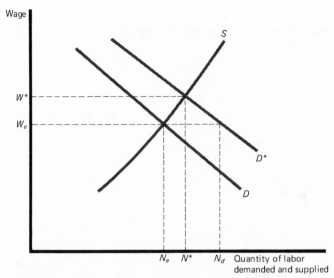

Figure 6.1. Labor market equilibrium. The equilibrium wage rate W_e and the level of employment N_e are determined by the interaction of demand D and supply S. If the demand for labor increases to D^*, there will be an excess demand for labor $N_d - N_e$ at the initital wage rate. A new equilibrium will be established at wage rate W^* and employment level N^*.

labor supplied, with the result that the wage rate will rise to W^*. Unlike our discussion in Chap. 3 where the quantity of labor supplied is assumed fixed, we find that the upward movement of the wage rate induces an increase in the quantity of labor supplied. In fact, the extent to which the wage rate must rise to eliminate the excess demand is determined by the elasticity of labor supply. We will have more to say about this point later in the chapter. For the present, one should note that the amount of employment that constitutes "full employment" is not fixed. While this point may seem obvious, much of the literature in economics assumes otherwise. For example, almost any textbook on principles of economics discusses the "GNP gap." The GNP gap, however, is calculated with the implicit assumption of a fixed labor force. The same point can be made regarding calculations of "hidden unemployment," a concept we presented in Chap. 4. The important point to be recognized is that the level of employment, in equilibrium, is jointly determined by the decisions of households and firms, both of which decisions are influenced by the wage rate.

The increase in the employment of labor that results from the increase in demand depicted in Fig. 6.1 can take two different forms: an increase in hours worked by a given number of employees (i.e., overtime) or, alternatively, an increase in the number of employees where all employees work the standard work week. We examine this employer choice now.

6.2

VARIATIONS IN AVERAGE HOURS OF WORK AND EMPLOYMENT

The length of the average work week has long been a subject of research among labor economists. The trend in hours of work had been downward in this century through World War II.[1] Yet in the postwar era, it appears that average hours of work have shown no trend. However, the appearance of no trend is subject to question because measurement of the trend is fraught with difficulties of an econometric nature. One of the problems deals with disentangling trend from the cyclical effects that we discuss in this section. Nonetheless, the evidence cannot support the hypothesis of a continuance of the strong pre-World War II decline in average hours of work.

The average hours of work, like employment, are jointly determined by demand and supply factors. The literature on hours of work for the most part does not recognize this joint determination. We provided the theory of the *supply* of hours of labor in Chap. 4. Most of the empirical literature treats actual hours of work as completely supply determined. In other words, employees are implicitly viewed as unilaterally deciding the hours they will work. There is a much smaller body of literature on the demand side which treats the employer as unilaterally deciding the length of the work week.[2] We examine now the employer's view of the optimal length of the work week.

Employers, when deciding to increase their employment of labor, are not indifferent between adding workers or lengthening the work week of their present employees, although both options are available. Several factors will influence their decision. First of all, beyond some length of the work week, worker efficiency will begin to decline so that an employer would not want an excessively long work week. Second, there are substantial "start-up" costs of employment. If an employer decides to expand the work force, there are expenses of recruiting, screening, and training which are incurred. The last element can be particularly expensive, especially for high-skilled jobs where the training required is specific to the firm. Further, individuals receiving or having recently completed on-the-job training will not produce at full efficiency although they may receive full pay. These start-up costs are incurred once, but only once, for each employee. The more hours of work that are obtained from any one employee, the lower will be the *per-hour* start-up costs.

---

[1] For a discussion of the trend in average actual hours of work, see the frequently cited article by E. B. Jones, "New Estimates of Hours of Work per Week and Hourly Earnings, 1900–1957," *Review of Economics and Statistics,* vol. 45, November 1963, pp. 374–385.

[2] The prime contribution to this literature is R. Ehrenberg, *Fringe Benefits and Overtime Behavior,* Heath, Lexington, Mass., 1971.

Besides the start-up costs, there are recurring fixed costs of employment. Fringe benefits such as employer-paid life and health insurance premiums represent an expense to an employer each pay period and do not vary with hours worked. In general, the dollar amount of such costs per employee is fixed and does not depend on the hours worked by each employee.

The presence of start-up costs and fixed costs of employment implies that the employer who wishes to increase his or her labor input would always prefer to work the existing work force more hours than to hire additional workers. Such would indeed be the case if employers never had to pay an overtime premium. However, owing to federal law and in some cases collective bargaining agreements, employers must pay at least time-and-a-half (150 percent of the straight-time hourly wage rate) for work in excess of the standard work week. The most typical standard work week is 40 hours per week.

The effect of fixed costs and the overtime premium on per-hour labor costs is demonstrated in Fig. 6.2. In this example we ignore start-up costs and the effect of the length of the work week on labor efficiency. We assume the straight-time wage to be $5 per hour with a time-and-a-half overtime premium for work in excess of 40 hours per week; fixed costs per employee are assumed to be $20 per week. As the work week lengthens, the average hourly labor cost declines, approaching the

---

Figure 6.2. The effect of fixed costs of employment on average hourly labor costs. The longer the length of the work week up to 40 hours, the lower the average hourly cost of labor. At 40 hours, the average hourly cost (including fixed costs and the wage rate) of any additional hours rises immediately and then begins to decline again.

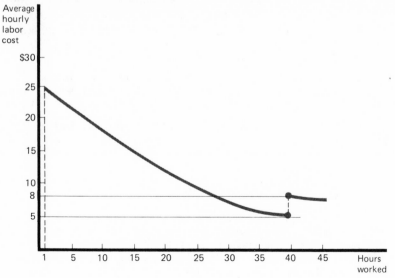

average hourly wage rate of $5. At 40 hours average hourly labor costs are $5.50. However, at 40 hours, the existence of the overtime premium causes average hourly labor costs to rise to $8. With further lengthening of the work week, average hourly labor costs approach $7.50. Under these circumstances it is not surprising to find that employers will prefer to employ whatever number of workers is necessary to provide the number of manhours of labor required, given that each employee works the standard work week. As a rule this is the path that employers will follow, provided that any increase in demand is seen by the employer to be reasonably permanent.[3]

If the increase in product demand is regarded as temporary, however, then start-up costs become very important. If an employer who is working his or her present work force at 40 hours per week experiences an increase in product demand, he or she may prefer to pay the existing work force the overtime premium rather than undergo the start-up costs involved in hiring new employees. In general, the employer will prefer to pay the overtime premium if the total amount of the overtime premium paid over the expected duration of the temporary increase in demand is less than the start-up costs that would be incurred by meeting the increased product demand by hiring new employees.

A similar principle applies in the case of a decrease in demand for the firm's product. If it appears that a decrease in demand is temporary, the employer may prefer to work the existing work force fewer hours per week rather than discharge workers, because discharged workers may not return to the firm, and the firm must incur start-up costs for their replacements. However, if the reduction in demand were perceived as permanent or of sufficiently long duration, employers would be inclined to discharge workers and work the remaining staff the standard work week. Thus, it is not surprising to find that in the face of a sudden growth of demand, the initial reaction of employers is to offer overtime hours. As the increased demand persists and employers become more convinced of its permanence, their delayed response will be to hire additional workers. For that reason, in the beginning of the recovery phase of a business cycle, we witness an increase in average hours worked. Only later do we see a significant increase in the number employed. In the beginning of a recession, we first see a decrease in average hours worked, followed later by a decrease in employment. Thus, any changes in manhours of labor will eventually take the form of changes in the number of persons employed rather than in changes in average hours of work.

In this presentation we have not discussed what determines the

---

[3] Figure 6.2 should be viewed as a planning curve, illustrating the factors influencing the choice of an employer as to whether to undertake fixed employment costs. Once those costs are borne, the employer's reaction to an inaccurate forecast of labor hours required will depend upon marginal, not average, hourly labor costs.

length of the standard work week. The issue is quite complicated—at least as much so as the determinants of the length of the actual work week. In general, we can expect that any explanation of the process by which the standard work week is determined must include both demand and supply considerations. That explanation has not as yet been formally developed. However, the length of the standard work week is a matter of collective choice and goes beyond the scope of this text. Similarly, labor economists have not yet formally integrated the demand and supply sides of the actual hours of work question.

6.3

THE DETERMINANTS OF THE ELASTICITY OF DEMAND FOR LABOR

We indicated in Chap. 2 that the effect of a change in the wage rate on the quantity demanded of labor depends on the elasticity of the demand for labor. We examine here the determinants of the elasticity of demand for labor. This will aid our discussion in a later section of this chapter. Further, we will see in Chap. 13 that the ability of a union to raise wages above the competitive level depends partially on the elasticity of labor demand.

The demand for labor will be more elastic:

1. The more elastic the demand for the product
2. The greater the ratio of labor costs to total costs
3. The greater the ease of substitution between labor and other factors of production
4. The more elastic the supply of substitute factors of production

6.3a
Elasticity of product demand

The elasticity of labor demand is influenced by the elasticity of the product demand in the market in which the firm produces and sells its output. We explained in Chap. 3 that as each firm in an industry reacts to a lower wage rate, industry output is increased. We also indicated that the additional output could be sold only at a price lower than the original price, and that the lower price shifted downward the firm's VMPP schedule. It is important to know *how much* product price falls, because this will determine how much each firm's VMPP schedule will shift downward, and this in turn will determine the elasticity of the industry's demand curve for labor.

We can illustrate the effect of the industry's increased supply of output on product price by examining two industries, A and B, in a single graph. For simplicity suppose that, by coincidence, both industries initially face identical product supply curves and identical MPP schedules, and face the same initial price, $P_1{}^{A,B}$. Their situation is depicted in Fig. 6.3. Now suppose that the wage rate is lowered in both industries

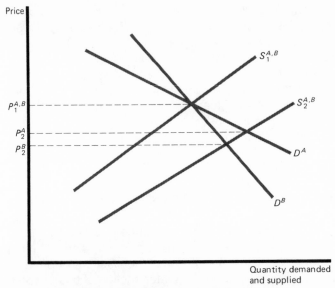

Figure 6.3. The effect of increased supply on product price. Two industries A and B initially face the same supply schedules $S_1^{A,B}$ and product price $P_1^{A,B}$. If supply increases for both industries to $S_2^{A,B}$, the fall in price will be greater in industry B than in A, since in industry A demand D^A is more elastic than demand in industry B, D^B.

resulting in an increase in the supply of output of both industries to $S_2^{A,B}$. Industry A faces the more elastic product demand curve. Its price must fall to P_2^A. Industry B faces a much less elastic demand curve, and so its price must fall to P_2^B. Other things being equal, the VMPP curves of the firms in industry B will shift downward to a greater extent than the VMPP schedules of the firms in industry A. Hence the increase in the quantity of labor demanded in response to a lower wage rate will be greater in industry A than in industry B. If the wage rate had *increased,* price would have risen more in industry B than in industry A. The resulting *decrease* in the quantity of labor demanded would have been greater in industry A than in industry B. Thus, we see that the elasticity of the demand for labor will be greater the more elastic the demand for the product.[4]

6.3b
The ratio of labor costs to total costs
The elasticity of a firm's demand for labor is also affected by the percentage of total costs made up by labor costs. If labor costs were the

---

[4] The student having difficulty with this argument should review Sec. 3.1, particularly the discussion concerning Figs. 3.1 and 3.2.

only costs of production, then a 10 percent rise in the wage rate would cause the firm's cost curves to shift upward by 10 percent. But if labor costs made up only half of the costs of production, then a 10 percent wage increase would cause production costs to rise by only 5 percent, i.e., by 10 percent of 50 percent. Now imagine two firms facing a 10 percent wage increase, where total costs consequently increase by 10 percent in firm A and by 5 percent in firm B. Which firm will choose the greater reduction in its employment of labor? We should expect that firm A will reduce employment more than firm B because firm A's costs have been more noticeably affected. Firm A's demand for labor will thus be more elastic than firm B's. In general, the firm's demand for labor will be more elastic the greater the percent of total costs made up by labor costs.

6.3c
The degree of substitutability between labor and capital
A third factor influencing the elasticity of labor demand is the degree of substitutability between labor and capital. As we pointed out in our discussion of isoquants in Chap. 2, a firm can produce a given quantity of output with any of a number of combinations of labor and capital. If a firm is using a particular combination of these inputs, it can produce the same level of output using one less unit of labor if it increases its use of capital. Given the price of capital, it makes a difference to the firm whether the increase in capital must be, say, one unit or three units. If it takes three more units of capital to compensate for one less unit of labor, it is more expensive to substitute capital for labor than it would be if only one more unit of capital were required. It should then be obvious that in response to a rise in the wage rate, the less is the amount of capital necessary to replace a unit of labor, the more greatly will the firm reduce the quantity of labor it demands. Hence, the elasticity of labor demand will be greater the easier it is to substitute capital for labor.

6.3d
The elasticity of supply of capital
The fourth factor that influences the elasticity of demand for labor is the elasticity of supply of capital or of any other factor that can be substituted for labor in production. In our discussion of the ease of substitution of capital for labor, we pointed out that a rise in the wage rate would lead the firm to substitute capital for labor. We implicitly assumed that the resulting increase in the firm's demand for capital did not affect the price of capital. If the firm faces a perfectly elastic supply of capital, then of course the price of capital will not rise. Keep in mind, however, that if an entire industry is experiencing a wage increase and consequently each firm's demand for capital increases, then the effect of the increased demand on the price of capital equipment could be significant. A rising price of capital equipment will dampen the firm's tendency to substitute capital for labor—the steeper the price rise, the

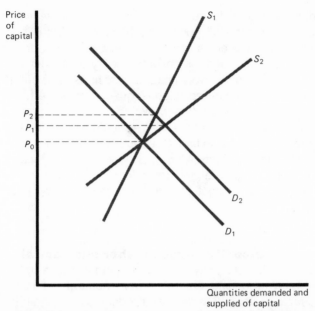

Figure 6.4. The effect of the elasticity of the supply of capital on the price of capital. If the demand for capital rises from D_1 to D_2, the price of capital will rise above its initial level of P_0. If the supply curve of capital is the more elastic one S_2, the price of capital will rise only to P_1. However, if the supply curve of capital is the relatively inelastic curve S_1, the price of capital will rise to P_2.

less the tendency to substitute capital for labor. In Fig. 6.4 we illustrate two hypothetical supply curves of capital—S_1 and the more elastic supply curve S_2. Note that an increase in the demand for capital (caused by a wage rate increase) will result in a greater price rise if S_1 is the supply curve than if S_2 is the supply curve. Because a rising price of capital dampens the tendency to substitute capital for labor, it should be apparent that the demand for labor will be more elastic if the supply curve of capital resembles S_2 than if it resembles S_1. The general principle is that the demand for labor will be more elastic the more elastic the supply of substitute inputs.

6.4

WAGE-PRICE-PRODUCTIVITY RELATIONS
The concept of elasticity is useful in analyzing the effects of productivity growth on the demand for labor and the allocation of labor across industries.[5] Product price is the link between productivity growth and

---

[5] Productivity is defined as average output per man. Productivity increases should be interpreted as shifting upward the MPP schedule of labor. This effect will also shift upward the schedule of average physical product (APP).

wage changes. Were it not for the effect of productivity change on product price, the productivity-wage relation would be quite straightforward. So let us begin our analysis by assuming in the first instance that changes in productivity have no effect on product price. In our example, we divide the economy into two industries: industry A, in which productivity is growing, and industry B, where productivity remains constant. Figure 6.5 shows sectors A and B as well as the aggregate market. We shall continue to assume that perfect information, mobility, and competition prevail.

Suppose that productivity grows in industry A, thereby raising the demand for labor in that industry from D_{A1} to D_{A2}. If industry A is large enough, the productivity growth will significantly raise the demand for labor in the aggregate, though to a relatively lesser degree than in industry A. The market wage rate will rise from W_1 to W_2 as industry A competes labor away from industry B. Note that employment grows in industry A where productivity has grown, but declines in industry B where productivity is stagnant. Note also that because the wage rate is determined in the aggregate labor market, the wage rate paid to workers rises in *both* industries. The extent to which the general wage level rises depends on the elasticity of the supply of labor. The more elastic the supply of labor, the less will be the rise in wages resulting from an increase in productivity. (We will explore this topic in greater detail in the section that follows.)

The industry's demand for labor at each possible wage rate must increase as in Fig. 6.5 if MPP rises and product price remains constant. We must recognize, however, that increased productivity in an industry will have an effect on product price. Increased productivity lowers average and marginal costs of production to an industry. This increases industry supply because each firm's supply curve is its marginal cost curve. The result will be a fall in product price, and a falling product

Figure 6.5. The effect of productivity growth on wage rates. If the demand for labor grows in industry A but not in industry B, the overall wage level will rise from W_1 to W_2. Employment will rise from N_{A1} to N_{A2} in industry A, and fall from N_{B1} to N_{B2} in industry B. The increase in employment in industry A exceeds the decrease in employment in industry B so that aggregate employment increases from N_{A+B1} to N_{A+B2}.

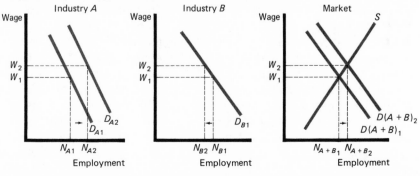

price acting alone reduces the demand for labor. The effect of a falling price will tend to offset somewhat or reverse the initial increase in the demand for labor occasioned by the increase in productivity. The extent to which this reversal takes place depends on the elasticity of product demand. The more elastic the demand for the product, the less will be the fall in price and thus the less will be the offsetting decrease in the demand for labor.

We might ask if it is possible for the demand for the product to be so inelastic that the *net* effect of an increase in productivity could be to *decrease* an industry's demand for labor. Clearly this outcome is a theoretical possibility, but we might also inquire about its empirical significance. Contrary to popular belief, the evidence shows that in all broad industries (with the exception of agriculture), productivity growth has in its final result brought about increases in the demand for labor and in industry employment. As for the general wage level, it will rise as we have illustrated in Fig. 6.5. Thus, even in agriculture, wages have risen over the long run even as the amount of labor that must be used to satisfy the nation's agricultural demand has decreased.

6.5

POPULATION, THE CAPITAL STOCK, AND TECHNOLOGY

In Chap. 5 we established that, *ceteris paribus,* increases in population will increase the supply of labor. We will now examine the effect of population growth on the labor market, as well as the effects of growth in the capital stock and changes in technology.

6.5a
Wage and employment implications for the aggregate economy

If population were to increase, so would the supply of labor to the market. Holding demand conditions constant, the result would be a fall in wages. On the other hand, an increase in the capital stock would enhance the productivity of labor. The rise in the schedule of the marginal physical product of labor will cause the demand curve for labor to increase, with the result that wages will rise. An improvement in technology will have the same effect on wages as an increase in the capital stock. By an improvement in technology is meant an increase in the output that results from any particular combination of labor and capital.

Of course, what we usually observe in most countries is a growth in the capital stock and population simultaneously, although history has provided us with a number of exceptions. If the rate of growth of a nation's capital stock is high relative to that nation's rate of growth of population, then wages and hence income will rise. That is why countries with the highest rates of saving (the source of investment in additional capital stock) also tend to experience the fastest growth of per capita income. The conclusion that capital growth causes wages to rise may be counterintuitive to some, as we tend to think of machines as *displacing* labor. In fact, much of Marxian economics is based on the premise that capital growth will result in a fall in the average wage level. Much of the concern shown by a large segment of the public for the effect of automation on jobs is based on such a misconception. But, given the time necessary for markets to adjust, capital growth will, in the aggregate, raise the demand for labor. Of course, automation may reduce the demand for labor in a specific broadly defined industry, but such a result is highly unusual. As we have already noted, agriculture is perhaps the only such broad industry where this has been the case.

The invalidity of the view that machines are the enemy of rising incomes can readily be seen if we ask what per capita income would be today if 200 years ago we had successfully brought a halt to technological progress. Of course, per capita income would not be significantly different than it was 200 years ago.[6]

6.5b
The elasticity of labor supply: The Lewis model

We mentioned in Sec. 6.4 that the extent to which the wage level will rise as a consequence of increases in the capital stock and/or improvements in technology depends on the elasticity of supply of labor. In particular, the more elastic the supply of labor, the less will the wage level rise given any increase in the demand for labor. Consider Fig. 6.6, panels *a* and *b*; in Fig. 6.6*a* we have illustrated the basic model that we discussed in Chap. 3. Because of the assumption we made there that the supply of labor is perfectly inelastic, an increase in the aggregate demand for labor has only one effect: it raises the wage level. Contrast this result of an increase in the demand for labor with that illustrated in Fig. 6.6*b*. An increase in labor demand there has no effect on the wage level. Because the supply of labor is perfectly elastic, the increase in labor demand causes only the level of employment to increase.

W. Arthur Lewis has developed a model of economic growth in which the key feature is a perfectly elastic supply of labor.[7] In the Lewis model, the increases in the size of the capital stock and improvements in productivity that are necessary ingredients for economic growth do not cause the wage level to rise. This has important implications for the continued speed of economic growth: if entrepreneurs are not forced by market conditions to offer higher wage rates as the aggregate demand for labor increases, they have more resources to reinvest in further capital formation.

---

[6] For documentation of the fact that rising productivity of labor has been the primary factor responsible for the rise in wages over the past century, see E. H. Phelps Brown and M. Browne, *A Century of Pay,* St. Martin's, New York, 1968.

[7] W. A. Lewis, "Development with Unlimited Supplies of Labor," *The Manchester School,* vol. 22, May 1954, 139–191.

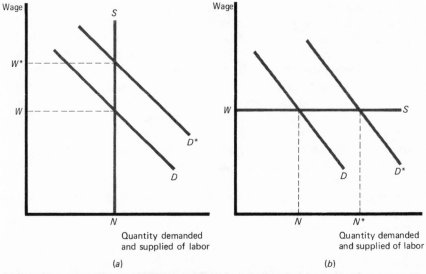

Figure 6.6. The effect of differences in elasticity of labor supply on wages and employment. If the supply of labor S is perfectly inelastic as in panel a, growth in the demand for labor will have its entire effect on wages. If the supply of labor is perfectly elastic as in panel b, growing labor demand will have no effect on wages; its entire effect is to increase employment.

We might ask how descriptively accurate such a model is. Are there any historical instances where the aggregate supply of labor has been so elastic that upward wage level movements have been significantly damped during a sustained period of economic growth? Two such instances come to mind and serve as good examples. One is the post-World War II period in Western Europe; the other is the period 1890–1914 in the United States. Both were periods of rapid capital formation and increases in the demand for labor. Charles P. Kindleberger has examined the postwar growth of Western Europe within the framework of the Lewis model with unlimited supplies of labor.[8] In the case of Western Europe, migrants from southern Europe constituted a huge pool of labor that became available to employers in developing Western European areas. In the case of the United States, immigration swelled during the period 1890–1914, with the result that real wages in the United States rose only at an annual compound rate of 1.3 percent, a rate considerably lower than that of post-1914.[9] It should come as no

[8] C. P. Kindleberger, *Europe's Postwar Growth,* Harvard University Press, Cambridge, Mass., 1967.
[9] A. Rees, *Real Wages in Manufacturing: 1890–1914,* Princeton University Press, Princeton, N.J., 1961.

surprise that organized labor fought hard (and successfully) to limit the immigration into the United States.

The Lewis model explores the implications for wage and income changes of a perfectly elastic supply of labor. The model does not envision the supply of labor being an initiating force in the process of economic development. Rather, labor supply is a passive element. Its existence, however, makes possible a higher rate of capital formation than would be the case if the supply of labor were inelastic. As we have seen, the more elastic the supply of labor, the less will be the upward pressure on the wage level of increases in the demand for labor.

We have presented and discussed in Part I the analytical tools of labor demand and labor supply, and have examined some important interrelationships among key variables such as wages, prices, productivity, and employment. We have been able to discuss some important issues concerning *overall* wages and employment while continuing to treat labor as homogeneous and possessing perfect information. However, some of the most important issues in labor economics stem directly from the nonhomogeneity of labor and the lack of perfect information. Both of these assumptions are relaxed in the following three chapters which constitute Part II of the book.

QUESTIONS AND EXERCISES

1. If fixed costs of employment continue to make up an increasingly larger portion of total labor costs, should we expect employment to become more or less stable over time? Should average hours of work become more or less stable?

2. Which would you expect to be more elastic, the demand for migrant grapepickers or the demand for airline pilots? Why?

3. In Sec. 6.4 we concluded that wages will grow over time even in industries where the demand for labor is not growing, given (*a*) perfect competition, mobility, and information, and (*b*) that the aggregate demand for labor is growing. Explain graphically and verbally what would happen under these conditions to wages and employment in an industry in which labor demand is actually declining.

4. The income elasticity of product demand is defined as the percentage change in quantity demanded in response to a 1 percent change in income. Given that income is rising over time, would you expect employment growth to be faster or slower than average in those industries that have a higher-than-average income elasticity of demand?

5. Many noneconomists view the tendency of the Indian economy to use labor-intensive methods of production as a hindrance to that country's development. The failure to mechanize is viewed as an irrational feature of a backward culture. How can the ideas presented thus far in the book be used to refute that argument?

REFERENCES FOR FURTHER READING

We have stated in Sec. 6.3 that the demand for labor will be more elastic the greater the ratio of labor costs to total costs. Under certain circumstances, the opposite is true. For a discussion of this point as well as a very thorough development of the concept of elasticity, see J. R. Hicks, *The Theory of Wages,* 2d ed., Macmillan, London, 1964.

For a full discussion of many of the points raised in this chapter, see E. H. Phelps Brown and M. Browne, *A Century of Pay,* St. Martin's, New York, 1968, and C. P. Kindleberger, *Europe's Postwar Growth,* Harvard University Press, Cambridge, Mass., 1967.

PART II

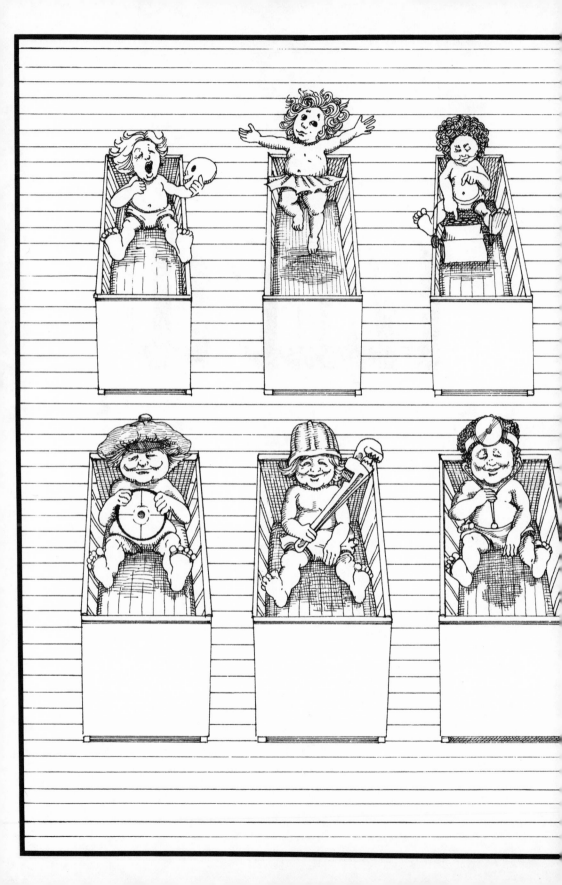

PART II

WAGE DIFFERENCES IN PURELY COMPETITIVE MARKETS

In Part I of this book we provided an explanation of how demand and supply factors interact to determine wage and employment levels in a simplified, frictionless, and perfectly functioning competitive world. We began in Chap. 4 the process of relaxing in sequence the simplifying assumptions we had made in our Chap. 3 basic model. In Part II we continue that process.

We have two major objectives in Part II. First, we examine the consequences of relaxing the assumption of homogeneous labor. One important sense in which workers are heterogeneous is with regard to their education and skills. In Chap. 7 we analyze the effect of education and skill on earnings. The "human capital approach" is taken there to explain the effects of demand and supply conditions on the earnings of workers in various educational categories. In Chap. 8 we analyze aspects of heterogeneity among workers other than their educational levels. Specifically, we examine the effects of differences in tastes and preferences among workers on occupational wages. When we acknowledge these differences together with differences in skill levels, and recognize further that the *demands* for various occupations also differ, we are led to conclude that there is no single labor market. Rather, there are as many labor markets as there are distinguishable occupations. However, these various occupational labor markets are very much interrelated: changes in the demand for or supply of any one occupation affect other occupations as well.

Our second major objective is to examine the consequences of relaxing the assumption that workers and employers have perfect knowledge or have costless access to perfect knowledge. We also relax the assumption that movement of workers between industries, occupations, and regions is costless. We see that the absence of perfect, costless information and the absence of costless movement give rise to industrial and regional differences in wages. Further, the absence of perfect and costless information and mobility gives rise to occupational wage differences beyond those discussed in Chap. 8.

It is important to distinguish ahead of time between the wage differences described in Chap. 8 and those in

Chap. 9. The wage differences discussed in Chap. 8 are attributable to the heterogeneity of labor and are permanent or equilibrium differences. Those described in Chap. 9 are attributable to information and movement costs and are transitory or disequilibrium differences, although the elimination of these differences may require a very long period of transition toward equilibrium.

Finally, it is most important to recognize that the wage differences described in Part II are differences that would exist even if the world were purely competitive in all respects. The fact that the world is not purely competitive means that there will be additional sources of wage differences beyond those described in Part II. Indeed, the labor market effects of imperfections in competition—monopoly, monopsony, labor unions, etc.—constitute the subject matter of Part III. However, even if the economy were dominated by market imperfections, the factors described in Part II would still be sources of differences in wages.

7

HUMAN CAPITAL

Up to this point we have treated labor as homogeneous. More specifically, we have regarded workers as though they were alike in their skill and training, as if any worker were a perfect substitute for any other worker. Many areas of labor economics can be discussed accurately and with relative ease if we employ the simplifying assumption that workers are homogeneous—e.g., the analysis of the effect of changing productivity on the demand for labor. However, many problems require a recognition of the fact that workers do differ in terms of skill, training, and other characteristics. One might reasonably argue that the problems that labor economists have found most interesting and most important during the last two decades have been predominantly concerned with differences among workers. Typical of the questions of concern are: Why do occupational wages differ? What explains the changes in the wages of blacks relative to the wages of whites? Are regional differences in wages getting smaller? Why do college graduates earn more than nongraduates? The answers to all these questions at least partially involve differences among individuals, or groups of individuals, in levels of skill and training—what economists have come to call *human capital*—and the extent to which society values those skills at the margin.

In this chapter we spell out more precisely the meaning of the term human capital. We proceed to analyze the decision to invest in human capital in very much the same fashion in which we might analyze the undertaking of any other type of investment: Does it pay or doesn't it? Both individuals as suppliers of labor and firms as employers of labor invest in human capital. While individuals tend to invest in formal schooling, on-the-job training is the predominant form of human capital investment by firms. Thus we examine in this chapter the investment behavior of both individuals and firms.

7.1

THE CONCEPT OF HUMAN CAPITAL

An individual may have skills and training that permit him or her to earn income each year. Hence these skills which provide a continual flow of income to the individual have value to the individual just as any form of tangible property which yields a monetary return has a present value to its owner. An individual may buy a bond yielding a 10 percent annual return for a price of $10,000. Alternatively, that individual may invest the $10,000 by putting himself through college so that each year following graduation he can earn a larger salary than he could earn if he had not gone to college. The higher salary is the return on his investment. In both cases the individual is investing a stock of funds, $10,000, in hopes of obtaining a periodic return, or flow, of income. In the latter case, the individual's funds are invested in his stock of "earning power" or human capital.

Much of human behavior can be understood and explained if we view individuals as making investment decisions with regard to their stock of human capital. Unfortunately, there has been a resistance to the human capital approach in some quarters. A typical criticism of the human capital approach is that it "treats workers as if they were machines instead of people." Despite the apparent humanistic sentiment expressed in this criticism, it is based on a failure to understand what is accomplished through the human capital approach. More correctly, the human capital approach treats human beings as if they invested in their own earning power as well as in physical capital. Traditionally, economists have viewed labor as a passive agent in the production process, with the capitalist entrepreneur being the decision maker and risk taker. The human capital approach, on the other hand, conditions us to the fact that we are all entrepreneurs to varying degrees, and that we all make investment decisions under uncertainty. Consequently we all take risks. The individuals who invested in advanced training in nuclear biology in the 1950s no doubt expected to earn very high returns on their investments. They took the risk that the demand for persons trained in this highly specialized field might collapse precipitously, as in fact it did in the early 1970s. Aside from the influence of luck, the highest returns will go to those investors in human or physical capital who are best able to foresee changing circumstances and to adjust rapidly to them. This ability to adjust to disequilibrium influences an individual's choices with respect to investment in education, and in turn is influenced by those past educational investments.

7.2

INVESTMENT VERSUS CONSUMPTION

An individual making an investment with his own funds, be it in an apartment building or in a college education, must sacrifice consumption (or at least the ability to consume). If the individual is rational, he will sacrifice present consumption only if he expects to become better off in some sense in the future. For example, an individual would not likely deposit a sum of money, say $10,000, in a savings account for a year unless that individual expected to receive something in excess of $10,000 at the end of the year. Why? Because everyone would prefer to have $10,000 in the present rather than the same amount 1 year from now. How much more would be required at the end of the year will vary among individuals. If one individual would be willing to give up $10,000 only if she receives no less than $11,000 (her original $10,000 plus 10 percent extra) at the end of the year, we would say that the minimum rate of return that she will accept is 10 percent. We might also say that a given sum of money a year from now is worth 10 percent less to her than the same sum of money is worth to her at present. In the terminology of economics, she has a 10 percent "internal rate of time preference." It is an internal rate in the sense that it describes a characteristic of an individual (the degree to which the individual is future-oriented) as opposed to a market-determined phenomenon such as the interest rate. We can also say that for an individual with a 10 percent internal rate of time preference, the present value of $11,000 to be received 1 year from now is $10,000. This present value will be found by dividing the future sum ($11,000) by $(1 + i)$, where i is the internal rate of time preference. In terms of a formula, $PV = S_1/(1 + i)$, where PV is the present value of a sum S_1 to be received 1 year from now.

If the $11,000 were to be received 2 years from now, its present value must be less than $10,000 for our individual with a 10 percent internal rate of time preference. The present value of $11,000 is determined by the process of compound discounting, the inverse of compounding of interest. The future sum of $11,000 must be divided by $(1 + i)^2$ to determine a present value of approximately $9,091. In other words, $PV = S_2/(1 + i)^2$, where S_2 is the sum to be received 2 years from the present. If the $11,000 will be received by our individual 3 years from now, its present value would be $11,000 divided by $(1.10)^3$, or $PV = S_3/(1 + i)^3$, which is approximately $8,264.

If a sum of $11,000 were to be received for each of the next 3 years, the present value of the future sums, S_1, S_2, and S_3, would be $PV = S_1/(1 + i) + S_2/(1 + i)^2 + S_3/(1 + i)^3$, or approximately $10,000 + $9,091 + $8,264 = $27,355. In statistical shorthand, the present value formula is

$$PV = \sum_{j=1}^{3} \frac{S_j}{(1 + i)^j}$$

where the Greek letter sigma is used to indicate a summation process. The subscript j designates the year in which each sum is to be received and takes on the values of 1 to 3.

7.3

INDIVIDUAL BEHAVIOR: INVESTMENT IN SCHOOLING

One of the reasons for which an individual may choose to obtain a college degree is that he expects to earn a higher wage with a college degree than he would be able to earn with a high school diploma. The higher earnings that may be received in the future must be balanced against the sacrifice of present consumption necessitated by the cost of attending college. The fact that the financial benefits of college graduation in the form of higher earnings are received *after* the investment in college is made is accounted for by finding the present value of those future earnings increases. For example, let us take the perspective of an 18-year-old who has just graduated from high school and is contemplating 4 years of college. For the time being let us consider only the dollar costs and benefits and ignore any nonfinancial considerations that may affect the decision to enter college. The financial benefit to college will not begin until the individual is at least 22 years old. The dollar benefit for her first year out of college is the difference between what she could earn if equipped with her college education and what she could have earned at age 22 had she stopped her schooling upon graduation from high school. The present value of the first year's benefit is found by dividing that benefit by $(1 + i)^4$ because it will not be received for 4 years. There will probably be a benefit to a college degree for each year that our individual expects to work, perhaps to age 65. The present value of all future benefits PVB is:

$$\text{PVB} = \sum_{a=22}^{65} \left(\frac{Y_a^C - Y_a^{HS}}{(1 + i)^{a-18}} \right) \tag{7.1}$$

where $Y_a{}^C$ represents the earnings that can be achieved by our individual at age a if she obtains a college degree, and Y_a^{HS} represents the earnings that our individual can expect at age a if she does not proceed to college and obtain a degree. From a strictly financial point of view, the investment in a college degree cannot be worthwhile unless the present value of the benefits exceeds or at least equals the present value of the costs of obtaining that degree. These costs will include tuition, the cost of textbooks, etc. They will not include room and board since these are costs of living and would have been incurred whether or not she chose to attend college. The most significant cost is in the form of earnings forgone in order to attend college. If a high school graduate can earn $6,000 per year working full time, then a college student is sacrificing $6,000 each year for 4 years in order to obtain a degree. The earnings forgone will be lessened to the extent that the student is able to work part time. Nonetheless, forgone earnings completely overshadow tuition costs, particularly among students of state-supported institutions. The costs of obtaining a college degree should also be stated in present value terms, since they are spread out over several years. For our hypothetical 18-year-old who will attend college for 4 years, the present value of the costs will be:

$$\text{PVC} = \sum_{a=18}^{22} \frac{C_a}{(1+i)^{a-18}} \tag{7.2}$$

where C_a represents the total costs of college incurred at age a.

We have said that an individual whose decision is based strictly on financial considerations should choose to attend college if the present value of expected increased earnings exceeds the present value of the costs of college. (We are implicitly assuming that the potential college student either has the funds necessary to attend college, or can borrow them at a rate no higher than his internal rate of time preference.) We could also say that such a person would make the investment in a college education if the rate of return on that investment exceeded his internal rate of time preference. The rate of return on the investment can be determined by solving the following equation for r, the rate of return:

$$\sum_{a=18}^{22} \frac{C}{(1+r)^{a-18}} = \sum_{a=22}^{65} \left(\frac{Y_a^C - Y_a^{HS}}{(1+r)^{a-18}} \right) \tag{7.3}$$

In other words, the rate of return on the investment is that rate of return which equates the present value of the benefits with the present value of the costs. If the rate of return is less than the individual's internal rate of time preference, the investment is not worthwhile since the internal rate of time preference in effect shows the minimum rate of return that the individual is willing to accept. An 8 percent rate of return on an investment is financially attractive to an individual with a 5 percent internal rate of time preference, but not to a less future-oriented person with a 10 percent internal rate of time preference.

Granted that the above decision rule as to whether or not to attend college applies without serious qualification in a world where financial considerations alone are considered and where the financial benefits are known, a number of questions can nonetheless be asked: (1) Are there really financial benefits to obtaining a college degree? (2) Do people know (or at least act as if they know) what these benefits are? (3) How do labor markets affect, and how are they affected by, the return on investment in education? (4) How is the analysis affected by all the other factors that typically influence a person's educational choices, such as the prestige of a degree, the attractiveness or unattractiveness of college

Table 7.1
Mean annual incomes in 1970 of males by age and education

Education	Age			
	25–34	**35–44**	**45–54**	**55–64**
Elementary school graduates	$6,235	$7,393	$7,384	$6,745
High school dropouts	6,970	8,292	8,507	7,891
High school graduates	8,138	9,673	10,201	9,466
College dropouts	8,773	11,551	12,847	12,011
College graduates	10,679	15,714	17,668	17,004
5 or more years of college	10,891	17,930	20,808	20,708

SOURCE: *1970 Census of Population*, vol. 1, *Characteristics of the Population*, pt. 1, U.S. Summary, U.S.G.P.O., June 1973.

life, the degree of security that is perceived as accompanying a college degree, and other such questions?

Table 7.1 provides some U.S. evidence on the first question. The table shows higher earnings for each successively higher level of educational attainment. Note that the differences between earnings for any one educational level and the level below it tend to increase with age. For each educational level, income peaks in the 45–54 age bracket. The increasing income up to that bracket is the result of on-the-job training and experience. Experience is, in a crude way, a type of on-the-job training, although it is not the result of conscious plans toward that end. Experience does tend to increase a worker's productivity, and this increase is reflected in earnings.[1] We caution that not all the apparent gain from acquiring additional education revealed by Table 7.1 can really be attributed to additional schooling. For one thing, the average native ability of college graduates is higher than that of high school graduates. Thus part of the higher incomes of college graduates is really a return to ability, not a return to educational investment. However, studies which have held ability constant still report the same type of positive relationship between education and earnings demonstrated in Table 7.1. Another possible distortion involves what is called

---

[1]Females have not been included in Table 7.1 because of the high percentage of females who are out of the labor force or participate irregularly but who nonetheless are averaged into the census data. The inclusion of all females distorts the picture of earnings that females could receive if they chose to remain steady participants in the labor force. On the other hand, a very high and consistent percent of males ages 25 to 64 are members of the labor force.

the "screening hypothesis."[2] According to this hypothesis, education does nothing to improve the skills of individuals, but it does provide a signal to a potential employer that the individual who holds the degree possesses the personal characteristics (intelligence, motivation, perseverance, etc.) that will probably enable him to be successful in the world of work. While college degrees undoubtedly do provide some information of this type to potential employers, it is unlikely that screening accounts for a great deal of the return to higher education.[3] In any event, the benefits to private individuals from acquiring education are unaffected by the validity of the screening hypothesis. The higher earnings for college graduates reported in Table 7.1 do exist, whether they are attributable to higher productivity or to the necessity of acquiring a college degree in order to convince potential employers of one's worthiness of a high-paying job.

While Table 7.1 provides evidence of a benefit to higher education, it does not tell us whether the benefits sufficiently exceed the costs. For that information we must know something of the rates of return to investment in college education. Although there have been numerous studies that have calculated rates of return to higher education, we will refer to the study by Richard Freeman. Table 7.2 shows Freeman's calculation of the rates of return to obtaining a college degree. The private rates of return calculated for 1959, 1969, and 1972 exceed 10 percent and thus conform to the rates of return found in other studies, but

---

[2] See Kenneth Arrow, "Higher Education as a Filter," *Journal of Public Economics,* vol. 2, July 1973, pp. 193–216.

[3] For some of the evidence against the screening hypothesis, see R. Layard and G. Psacharopoulos, "The Screening Hypothesis and the Returns to Education," *Journal of Political Economy,* vol. 82, September/October 1974, pp. 985–998; and K. Wolpin, "Education and Screening," *American Economic Review,* vol. 67, December 1977, pp. 949–958.

Table 7.2
Private rates of return to a college degree

Year	Private rate of return, %
1959	11.0
1969	11.5
1972	10.5
1974	8.5

SOURCE: Richard Freeman, "Overinvestment in College Training," *Journal of Human Resources,* vol. 10, summer 1975, table 4, p. 296.

in Freeman's estimates we see that the rate of return had fallen to 8.5 percent by 1974.

The rates reported above are labeled private rates of return because they reflect only those measurable benefits received by the individual making the investment and only those costs borne by that individual. To the extent that the cost of education is subsidized by government, alumni, contributing corporations, or other third parties, the true social cost of higher education will be higher than the private cost. Social benefits may also be higher than private benefits. While the distinction between private and social rates of return is important for public policy decisions about educational subsidization, we have confined our analysis to private rates of return because it is to private rates that participants in the labor market react.

With regard to whether individuals know what these rates of return are (or act as if they knew), it should immediately be obvious that people cannot know what they will earn each year until retirement if they obtain degrees or what they will earn if they do not. Nonetheless, individuals can form expectations about the relationship between earnings and education, however rough those notions may be. Of more importance is whether or not people respond to changes in rates of return to education. A number of studies confirm that the decisions of persons to enter college are very much affected by changes in the rates of return to human capital. Table 7.3 shows Freeman's calculation of the percentage of 18- and 19-year-olds who had chosen to enroll in college for 1969 and 1974. The data on enrollment can be compared to Freeman's rate of return data in Table 7.2. The data show a steep drop in enrollment rates for males. The decline for females is quite minor, but it brought to a halt what had been a strong upward trend in female enrollment rates. While Table 7.3 is only suggestive of a supply response, Freeman presents more sophisticated econometric evidence of a close relationship between the relative earnings of college graduates and college enrollment rates. When the effect of the military draft is controlled for, Freeman

Table 7.3
Percentage of 18- and 19-year-olds enrolled in college

Year	Sex	
	Male	**Female**
1969	44.0%	34.4%
1974	33.4%	33.0%

SOURCE: Richard Freeman, *The Over-Educated American*, Academic, New York, 1976.

estimates that a 1 percent change in the ratio of college to high school wages will induce an increase of about 3.71 percent in the proportion of 18- and 19-year-olds who enroll in college.

7.4

THE OPERATION OF THE MARKET FOR HUMAN CAPITAL

We examine now the operations of the labor market in which labor is not homogeneous. However, to illustrate the importance of human capital, we need to relax the assumption of homogeneity of labor only partially. Specifically, we assume that there are two types of labor: those with high school diplomas and those with a college degree. For the sake of manageability, we shall assume further that a high school graduate is not a perfect substitute in the production process for a college graduate, but that all high school graduates are perfect substitutes for each other, as are all college graduates.[4]

If potential college enrollees decide to obtain a degree so long as the rate of return on the degree exceeds their internal rate of time preference, and if people differ significantly in their internal rates of time preference, then the quantity of college graduates supplied to the labor market will be positively related to the rate of return to a college degree. The rate of return to a college degree will in turn be greater the higher the wage of college graduates relative to high school graduates. A long-run *relative* supply curve of college graduates can thus be constructed as in Fig. 7.1. The wage of college graduates relative to high school graduates is labeled W_c / W_{hs} along the vertical axis. When rates of return and hence the relative wage of college graduates are low, only those with low internal rates of time preference will be attracted to the degree-requiring occupations. As the relative wage of (and rate of return to) college graduates increases, the quantity of degree holders will increase as persons of successively higher rates of time preference find the rate of return to be sufficiently high to induce their entry. Note, however, that as long as there is an investment required to obtain a college degree, the supply curve will be entirely above a relative wage of 1.00, since a relative wage below 1.00 implies a negative rate of return. If the financial inducement were the only inducement to investment in higher education, then a short-run negative return would in the long run result in a discouragement of college attendance until the rate of return was once again positive.

In Fig. 7.2 we superimpose a demand curve for college graduates. Given that there is diminishing marginal productivity for both types of

---

[4] Thus, college graduates are still treated as homogeneous with respect to each other, as are high school graduates. In the next chapter, when we analyze supply to and earnings in various occupations, we relax completely the assumption of homogeneous labor.

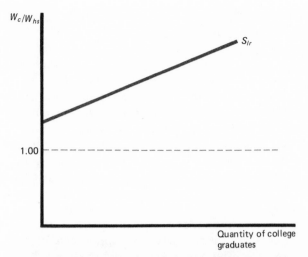

Figure 7.1. The long-run supply of college graduates. The higher the ratio of wages of college graduates to the wages of high school graduates W_c/W_{hs}, the greater will be the quantity of college graduates supplied to the labor market in the long run, as illustrated by the supply curve S_{lr}.

labor, the demand curve for college graduates will be a negative function of the relative wage. The interaction of the long-run demand and supply of college graduates determines the equilibrium relative wage, $(W_c/W_{hs})_e$, and consequent rate of return.

Figure 7.2. The equilibrium relative wage rate of college graduates. The equilibrium relative wage of college graduates $(W_c/W_{hs})_e$ is determined by the interaction of the relative demand D and supply S_{lr} of college graduates.

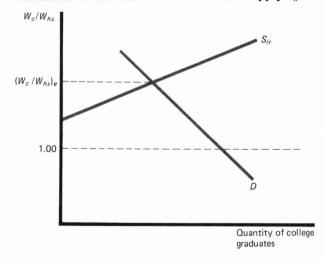

We might ask how long is the long run of our analysis. Given that it takes 4 years to produce a college graduate from a high school graduate, the complete adjustment to long-run equilibrium in response to a change in demand may require the passage of a considerable length of time. This is not to say that there won't be a short-run supply response, however. In Fig. 7.3 we analyze the consequence of an increase in the demand for college graduates from D_1 to D_2. The market is initially in both short- and long-run equilibrium at the intersection of D_1, S_{lr} (the long-run supply curve), and S_{sr1} (the initial short-run supply curve). The equilibrium relative wage is W_1. The short-run supply will probably be quite inelastic, but not perfectly inelastic. In response to the higher wage W_2 resulting from the shift in demand to D_2, some college-educated persons not in the labor force (such as married women working in the home) will enter the labor force because the return to market work is now higher. To put it otherwise, the opportunity cost of household work will have risen. The higher wage will induce a greater number of high school graduates to seek college degrees so that the

---

Figure 7.3. Long- and short-run responses to changes in the relative demand for college graduates. The market is initially in both short- and long-run equilibrium at the intersection of D_1 (the initial demand curve), S_{lr} (the long-run supply curve), and S_{sr1} (the initial short-run supply curve). The initial equilibrium relative wage is W_1. As demand shifts to D_2, the relative wage rises in the short run to W_2 which then induces an increase in short-run supply. The market is again in long-run equilibrium when the short-run supply curve shifts out to S_{sr2} and the equilibrium relative wage is W_3.

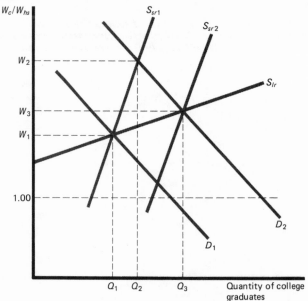

short-run supply curve shifts to the right. In the absence of further disturbances, the increased supply of college graduates will move the relative wage rate downward. The increases in the supply of college graduates will continue, and continue to cause the relative wage of college graduates to fall until a long-run equilibrium is achieved at the relative wage W_3. W_3 must of necessity be higher than W_1 because the increase in the quantity of labor demanded from Q_1 to Q_3 can only be forthcoming if the relative earnings of college graduates are higher than initially so that persons of higher internal rates of time preference are attracted into seeking a college degree. In this manner the changing demands of the economy are met.

But what if the choices of individuals with respect to college attendance are affected by numerous other factors besides financial returns and costs, as of course they are? One of the factors that leads people to choose college is the increase in prestige from having a degree. There is also the status enjoyed by people in occupations that require a college degree, independent of the status derived from the higher incomes of those occupations. In addition, education may improve the efficiency of consumption, or in other words, enable consumers to allocate their budgets more effectively than those with less information. Prospective college students may give consideration to the greater security in the form of lower unemployment rates that are experienced by college graduates. If an individual values these non-wage benefits, their value must have a dollar equivalent—the amount of wages the individual would be willing to give up each year in order to enjoy these nonwage benefits. If an individual considers these benefits to be equivalent to, for example, a 2 percent return on investment, then that individual would be willing to invest in a college education yielding a financial return of 8 percent even if his or her internal rate of time preference were as high as 10 percent. If everyone viewed the benefits as being worth an additional 2 percent, then the supply curve of college graduates depicted in Fig. 7.1 would shift downward: each quantity of college graduates (given along the horizontal axis) would be forthcoming at a relative wage for college graduates that would yield a 2 percent lower rate of return than would be observed if wage considerations alone were considered. Of course, people differ widely in the value that they place on the nonwage aspects of receiving a college degree. The prestige afforded by entrance into college-level occupations, for example, is highly subjective. While a bank teller's status and working conditions may be considerably valued in some segments of society, they are not so envied in others. One can hardly imagine the bank teller being held in high esteem in a ghetto where the local hero is a gang leader. The problem of peer rejection is a very real (though seldom discussed) disincentive to the acquisition of human capital among poverty-level groups.

The effect of widely varying valuations of nonwage aspects is to make the slope of the supply curve of college graduates steeper. Toward the lower end of the supply curve will be concentrated those individuals who not only have low rates of time preference but also place a particularly high value on nonwage aspects of obtaining a degree. The upper extreme of the supply curve will contain those persons with very high internal rates of time preference and very low, or possibly negative, valuations of nonwage considerations.[5]

Even the costs of acquiring a college degree have a subjective or nonfinancial element. There is a psychic cost to attending college. The effort required to obtain a degree may be a substantial cost to some, particularly those whose abilities and inclinations do not lean so heavily in the academic direction. On the other hand, what is pain to some may be perfectly enjoyable to the proverbial "true scholar." Attendance at college is at least partially a consumption good for such an individual. Further, there are some aspects of college life, such as an enjoyable atmosphere and the postponement of market work, that to varying degrees are consumption benefits which reduce the true investment cost of obtaining a college degree. The nonfinancial costs of education are particularly subjective and hence highly variable from person to person. We cannot say whether on balance they are positive or negative. We can say, however, that the individual who regards the costs as substantial will require a higher financial rate of return, *ceteris paribus,* in order to be induced to attend college. The individual who regards these nonfinancial costs as negative—i.e., as providing positive utility and thereby reducing the true cost of education—will settle for a smaller financial return.

In summary, the subjective nature of certain costs and benefits does not diminish the link between labor markets and the behavior of individuals in the acquisition of human capital. An increase in the economy's demands for college graduates relative to high school graduates, for example, will still result in an increase in the wages of college graduates relative to high school graduates. The higher relative wage of college graduates will still result in a higher relative quantity of college graduates being supplied to the market, as depicted in Fig. 7.3. Further, any change in the costs of acquiring a college degree will have a predictable effect. A decrease in the cost of education to individuals, given a particular demand schedule for graduates and its resulting equilibrium relative wage, will initially raise the rate of return to a college degree. The higher rate of return will result in a rightward shift of the supply curve of college graduates because now at each possible relative wage the higher rate of return will induce more individuals to

---

[5]The effect of interpersonal variations in valuations of nonwage aspects is discussed in much greater detail in the next chapter, in our presentation of occupational wage differences.

seek a degree. Given the negative slope of the demand curve, the new equilibrium relative wage will be lower than before and the equilibrium quantity greater than before.

Because forgone earnings make up the greater part of the costs of schooling, changes in unemployment rates among high school graduates should affect college enrollment rates. During a recession many high school graduates will be unable to find jobs, or will only be able to find jobs that pay less than they could obtain under more normal circumstances. Thus the forgone earnings component of schooling costs may be eliminated or significantly reduced. In fact, school enrollment rates do tend to be higher during recessions and lower during expansionary periods, the opposite of the relationship of the business cycle to labor force participation rates of youth.[6]

We can also examine the effects of any changes in the subjective factors that influence individual behavior. Collegiate football may serve as a minor illustration. Presumably, collegiate football is a positive side benefit to many who attend college, and can, *ceteris paribus,* yield more utility to a student than to someone with no emotional tie or identification with the college. Further, this utility is provided at a significantly lower cost than to regular ticket purchasers. Now suppose that collegiate football is abolished. Let us assume that its abolition does not lower the cost of education to individuals.[7] Since one of the nonfinancial benefits to higher education will now be gone, the long-run supply curve of college graduates will eventually decrease, resulting in a higher relative wage for college graduates and a correspondingly higher financial rate of return.

We might like to think that the existence of collegiate football is a relatively trivial consideration affecting the decision to attend college; if so, the effect of its abolition on supply, relative wages, and rates of return will also be trivial. Other nonfinancial considerations are not so trivial. The ending of the Vietnam War and the draft (and consequently the ending of the value of the college deferment from the draft) had a substantial effect. As we have shown, the percentage of high school graduates choosing to attend college ceased its upward trend and appears to have slightly reversed itself in the early and mid-1970s. While a falling financial rate of return can explain the lower rates of college enrollments, the ending of the draft undoubtedly contributed to declining enrollment among males.

---

[6]For an empirical analysis of the inverse relation between labor force participation rates of youth and their school enrollment rates, see R. Fearn, "Labor Force and School Participation of Teenagers," Ph.D. dissertation, University of Chicago, 1968.

[7]This assumption seems reasonably valid on balance, since at the larger universities revenues from football programs generally exceed costs while at smaller schools the reverse tends to be true.

In this section we have limited the analysis to but one type of human capital investment, the acquisition of a bachelor's degree. The principles involved can be easily generalized to other investments in formal education. An individual with a bachelor's degree can evaluate the benefits and costs of obtaining a master's degree, and an individual with a master's degree can evaluate the desirability of obtaining a Ph.D. From the perspective of a 16-year-old who is no longer legally obliged to remain in school, a decision will be made as to whether to proceed on to graduation from high school. Just as there are shifts in the economy's demands for and supplies of four-year college graduates relative to high school graduates, there are shifts in the economy's demands for and supplies of master's degree holders relative to those with a bachelor's degree. The method of analysis is the same.

Further, formal education is not the only type of investment in human capital. Indeed, any expenditure to raise future wages can be viewed as an investment. An expenditure on health may have an investment aspect that can be analyzed within the framework presented here. The decision to migrate from one area to another also can be analyzed within a human capital framework. Nor are individual household members the only investors in human capital. Governments, acting partially out of the conviction that formal education bestows benefits to society beyond those accruing to the individuals receiving the schooling, have heavily subsidized the education industry in order to increase the supply of human capital. Firms also make investments in human capital. Let us now turn our attention to the decision-making process of the firm with respect to its investment in human capital.

7.5

FIRM BEHAVIOR: ON-THE-JOB TRAINING[8]

When in a free market we observe that there is a positive return to investment in human capital, it must be the case that supply-and-demand conditions dictate that persons with a higher degree of education receive higher wages. If we discount the "screening hypothesis," the most important reason for the higher wages must be that human capital investment raises productivity. Suppose that a firm is in the position to raise the value of marginal product of a worker from $VMPP^b$ (before training) to $VMPP^a$ (after training) through the expenditure of funds on training. The difference between $VMPP^a$ and $VMPP^b$ is the return to the firm for having made the investment. The return is received not just once,

[8] With modification, our treatment of on-the-job training follows the analysis developed in G. S. Becker, *Human Capital,* 2d ed., National Bureau of Economic Research, New York, 1975; and in W. Oi, "Labor as a Quasi-Fixed Factor," *Journal of Political Economy,* vol. 70, December 1962, pp. 538–555.

but during each period for which the employee remains with the firm. Let us take each period to represent a year and assume that the firm completes its training of the worker within 1 year at a particular cost C, which is borne by the firm. The firm will have made a good investment if the discounted present value of the returns to training exceeds the cost of training, i.e., if

$$C < \sum_{i=1}^{n} \left(\frac{\text{VMPP}_i^a - \text{VMPP}_i^b}{(1 + r)^i} \right) \tag{7.4}$$

where in this case i represents the year in which the benefit is received, with $i = 1$ in the first year following the investment; n is the number of years for which the worker can be expected to remain with the firm; and r is the opportunity rate of return to the firm (the rate of return it can receive on its best alternative investment). In equation (7.4) we can see the similarity between the human capital investment decision process of the firm and that of the individual.

The nature of the costs of training vary greatly with the type of training. These costs may include materials used up in the production process, the wages of those conducting the training, and the extent to which the trainee's output is reduced during the period of training. The question arises: What is the optimal amount of training that a firm will undertake for a given individual? Where there are potential returns to training, the returns will diminish with increased investment. The marginal returns will diminish if for no other reason than that increasing the period of investment decreases the number of remaining periods over which the return can be received. The optimal amount of investment, therefore, will be that amount for which the *marginal* present value of returns is equal to the *marginal* cost of additional training.

Where employers do not engage in on-the-job training or incur other "start-up" costs of employment, the firm will be willing to retain a worker in a given period only if the VMPP during that period is at least as high as the wage for that period. When employers have made investments in training, however, the criterion changes. Labor becomes a "quasi-fixed" factor of production and the investments become sunk costs. The firm that lays off a worker because her VMPP in the present period is below her wage runs the risk of not being able to rehire the worker when in the future its employment expands. The firm will then have to invest in the training of new workers. When employers have already invested in a worker, the necessary condition for her retention is that the present value of her future VMPPs equals or exceeds the present value of her future wages, i.e.,

$$\sum_{i=0}^{n} \frac{W_i}{(1 + r)^i} \leq \sum_{i=0}^{n} \frac{\text{VMPP}_i}{(1 + r)^i} \tag{7.5}$$

where $i = 0$ in the current year and n is again the number of remaining years of worklife of the employee. In periods of slack business activity (when current value of marginal product will fall below the current wage for many workers), employers will be reluctant to release workers if employers see the slack as temporary. With fixed costs of employment, particularly training costs, it should be apparent that investments by firms in human capital will, *ceteris paribus,* lead to greater stability of employment for those workers receiving training. One example, although somewhat dated, illustrates the importance of the fixed costs of employment to firms. In his previously cited work, Walter Oi found one firm (International Harvester in 1951) to have invested in workers amounts ranging from $125 on average for a common laborer to nearly $19,000 for a highly skilled craftsman.

7.6
GENERAL VERSUS SPECIFIC TRAINING

We have thus far ignored the problems that employers might have in the retention of workers. If a firm invests in a worker under the expectation that the worker will remain until retirement, the firm may not recoup its entire investment if the worker quits prematurely. If a firm expended $10,000 to train one of its workers as an electrician, the worker's VMPP would be raised not only for his present employer but for anyone else who might employ him. What would prevent the worker from quitting the day after finishing his training in order to go to work for another employer willing to pay a higher wage than the worker's present employer has been paying him? While the present employer could raise the employee's wage to meet the competition, he would engage himself in a losing battle. He would be acting irrationally to pay the worker a wage higher than his VMPP, but every other potential employer would be willing to pay him his VMPP. In such a competitive situation the firm that engages in the training of electricians will not receive any return on its investment at all, since it would have to raise the wage to the same extent that the worker's productivity has been raised. Other firms would have to pay the same higher wage, but will operate more profitably because they bear no training costs. It should then not be difficult to understand why firms do not usually train their own electricians. This type of training is referred to as "general training." By general training, we mean any type of training which raises the marginal product of a worker not only to his firm but to other firms as well. Besides our electrician, other examples would be machinists, accountants, typists, and many others. By contrast, what is referred to as "specific training" involves types of training which are of value only to the employing firm or, at most, to the industry of the employing firm. For the reason given above, firms will not provide general training unless workers pay for the training by accepting a wage below their marginal products during the training period. Some firms such as plumbing contractors will operate apprenticeship programs.

The cost is borne by the apprentices in the form of very low wages as compared to those received by journeymen. Where there is a zero or near-zero marginal product during training, firms providing general training will actually charge for it. For example, many hospitals operate nursing schools, but the nursing students pay the cost of their training. More typically, general training is the specialty of vocational schools, colleges, and universities.

By virtue of the very nature of specific training, it is difficult to give recognizable examples, but some illustrations are possible. Telephone linemen have received training that is largely specific, and hence of value only to one company in a given area. Some firms have developed cost accounting techniques that are particular to their firm or industry. Even firms that engage in highly specific training will have some problem with employee turnover. Training is more likely to be specific to the industry than to the firm, so that other firms in the industry may reap the benefits of training expenditures. However, rival firms within an industry may be widely separated geographically so that they exert a minor influence. Yet not even the firm with perfectly firm specific training is immune from employee turnover. If such a firm pays the trained worker the equivalent of his productivity value elsewhere, any number of nonwage reasons might attract the worker elsewhere. Thus, it is in the interest of the firm offering specific training to pay a wage somewhat higher than what the worker could obtain elsewhere, but below his marginal product with his present firm. The higher wage will not only discourage the worker from leaving after the training is received, it will also provide an incentive for him to undergo the training in the first place.[9] John Pencavel has argued and shown empirically that there is a negative relation between quit rates and the size of the wage premium that firms pay to workers with specific training. In effect, a firm simultaneously chooses the wage premium that it will pay and the quit rate that it is willing to accept. The firm's choice of a quit rate will depend on the extent of its investment in specific training. As expected, higher wage premiums are paid by firms with higher investments in specific training.[10]

Other nonwage inducements such as seniority recognition and nonvested pension plans serve to reduce turnover.[11] A firm will be more interested in these types of inducements the more involved it is in

---

[9]For a comprehensive analysis of the relation between specific investment and quit and layoff rates, see D. Parsons, "Specific Human Capital: An Application to Quit Rates and Layoff Rates," *Journal of Political Economy,* vol. 80, November/December 1972, pp. 1120–1143.

[10]J. Pencavel, "Wages, Specific Training, and Labor Turnover in U.S. Manufacturing Industries," *International Economic Review,* vol. 13, February 1972, pp. 53–64.

[11]A pension is vested if an employee retains rights to the pension even though he leaves the company. A pension is nonvested if the employee loses rights to the pension upon leaving the firm.

on-the-job training and other investments in its workers. While the public is accustomed to thinking of seniority arrangements as something that firms reluctantly give in to in their negotiations with unions, the truth is that firms generally see such arrangements as in their interest. As for pension plans, we may see employers grow less interested in them since the drift of recent "pension reform" law seems to be away from nonvested pensions. Vested plans, of course, would not serve the function of reducing turnover.

Much has been said in recent years about the Occupational Safety and Health Act which Congress passed in the hopes of significantly reducing industrial accident rates. Yet the statistical evidence does not suggest that the act has had a measurable effect despite the vast enforcement powers granted to the administrators of the act.[12] The costs of training and other investments in workers may explain this. Congress apparently acted under the assumption that the profit motive does not induce employers to provide reasonably safe working conditions, but that it in fact works in the opposite direction. But no employer who has invested $20,000 in a worker (as many have), who has to purchase experience-rated Workmen's Compensation Insurance, and who is subject to lawsuit by injured workers can be indifferent to the safety of his workers. Such employers have at least as much incentive to protect their workers as their machines. Consequently, there may have been little improvement that could likely have resulted from the Occupational Safety and Health Act.

If the trend toward heavy investment in workers has led to greater employment stability and the provision of safer worker conditions, it has perhaps made more difficult the plight of the older worker who loses his job. If the jobs that are available require heavy fixed investments, employers will be reluctant to employ older workers because, whatever the investment cost, the return on that investment will be larger the greater the number of working years that the employee has left. Employers will demonstrate a similar reluctance to employ and invest heavily in female workers because they expect women to withdraw periodically from the labor force to marry or bear children. As a result, women have not been given the same opportunities as men to receive on-the-job training.

7.7

HUMAN CAPITAL AND ADJUSTMENTS IN THE LABOR MARKET

We have documented the existence of a financial return to investment in human capital. We have also established that individuals do respond in

---

[12]See R. Smith, *The Occupational Safety and Health Act,* American Enterprise Institute for Public Policy Research, Washington, D.C., 1976.

a predictable fashion to changes in the rate of return on investment in human capital. We should also point out that, as expected, the relative wage of college graduates is in turn affected by the changes in the supply of college graduates. Freeman, in the studies reported above, finds that a 1 percent shift in the supply of college graduates leads to a 0.39 percent change in the opposite direction of the relative wage of college graduates.

Despite the apparently straightforward arguments presented in this chapter, we should stress that we have dealt in the main with long-run equilibrium in the market for human capital, having glossed over the process of adjustment from one long-run equilibrium to another. The adjustment process is lengthy, somewhat complicated, but very important. We postpone a more comprehensive discussion of this adjustment process until Chap. 9.

We note again that we have gone but part of the way in relaxing our earlier assumption of the homogeneity of labor. Up to this point it has been sufficient for our purposes to consider the existence of but two grades of labor—college graduates and high school graduates. Such a treatment is illustrative, but highly aggregated and thus somewhat superficial. The markets for engineers, elementary school teachers, physical therapists, and accountants are in important respects distinct from each other, even though all four occupations require a college degree. It is for this reason that we postpone any further discussion of the adjustment process in labor markets until after we have analyzed the long-run supply to specific occupations, the subject matter of the following chapter.

QUESTIONS AND EXERCISES

1. Our analysis of the human capital investment decision implicitly assumes that the individual already has the funds necessary to attend college and that present consumption is the only alternative use of the funds. How would the analysis change if (*a*) the individual has to borrow funds at the going interest rate in order to attend college, or (*b*) if the individual has the funds but can invest them at the going interest rate?

2. In light of your answer to the above question, how would you expect a change in the interest rate to affect the supply of college graduates?

3. How would the supply curve of college graduates be affected by a change to a more progressive income tax system? How would the relative wage of college graduates be affected?

4. Why does the fact of diminishing marginal productivity of both high school and college graduates lead to the negatively sloped relative demand curves for college graduates in Figs. 7.1 and 7.2?

5. Investment tax credits have not been applicable to firms' investments in on-the-job training. If they were applicable, would they influence the amount of human capital investment that firms would undertake?

Does the current system of investment tax credits discourage human capital formation?

6. It is often argued that education bestows benefits upon society at large for which the recipient of education is not compensated in the form of higher wages. What might these benefits be? These benefits have provided an economic justification for the public subsidy of education. Can we conceptually determine the optimal extent of subsidization?

REFERENCES FOR FURTHER READING

An excellent introduction to the concept of human capital is T. W. Schultz, "Investment in Human Capital," *American Economic Review,* vol. 51, March 1961, pp. 1–17. For a discussion of social versus private benefits and costs associated with education, see B. A. Weisbrod, "Education and Investment in Human Capital," *Journal of Political Economy,* vol. 70, October 1962 (supp.), pp. 106–123. In the same issue, see the article by J. Mincer, "On-the-Job Training: Costs, Returns, and Some Implications," pp. 50–79. A discussion of the human capital approach to health (also in the same issue) is S. J. Mushkin, "Health as an Investment," pp. 129–157.

LONG-RUN EQUILIBRIUM WAGE DIFFERENCES

The purpose of this chapter is to analyze permanent differences in average wages across various occupations. We are particularly concerned with those differences that exist in long-run equilibrium and not so much concerned with transitional differences, the subject of the following chapter. Nor are we concerned with wage differences that may be attributable to labor market imperfections such as discrimination or monopsony. More specifically, we are concerned with the major factors that account for equilibrium differences in occupational wages and with the ways in which changes in these factors alter the structure of occupational wages.

8.1

WHY DO OCCUPATIONAL WAGES DIFFER?

In equilibrium, occupational wage differences will exist because of the following reasons: (*a*) the costs of acquiring the skills necessary to enter the various occupations differ; (*b*) people differ in their internal rates of time preference; (*c*) nonwage aspects of occupations (such aspects as prestige, working conditions, etc.) are considerably varied; (*d*) people differ in their evaluations of, or tastes for, these nonwage aspects; (*e*) occupations differ with respect to the variability of earnings (the degree of riskiness) of the occupation; (*f*) people differ significantly in their willingness to expose themselves to risk. Each of these factors affects the supply of workers to an occupation, and we examine the effects of each below. In the process we shall have almost completely relaxed the assumption of homogeneity of labor. As a result we will have replaced our concept of "the labor market" with a realization that in the real world, there are at least as many distinct but interrelated labor markets as there are occupations.

8.1a
Differences in the costs of acquiring skills

Occupations differ in the amount of money that individuals must spend in order to acquire the skills necessary to enter an occupation. Let us consider two hypothetical occupations: entrance into occupation A, a skilled occupation, requires costly training; entrance into occupation B, an unskilled occupation, requires no training. If the jobs were comparable in all other respects, and if all workers had the same tastes and the same internal rates of time preference, then the fact that occupation A requires a human capital investment will result in workers requiring a wage premium in order to be induced to enter occupation A. It doesn't matter whether the investment required is in the form of a college degree, a trade school course, an apprenticeship program partially financed by the worker, or in some other form. As long as there is some investment cost to the worker, he or she has no incentive, given our assumptions, to enter occupation A unless it pays better than occupation B. Figure 8.1 illustrates the resulting supply curve to occupation A relative to B. The relative supply of persons to A will be perfectly elastic at the wage ratio W_e. W_e must be greater than 1.00, but how much greater than 1.00? Our analysis of the human capital decision in the previous chapter provides the answer. The wage ratio must exceed 1.00

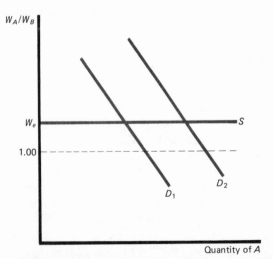

Figure 8.1. Occupational wage differences attributable to differences in the cost of acquiring skills. If occupation A is more costly to enter than occupation B, then the equilibrium ratio of wages in A to wages in B, W_e, must be greater than 1.00. Changes in demand from D_1 to D_2 will not change the long-run equilibrium wage ratio.

by just enough to equate the rate of return on the investment with the internal rate of time preference that we assume here to be the same for everyone. If the ratio were to go above W_e, persons would leave occupation B to enter A, causing the wage to rise for B but to fall for A. The movement of persons from occupation B to occupation A would continue until the wage ratio returned to W_e, leaving everyone indifferent as between the two occupations. By the same reasoning, a fall in the relative wage below W_e would induce people to leave the skilled occupation A for the unskilled occupation B, eventually causing the relative wage ratio to rise to W_e. Hence we have the perfectly elastic supply of persons to occupation A at the relative wage W_e. Under our assumed conditions, changes in demand will not affect the equilibrium relative wage.

8.1b
Differences in internal rates of time preference
The effect of differences in costs of acquiring skills becomes more complicated when we recognize and take account of the fact that people differ in their internal rates of time preference. Relying again on our discussion of the previous chapter, we can see that differences in internal rates of time preference will result in the supply of persons to occupation A being less than perfectly elastic. Hence the supply curve will have an upward slope as depicted in Fig. 8.2, with persons of low rates of time preference being located toward the lower end of the supply curve. Because people differ in their internal rates of time preference, the equilibrium wage ratio will depend on the state of demand. But at every level of demand some wage premium exists—the

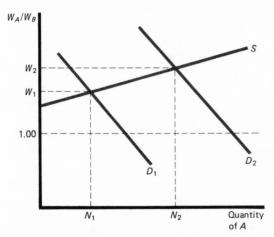

Figure 8.2. Occupational wage differences associated with differences in internal rates of time preference. When internal rates of time preference differ, the supply curve S to a skilled occupation A will be a positive function of the relative wage. Hence, a change in the relative demand for A from D_1 to D_2 will raise the equilibrium relative wage from W_1 to W_2.

wage ratio is greater than 1.00. Figure 8.2 illustrates the fact that if the demand for skilled occupation A were to increase from D_1 to D_2, the ratio of wages in occupation A to those of occupation B must rise from W_1 to W_2 in order to induce a larger flow of persons into occupation A. The higher relative wage would have at the margin induced into occupation A persons whose internal rates of time preference are higher than those who would have been attracted at the wage W_1. Thus, while it is true that differences among occupations in costs of acquiring requisite skills will result in the existence of a wage premium for more skilled occupations, the size of that premium will be affected by the level of demand.

8.1c
Nonwage aspects of occupations

The above discussion might lead one to believe that two occupations requiring the same pattern of human capital investment must in equilibrium pay the same wage, but such is not the case. Occupations do differ in terms of their nonwage aspects, and these differences will be reflected in relative wages. Working conditions, most people will agree, are more pleasant for a retail clerk than for a coal miner, and this difference in working conditions will affect the equilibrium difference in wages between the two occupations. The prestige of a job will affect its attractiveness and hence its wage. Some occupations provide more opportunities than others for moving into better-paying occupations. Accountants, for example, have a better opportunity to move into executive positions than do persons trained in pharmacy. In fact, any aspect of a job which affects its attractiveness will affect its relative wage. (The degree of security of an occupation also affects its attractiveness, but we shall discuss that nonwage aspect separately.)

To illustrate the effect of nonwage aspects of jobs, let us take as examples two occupations which require no human capital investment. However, one of the jobs is more prestigious than the other. We shall label the high-prestige occupation as H, the low-prestige occupation as L. If everyone had exactly the same taste for the added prestige of occupation H, then the supply of persons to occupation L will be perfectly elastic at a wage ratio W_L/W_H, that is just enough to compensate individuals in occupation L for the lower prestige of their jobs. Thus, the wage ratio must exceed 1.00, as in Fig. 8.3. The excess of W_L over W_H is called an "equalizing difference," because it is a premium which must be paid in order to equalize the net advantage of the two occupations when both pay and prestige are taken into account. For that matter, equalizing differences must exist in order to compensate for *any* nonwage differences among occupations. Any short-term deviation of the relative wage from the equilibrium ratio will induce movement of workers until the equilibrium relative wage is restored. Viewed from the perspective of the more attractive occupation, its members can be thought of as receiving a "psychic wage," i.e., the converse of an equalizing difference.

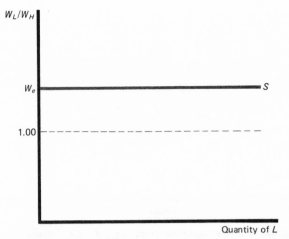

Figure 8.3. Occupational wage differences attributable to differences in nonwage aspects of jobs. As between two jobs, one of which is a high-prestige job H and the other a low-prestige job L, the wage to L must be higher. The long-run supply curve S to occupation L will be perfectly elastic at the relative wage W_e if the two jobs are alike in all other respects and workers have the same tastes.

8.1d
Differences in tastes for nonwage aspects of jobs

The explanation of equalizing differences would be fairly straightforward if workers all had the same tastes for nonwage aspects of jobs as we assumed them to have in our preceding explanation. To approach reality we must take our analysis one step further and account for the fact that people differ in their tastes: what is a highly attractive aspect of a certain occupation for one person may be substantially less attractive for another. This being the case, a low relative wage ratio for occupation L will tend to bring to that occupation those potential workers who place the least value on the nonwage attributes of occupation H or other reference occupations. A higher relative wage for L will attract workers who are less inclined toward occupation L. As in Fig. 8.4, the supply of persons to occupation L will be a positive function of the relative wage for L. Note that it is not necessary that the entire supply curve to occupation L lie above a wage ratio of 1.00. Not only do people place different values on the nonwage aspects of jobs but also an attribute may have a positive value for some and a negative value for others. One intuitively apparent example is the military service; the military way of life is very appealing to some but repugnant to others. When demand is appropriately low enough, say D_1 in Fig. 8.4, a wage ratio below 1.00 may attract a sufficient number of persons into occupation L to meet demand, even if *most* people find occupation L to be relatively unattractive. If relative demand were to increase to D_2, the additional labor will be forthcoming only as the wage ratio rises above 1.00 to W_2. It is safe to say that the additional entrants into occupation L will enjoy

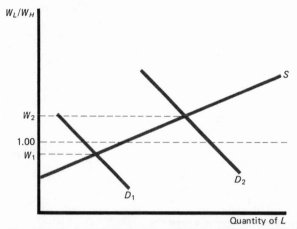

Figure 8.4. Occupational wage differences attributable to differences in tastes for nonwage aspects of jobs. When workers differ in their tastes for nonwage aspects of jobs, the supply curve to an occupation S will be upward-sloping. In this example the equalizing difference is negative when demand is D₁, but positive when demand is D₂.

their work less than those who chose the occupation when the relative wage for L was W_1.

There is one striking example of the way in which changing occupational demands will alter not only wage rates but also the typical characteristics of persons in that occupation. Most people would find the work of steel workers (those who rivet girders in skyscraper construction) to be frighteningly unattractive, since they must walk in open air on narrow girders many hundreds of feet above the ground. Some of us are more fearful than others and would require a huge premium in order to do this kind of work. When skyscrapers first began to appear in Manhattan, not many riveters were demanded. Most of the work was done by Mohawk Indians, who have the quality of being relatively unafraid of heights. Thus, not much of an equalizing difference had to be paid. However, as demand for this type of labor increased, a much higher relative wage was necessary in order to attract persons less unafraid of heights, since there was a limited supply of Mohawk Indians. An insignificant fraction of this work is now done by Mohawks, as the wage is now high enough to attract a demographically more representative segment of the labor force.

8.1e
Occupational variability of earnings
Two occupations may have the same average annual wage but differ in the variability of earnings within the occupation. In some occupations such as high school teaching, an individual can with virtual certainty come within several thousand dollars of the mean annual earnings of the occupation. But should an individual decide to enter the acting profes-

sion, he or she may earn an income anywhere from zero to a million dollars or more per year. Knowledge of the average annual earnings of actors is not very helpful in allowing an individual to form an expectation of what annual income may be because the dispersion of earnings among actors and actresses is so great. A person who chooses acting is subjected consequently to considerable risk because of not being able to determine in advance how well he or she will fare. Further, wide dispersion of earnings among members. of an occupation is not the only type of risk. Earnings of an individual may vary considerably over a lifetime in one occupation but less so in another occupation. For one thing, the risk of unemployment varies considerably among occupations, and the security of an occupation undoubtedly affects the decision of people to enter it. Those in self-employed occupations can be particularly subject to considerable year-to-year variation in earnings.

Risk—i.e., variability of earnings both at a point in time and over time—will affect the supply of persons to an occupation. Most people are risk averters in that if two occupations were identical in every respect, including average earnings, but one occupation were riskier, they would choose the less risky occupation. If all people were equally averse to risk, then the supply of persons to the risky occupation would be perfectly elastic at a wage ratio that contained a premium just high enough to compensate for the added risk. A graph of the supply curve would look like Fig. 8.1, where occupation A is the riskier occupation. We know, however, that some people are more willing than others to subject themselves to risk. Accounting for this fact, we can expect that individuals who are less risk averse will be willing to enter occupation A at a relatively low compensation for risk (that is, at a lower relative wage) than those less willing to take risks. The result would be an upward-sloping supply function as in Fig. 8.2. The supply curve to occupation A may even have a segment below a wage ratio 1.00, as in Fig. 8.4, if there are some potential entrants to A who actually seek risk rather than avoid it. This possibility is plausible because some people probably have an unrealistic faith either in luck or in their ability to end up on the upper end of a widely scattered distribution of earnings. The question is largely moot, however, since empirical evidence strongly suggests that occupational labor markets are dominated by risk averters.[1]

8.2

OCCUPATIONAL WAGE DIFFERENCES IN PERSPECTIVE
Having discussed individually the factors that influence permanent occupational wage differences, we should pause and reflect upon the significance of all factors influencing occupational wage differences.

---

[1]For a more advanced analysis of risk aversion and risk preference, see M. Friedman, *Price Theory,* Aldine, Chicago, 1976, chap. 4, pp. 76–84.

First, we should recognize what factors give the supply curve to an occupation its upward slope: they are the interpersonal differences in internal rates of time preference, tastes, and degree of risk aversion. Differences among occupations in terms of necessary human capital investment, nonwage attributes of jobs, and the riskiness of jobs give rise to occupational wage differences by shifting occupational supply curves upward or downward, but do not give the supply curves their upward slope. Second, one should recognize that in all our explanations we have analyzed occupational wage differences as though workers had only two occupations from which to choose. Had we attempted more realism in our analysis, we would have compared an occupation's wages, human capital investment, nonwage aspects, risk, etc., with an index of these same factors for all other relevant occupations combined. Such an explanatory procedure would have been tedious and would not have added any information or altered the conclusions or generalizations that we have drawn, however. Third, the dominant influence of differences in human capital should be recognized. There have been numerous studies of differences in earnings levels among individuals, and the difference in human capital endowment is invariably the single most significant factor explaining variability in earnings. The link between human capital investment and occupational wage levels is multifaceted. A large part of the private return to investing in higher levels of education comes from the fact that acquisition of a certain level of education enables an individual to enter higher-paying occupations where some minimum educational requirements exist. Yet even *within* occupations much of the variation in earnings is explained by differences in human capital.[2]

We have stated that employers are willing to pay a higher wage for persons with greater human capital because they are more productive. But it is not the higher productivity per se that causes the wage to be higher. A firm can vary the combination of skilled and unskilled labor with which it can produce a given output, just as it can vary the mix of labor and capital. Given that the marginal productivity of both skilled and unskilled labor diminishes, the firm will have reached the optimal combination of skilled and unskilled labor when each group's marginal productivity is equal to its wage rate. It then must also be true that the ratio of the value of marginal products for the two groups be equal to the ratio of relative wages, i.e., $\text{VMPP}_s / \text{VMPP}_u = W_s / W_u$, where the subscripts s and u represent skilled and unskilled workers respectively. If the wage rate for skilled workers were to fall, employers would produce a given output with a different mix of labor, using more skilled labor (thereby lowering its VMPP) and less unskilled labor (thus raising its

[2]A. Mayhew, "Education, Occupation, and Earnings," *Industrial and Labor Relations Review,* vol. 24, January 1971, pp. 216–225.

VMPP). Once again, the ratio of values of marginal product would be equal to the wage ratio. In fact, all the relative demand curves in this and the preceding chapter can be derived along these lines. The important point to note here is that the marginal productivity of more highly educated occupations is higher because their wage is higher, and not vice versa. In long-run equilibrium, their higher wage is the result of the costs of acquiring the necessary skills, together with the other supply-determining factors considered in the first part of this chapter.

The significance of this point can be grasped readily if we assume that the only difference between two occupations is that one occupation requires an expenditure on acquiring skills while the other is unskilled. For simplicity we assume that all workers have the same internal rates of time preference. We can use Fig. 8.1 for this case, with A representing the skilled occupation. Under our assumptions, the supply to skilled occupation A (and, by inference, the supply to occupation B) will be perfectly elastic at the wage ratio W_e. Now assume that for some reason the entire marginal productivity schedule for occupation A shifts outward. The increased schedule of marginal productivity for skilled workers will shift the demand schedule for occupation A outward, say from D_1 to D_2. In final equilibrium the wage ratio will not have changed and the value of *marginal* product will, given the increased employment of skilled workers, return to its original value. The wage ratio continues to be that ratio which provides a high enough rate of return to compensate workers for the costs of acquiring the requisite skills of occupation A. (This is not to say, however, that relative wages cannot permanently change in response to a change in the schedule of marginal productivity.) Now relax the assumption that workers have identical internal rates of time preference. Figure 8.2 becomes the appropriate graph, and the supply curve to occupation A becomes upward sloping. A rise in the productivity schedule and the consequent increase in the demand for skilled occupation A will result in a relatively higher wage for skilled workers, but their relative wage rises because a higher wage is necessary to attract the requisite number of persons to skilled occupation A. (Recall that interpersonal differences in internal rates of time preference is one factor which causes the supply curve to have an upward slope.)

The response of individuals making occupational choices to differences in private rates of return is well documented. One particularly interesting study by James Koch finds that college student choice as to academic major is significantly responsive to changes in rates of return to various majors.[3] Economists have also given a considerable amount

[3]J. V. Koch, "Student Choice of Undergraduate Major Field of Study and Private Internal Rates of Return," *Industrial and Labor Relations Review,* vol. 26, October 1972, pp. 680–685.

of attention to medical economics in the last decade, resulting in a number of studies dealing with the supply of medical personnel. F. A. Sloan has found that student applications to medical schools are strongly related to interoccupational differences in expected incomes and tuitions.[4] In another study Sloan has found that among doctors who choose to specialize, the supplies to the various specialties respond significantly to differences in incomes generated by the various specialties.[5] There have also been studies of other occupations such as engineering. For example, E. H. Mantell has compared the rates of return to education among engineers with rates of return among members of other professions and concludes that over the long run, the labor market has tended to produce an equilibrium between the supply of and demand for engineers.[6]

Despite the overriding importance of human capital as an explanation of occupational wage differences, we should recognize that it is other factors discussed that give the supply curves to occupations their upward slope. An appreciation of these factors is important in understanding the nature of supply to an occupation. Yet few economists have attempted to study empirically the effects of these factors. One exception is a study by A. G. King which verifies our prediction that the greater the dispersion of income within an occupation, *ceteris paribus,* the greater will be the wage that must be offered to entrants into that occupation.[7] Another exception is a study by R. E. B. Lucas.[8] Lucas finds that, as predicted, equalizing differences are in fact contained in occupational market wages for jobs involving repetitive routines and obnoxious physical environments, holding constant the amount of human capital associated with the jobs. However, because jobs requiring a compensating difference are more likely to require lower skill levels, it can be inferred that studies of rates of return to investment in education underestimate the rate of return. The underestimation takes place because highly educated persons are more likely to be in jobs that are attractive and thus provide a psychic wage—the converse of a

[4] F. A. Sloan, "The Demand for Higher Education: The Case of Medical School Applicants," *Journal of Human Resources,* vol. 6, fall 1971, pp. 466–489. A similar study of the decision to enter dental school is examined in A. Maurizi, "Rates of Return to Dentistry and the Decision to Enter Dental School," *Journal of Human Resources,* vol. 10, fall 1975, pp. 521–528.

[5] F. A. Sloan, "Lifetime Earnings and Physicians' Choice of Specialty," *Industrial and Labor Relations Review,* vol. 24, October 1970, pp. 47–56.

[6] E. H. Mantell, "Labor Markets for Engineers of Differing Ability and Education," *Industrial and Labor Relations Review,* vol. 27, October 1973, pp. 63–73.

[7] A. G. King, "Occupational Choice, Risk Aversion, and Wealth," *Industrial and Labor Relations Review,* vol. 27, July 1974, pp. 586–596.

[8] R. E. B. Lucas, "Hedonic Wage Equations and Psychic Wages in the Returns to Schooling," *American Economic Review,* vol. 67, September 1977, pp. 549–558.

compensating wage difference. Of course, it has not been possible to account for psychic wages in studies of the rate of return to investment in education.

There are two good reasons why economists have focused their attention on human capital considerations to the neglect of the other factors. First, data on such factors as internal rates of time preference, tastes for nonwage aspects of jobs, and degree of risk aversion are theoretically measurable, but in practice most infeasible to obtain. Second, and more important, is the fact that changes in tastes, time preference, and risk aversion occur very slowly, so their *changes* exert very little effect on *changes* in relative occupational supply. Changes in costs and returns tend to swamp other influences. It is very rare, for example, for the prestige of a profession to rise or fall dramatically within a short period of time. Nonetheless, such a change did seem to occur in the case of the journalism profession in response to the role played by investigative journalists in the Watergate scandal. When such rarities do occur it is possible to use the theory we have developed to predict the consequences of a rapid increase in prestige. We would predict that the relative wage necessary to induce any given number of persons into journalism would decrease, or in other words, the supply of journalists would shift outward. As a matter of fact, enrollment in journalism schools increased dramatically in the mid-1970s. Our theory also leads us to predict that the effect of Watergate on journalism's prestige, instead of increasing the relative wage of journalists as some might expect, will actually decrease it because of the increase in the supply of journalists.

It is also true that a knowledge of the way in which the other supply-determining factors interact with human capital considerations makes us able to explain phenomena that will appear as anomalies to those taking too simple a view of labor markets. For example, it is sometimes alleged that high school teachers do not make a fair return on their investment in human capital because, despite their years of education, their average wages are substantially below those of long-haul truck drivers or others who require less than a college level education in order to gain entry into their occupation. While it is difficult to be precise about the appropriate definition of "fairness," it is reasonable to ask whether the return on human capital investment is fair in the sense that teachers are receiving a positive rate of return high enough to induce a sufficient number of them to choose to stay in the teaching profession. But can teachers be receiving a positive rate of return if their wages are below those of truck drivers, whose human capital investment is so much less? If working conditions, job status, and risk were identical between the two jobs, our theory would predict that the wages of teachers would always be above those of truck drivers regardless of the levels of relative demand (as in Fig. 8.2) if occupations A and B are teachers and truck drivers respectively. Of course, few would argue that the working conditions, job status, and job security of truck drivers are no worse than those of teachers. If there were no differences in the amount of investment necessary to enter either occupation, then our theory would predict that over a significant range wages would be lower for teachers than for truck drivers. Figure 8.5 depicts the effects of human capital investment in combination with job characteristics for teachers that are regarded as superior to those of truck drivers. W_{te} and W_{tr} are the wages of teachers and truck drivers respectively. S_{te} is the actual supply curve of teachers. S'_{te} is the hypothetical supply curve of teachers that would exist if there were no differences between the two occupations in required human capital investment. The line S''_{te} is the hypothetical supply curve that would exist if the *only* difference between the two jobs were the heavier investment necessary to enter the teaching profession. The actual supply curve shows a wage ratio below 1.00 except at a high relative demand for teachers. The difference between S_{te} and S'_{te} represents the compensation that teachers receive in order to make them willing to make the investment necessary to enter the teaching profession. The difference between S'_{te} and S''_{te} measures the effect of the equalizing difference that must be paid to truck drivers to make them willing to enter that occupation, or conversely, can be considered the premium (in the form of a reduced wage) that teachers would willingly pay for the superior nonwage factors that they enjoy. The two forces of cost of investment and nonwage aspects pull the supply curve in opposite

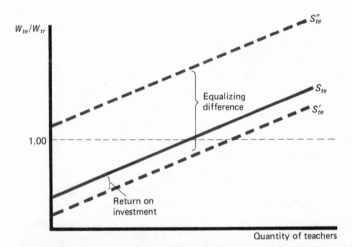

Figure 8.5. Equilibrium pay differences between teachers and truckdrivers. The vertical axis measures the ratio of teachers' wages to truckdrivers' wages W_{te}/W_{tr}. The supply curve S_{te} is the actual supply curve of teachers. S'_{te} is the hypothetical supply curve of teachers that would exist if both occupations required the same human capital investment. S''_{te} is the hypothetical supply curve of teachers that would exist if the only difference between the two occupations were the heavier investment that is necessary to enter the teaching profession.

directions, with the net result that teachers' wages are below those of truck drivers over a large range of the supply curve, but teachers are being sufficiently compensated for their investment costs to make them willing members of the profession. Were it not for their educational costs, teachers would receive a lower wage than they do receive at every level of demand. Of course we cannot observe hypothetical supply curves such as S'_{te} and S''_{te}. How, then, can we verify empirically that teachers are receiving the wage that compensates them for their investment? Almost any member of the labor force would claim, if asked, that he or she should be receiving a higher pay. If we are to determine whether or not members of a particular occupation are being paid what they regard as a fair wage, we must observe what they do rather than what they say. For example, suppose that truck drivers through a very strong union are able to obtain a much higher than equilibrium wage, and that market forces are unable to drive the wage downward. At the existing above-equilibrium wage for truck drivers, there would be an excess supply of truck drivers. If we witnessed a large number of teachers trying unsuccessfully to leave their jobs and become truck drivers, we would then have evidence that teachers were not receiving what they regarded as a fair return. There is little evidence that the pay of truck drivers, high though it may be, has induced an excess supply of persons waiting in line for the available jobs. On the other hand, there is evidence that there has in recent years been an excess supply of teachers at recent relative wages for teachers, possibly indicating that the relative wage of teachers is not yet low enough to restore equilibrium in that market. In any market, in fact, an extended period of excess supply is the only true evidence that the wage is higher than what would be required to both meet the demands of the economy and provide a wage that is regarded as satisfactory by the people who have freely chosen that occupation. Conversely, a persistent excess demand is the only evidence that the existing wage rate does not provide satisfactory compensation to enough people to meet society's demands.[9]

A lack of understanding of the principles demonstrated in this chapter has led to the development of a number of misguided public policies. For example, many municipalities have adopted the policy of establishing equal pay scales for police and fire department workers. The result has frequently been that it is difficult for these cities to attract enough competent individuals into police work at the same time that long waiting lists develop for positions in their fire departments. Equal

---

[9]One should be cautioned not to read too much into this line of reasoning. If by virtue of racial or sex discrimination a person is blocked from entering an occupation that he or she is or can become qualified for, then an individual's presence in some other occupation may indicate only that the occupation presented the best net advantage among those jobs to which the individual was restricted. We postpone a comprehensive analysis of discrimination until Chap. 11.

pay policies are no doubt motivated by a desire for equity, but the excess demand for police and excess supply of fire department workers indicate that equity requires an equalizing difference be paid for police work.

Another example is the case of university faculties. There is always some pressure in universities to equalize pay across academic fields rather than to pay the salaries determined by conditions of demand and supply for the various academic specialties. Yet the tastes and preferences of the population are distributed in such a way that some people find certain fields, particularly in the humanities, to be so intrinsically interesting and rewarding that an abundant number are attracted to those fields even at relatively low salaries. A university offering equal salaries across all academic fields would soon find that it could choose from among the cream of the crop in some fields, while in others it would have to settle for an inferior caliber of scholar.

8.3
LONG-RUN CHANGES IN PERMANENT OCCUPATIONAL WAGE DIFFERENTIALS

While we have described as "permanent" those differences in occupational wages that would persist when occupational labor markets have adjusted to long-run equilibrium, the term permanent should not be taken to imply that equilibrium differences do not change over time. Both supply and demand conditions change over time, and these changes affect long-run equilibrium wage differentials. Economists have paid particular attention to historical changes in what is termed the "skill differential," meaning the differential between the wages of skilled and unskilled occupations in various industries. The studies uniformly show that the skill differential has narrowed substantially over the last century.[10] Table 8.1 shows the ratio of wages of skilled to unskilled labor for two groupings of workers in construction. The first is the ratio of wages for all journeymen to the wages of all building laborers. The second ratio is for a particular subset of construction labor, namely, the ratio of wages for bricklayers to those of bricklayer tenders. While both series have moved up and down at times, the long-run trend of both is clearly downward.

The reasons for the narrowing of skill differentials can be discussed

---

[10]Two of the most frequently cited studies of the narrowing skill differential are: P. G. Keat, "Long Run Changes in Occupational Wage Structure 1900–56," *Journal of Political Economy,* vol. 68, December 1960, pp. 584–600; and H. Ober, "Occupational Wage Differentials, 1907–47," *Monthly Labor Review,* vol. 67, August 1948, pp. 127–134. For a tabulation of more recent occupational wage comparisons, see "Occupational Rankings for Men and Women by Earnings," *Monthly Labor Review,* vol. 93, August 1974, pp. 34–51.

Table 8.1
Skilled-unskilled wage ratios for two groups of workers

Year	W^s/W^u Journeymen to building laborers	W^s/W^u Bricklayers to bricklayer tenders
1907	1.90	2.21
1914	2.17	2.35
1920	1.79	1.75
1923	1.97	2.10
1935	2.09	1.87
1941	1.93	1.74
1946	1.64	1.58
1953	1.49	1.56
1960	1.39	1.39
1968	1.36	1.31

SOURCE: A. Rose, "Wage Differentials in the Building Trades," *Monthly Labor Review,* vol. 92, October 1969, table 2, p. 16.

within the human capital framework. G. S. Becker has shown that technological progress will result in some narrowing of the skill differential.[11] To illustrate this argument, let us categorize labor into two types, skilled and unskilled, and define the individual's rate of return with respect to human capital investment:

$$C = \sum_{t=1}^{n} \frac{(W_t^s - W_t^u)}{(1 + r)^t} \tag{8.1}$$

where W_t^s represents the skilled wage level in time period t, W_t^u is the analogous wage for unskilled labor, and n is the number of years of remaining worklife. The discussion is simplified, with no loss of generality, if we assume that the costs of acquiring the requisite skills (C) are all incurred in the first year, $t = 0$, and that work begins in the following year, $t = 1$, for persons who acquire the skill. As before, r represents the individual's rate of return on acquiring skill. An individual would make the investment in skill if the rate of return equaled or exceeded his or her internal rate of time preference. Now assume that neutral technological progress occurs. By neutral we mean that the technological progress raises productivity of both skilled and unskilled labor to the same degree. Consequently, both W^s and W^u will rise by the same percentage

---

[11]G. S. Becker, *Human Capital,* 2d ed., National Bureau of Economic Research, New York, 1975, pp. 75–77.

amount. (Recall our discussion in Chap. 6 of the effect of increasing productivity on wages.) Now if both wage rates rise initially by the same percentage amount, then the ratio W^s/W^u will remain unchanged, and employers will have no incentive to change their relative employments of skilled and unskilled labor. However, the benefit to acquiring skill will have risen because the numerator of Eq. (8.1), $W^s_t - W^u_t$, will have increased. If C remains the same or, as is more likely, rises only for that proportion of C that is made up of labor costs, then the rate of return to investment in skill will have risen. The higher rate of return will induce a larger number of persons to make the investment in skill and fewer to remain unskilled. In fact the entire supply schedule will shift outward as in Fig. 8.6 from S_1 to S_2. The ratio of skilled to unskilled wages will fall from W_1 to W_2. In this manner, the skill differential will have been narrowed. The rate of return will also fall but not as low as its original value because no one's internal rate of time preference has been lowered.

The skill differential also will tend to narrow if real private costs of acquiring skill decrease. Albert Rees has argued that the cost of acquiring skill has decreased on two fronts: the age of mandatory school attendance has increased, thus lowering the forgone earnings cost of acquiring a high school diploma; increased public subsidization of higher education has probably lowered the real private costs of college and other postsecondary school forms of training, if not necessarily the

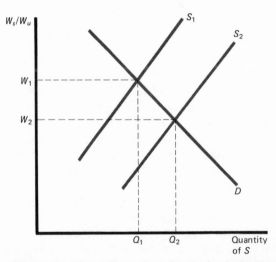

Figure 8.6. The effect of technological progress on the skill differential.
Technological progress may cause both skilled wages W_s and unskilled wages W_u to rise initially by the same percentage, which causes the rate of return on investment in skill to rise. The rise in the rate of return induces an increase in the supply of skilled workers from S_1 to S_2. The supply shift causes the ratio of skilled to unskilled wages to fall from W_1 to W_2.

social cost.[12] Of course, it is the private costs that influence individual decisions on human capital investment.[13]

8.4

A FINAL CAVEAT

The analysis of this chapter is intended to explain one part of the pattern of occupational wage differences. Specifically, we have sought to explain the occupational differences that would exist in long-run equilibrium under conditions of perfect competition. But the factors determining long-run equilibrium wage differences are not the only sources of occupational wage differences that we will observe at any time. In a purely (but not perfectly) competitive occupational labor market, adjustment to long run equilibrium is not instantaneous or costless. Hence some of the observed occupational wage differences are transitional in nature and tend to dissipate over time. It is also true that there are short-run occupational wage differences that occur in response to the business cycle. At any time, we may observe substantial regional or industrial differences in pay for the same occupation. These differences are for the most part transitional rather than permanent differences, and they will be discussed in the following chapter. Later in Part III we present the effects of market imperfections on wage differences. Limiting our analysis to competitive long-run equilibrium occupational wage differences has nonetheless yielded some fruitful insights that we have discussed throughout this chapter.

In Chap. 3 we assumed labor to be homogeneous in all respects. In the model of that chapter we came to the conclusion that, under our assumptions, all labor would everywhere earn the same wage. In this chapter, by relaxing the assumption of homogeneity, we have been able to identify certain factors that result in permanent occupational wage differences. These differences are entirely consistent with pure competition. Further, as society's demands for various occupations change, so too will occupational wage differences. Indeed, it is the same competitive forces discussed in Chap. 3 that bring about occupational wage differences and cause them to change.

---

[12]A. Rees, *The Economics of Work and Pay,* Harper, New York, 1973, pp. 170–172.

[13]Given the amount of attention that the media have given to the rising costs of education, one may be surprised to hear it argued here that the costs of education have fallen. But one should be aware that part of the publicized rise in costs reflects inflation, which is not germane to our argument because wages will also rise in the long run in response to inflation. Further, *average* private costs could have fallen because of the greatly increased proportion of students now receiving their education at subsidized public universities, even though real social costs at individual institutions, both public and private, have risen.

QUESTIONS AND EXERCISES

1. How should a progressive income tax system affect the pretax ratio of skilled to unskilled wages? How should it affect the ratio of wages in low-prestige jobs to wages in high-prestige jobs?

2. Under existing income tax laws, a person whose income fluctuates considerably from year to year will pay higher taxes than someone with the same average annual income whose income is more stable. How do you expect this feature of the tax laws to affect the relative wage in occupations subject to wide fluctuations in earnings?

3. The rapidly rising cost of medical care—particularly physicians' services—has led to increased interest in national health insurance. Explain why national health insurance cannot reduce the cost of physicians' services, but can only increase it.

4. What would be the effect on the skilled/unskilled wage ratio if everyone were compelled to serve for 4 years in the military without receiving skills that are useful in civilian employment? What if the military did provide skills that are in high demand in the private economy?

5. We have discussed in this chapter the presence of equalizing differences in wages. Because industries differ in their relative attractiveness, do you think that there may be equalizing differences in profit rates?

REFERENCES FOR FURTHER READING

A clear discussion of factors generating occupational wage differences is contained in M. Friedman, *Price Theory,* Aldine, Chicago, 1976, chap. 13, "Wages in Different Occupations." The interested student should also see the frequently cited article by M. Reder, "The Theory of Occupational Wage Differentials," *American Economic Review,* vol. 65, December 1955, pp. 833–850. For a presentation of statistical information on occupational wages, see the three articles cited in footnote 10 of this chapter.

TRANSITIONAL WAGE DIFFERENCES: OCCUPATIONAL, INDUSTRIAL, AND REGIONAL

There are differences in occupational wages that will exist in the long run. These are long-run *equilibrium* differences in that there will be no net tendency for these wage differences to change unless there is a change in the long-run demand for or supply to these occupations. The existence and explanation of these differences was the subject of Chaps. 7 and 8. Under perfect competition long-run or permanent occupational wage differences would be the only occupational wage differences that would persist for any length of time; the concept of the short run would be of considerably less significance than it is in the real world. There would be occupational wage differences of a short-run nature, but only because a certain amount of time is necessary for individuals to acquire the skills required to enter the occupations of their choice.

Industrial wages would then differ only to the extent that industries differed in their occupational mixes in employment. In turn, regional wages would differ only to the extent that industry mix differed across geographical regions.

We face several tasks in this chapter. The first is to explain why perfectly competitive theory leads to the predictions given above. Next we specify the extent to which such factors as incomplete knowledge, positive information and transportation costs, etc., act as impediments to the instantaneous achievement of the long-run equilibrium predictions of perfectly competitive theory. In other words, we will investigate the extent to which various impediments give rise to transitional (as opposed to permanent) wage differences. The last task is to describe the process of transition from short-run to long-run equilibria with respect to occupational, industrial, and regional labor markets.

9.1
PERFECT VERSUS PURE COMPETITION IN THE LABOR MARKET

To comprehend fully the distinction between permanent and transitional wage differences it is necessary to reiterate the distinction between perfect competition and pure competition. The most important assumptions of pure competition are that there are a large number of buyers and a large number of sellers in the market. In the case of the labor market, this means that there are a large number of employers and a large number of individual suppliers of labor, so that no employer or employee exerts a significant influence over the wage rate. Further, purely competitive labor market theory assumes that workers are free to change employers and that employers are similarly free to alter their levels of employment. Perfect competition includes the assumptions of pure competition, but adds other assumptions:

1. All buyers and sellers have perfect information about all aspects of the market, or can obtain information at zero cost.
2. Movement from one employment to another can be accomplished instantly and at no cost.[1]

The assumptions of pure competition can in principle exist in the real world. The additional conditions assumed in perfectly competitive theory cannot exist. Man is not capable of being perfectly knowledgeable, information cannot be costless to obtain, and movement between jobs cannot be accomplished entirely without cost. Of what value, then, is the perfectly competitive model if some of its assumptions are not only unrealistic but impossible? First, the model serves as a benchmark: we can appreciate the effects of information and movement costs only if we know what conditions would exist in the absence of such costs. Second, the *perfectly* competitive model does indicate the equilibrium values toward which a more or less *purely* competitive market will tend to move in the long run as the impediments to perfect adjustment are gradually overcome.

We now examine the general significance of information cost as it

---

[1]We are not assuming that the costs of acquiring skills necessary to change employment are zero, nor that the skills can be acquired instantaneously, but only that those costs that can be *directly* associated with changing employment (e.g., transportation costs) are zero.

relates to the labor market, after which we turn our attention to occupational, industrial, and regional wage differences.

9.2

THE ECONOMICS OF SEARCH AND INFORMATION COSTS

If workers can freely move from one employer to another, they would always tend to seek a job with the employer offering the highest wage, provided that the worker knows which employer will offer the highest wage. If every worker had perfect knowledge of all the wage offers that could be obtained and all employers similarly had perfect knowledge of the job market, then competition among employers and employees would quickly force a uniform wage rate for labor of a given type. Only in disequilibrium could a dispersion of wages exist, but the movement of workers would quickly eliminate the dispersion.

In the real world, information can be obtained but only at a cost. Job opportunities must be sought out. The costs of obtaining job offers vary considerably from one individual to another. Time is consumed in the search process. The opportunity cost of this time will be greater for an employed person (who must take time off from his present job) than for an unemployed person. The number of job offers that an individual can obtain will depend on the extent to which vacancies exist. When vacancies are plentiful, the time cost of obtaining an offer will on average be less than when vacancies are scarce. Transportation costs will also be less when vacancies are plentiful. Both the opportunity and transportation costs will be less the more easily potential employers can be identified. For example, construction workers can more easily identify employers who are likely to have vacancies for which they may be suitable than can general sales representatives. The geographical density of potential employers will affect search costs: maintenance workers may find hundreds of potential employers in a small city, while TV journalists might have to search over a large part of the country in order to locate the same number of potential employers. *Ceteris paribus,* search costs should be significantly greater for TV journalists than for maintenance workers.

Although the search for job information is costly, the process yields potential benefits. The more an individual searches, the greater will be the probability that the individual will locate the highest-paying job offer obtainable. Of course an individual can never know when the highest-paying job offer has been obtained, but the more the individual searches, the smaller becomes the probability of finding a job offer higher than the highest offer obtained so far. In other words, the search process yields marginally diminishing potential benefits. Within any labor market the potential benefits to search will also be affected by the degree of dispersion among wage offers: if all potential employers are paying about the same wage, there is little benefit to search.

An individual would tend to terminate the search process when it seems that the benefits to additional search are probably not worth the costs of additional search. Since the individual cannot know exactly the existing distribution of wage offers, the judgment that the probable benefits are less than the costs is a subjective one. Nonetheless, the more the individual has already searched, the better he or she can approximate the exact distribution of job offers. Hence the more extensive the search, the less subjective the judgment about the probable benefits of further search. The subjectivity is more easily reduced with additional search if market conditions are relatively stable, i.e., if the market's demand and supply curves "stay put" for some time.

The relationship between wage dispersion and job search is simultaneous. Let us say that a labor market is out of equilibrium and that a dispersion of wage rates exists. The greater the original dispersion of wages, *ceteris paribus,* the more incentive there is for individuals to engage in search. But the more search that is undertaken, the greater will be the gradual narrowing of the dispersion.

One should keep in mind two important implications of search theory for labor markets, the first referring to equilibrium and the second to disequilibrium situations. First, because search is costly and the returns to it diminishing, the equilibrium wages shown in all our previous and forthcoming graphs should be thought of as equilibrium mean wages. Even in equilibrium, there will be somewhat of a dispersion of wages around the mean. The dispersion that exists in equilibrium does not necessarily indicate inefficiency in the market, only that the economic benefits to search are no greater than the costs. In other words, further reduction of the wage dispersion would be inefficient, given the costs. Second, when equilibrium in a labor market is disturbed, lack of information and the costs of acquiring information will slow down the return to equilibrium. Depending on the costs of information and movement, the retarding effect, though transitional, may be of considerable duration. (One of the major factors impeding adjustments to a new equilibrium is a stickiness of wages: when conditions change, wages will not immediately adjust to their new equilibrium levels. The effect of information costs on wage changes constitutes one of the reasons for the existence of unemployment, a subject we will discuss in some detail in Chap. 15. For the time being, we are concerned about the effects of information costs on wages rather than on employment and unemployment.) Thus, one should keep in mind this important role of information costs in the following discussion of transitional occupational, industrial, and regional wage differences.[2]

---

[2]Much of what we discuss in this section is covered more formally in G. Stigler, "Information in the Labor Market," *Journal of Political Economy,* vol. 70, pt. II, October 1962, pp. 94–105.

9.3

TRANSITIONAL OCCUPATIONAL WAGE DIFFERENCES

With perfect, costless knowledge and mobility we would expect a one-time change in an occupation's demand to result in an adjustment process somewhat like the one depicted in Fig. 9.1. In this figure, W_a is the wage rate for the particular occupation of concern which we shall label occupation a. W_i is an index of wages in all other occupations; thus the ratio W_a/W_i is the relative wage of occupation a. In response to the shift in demand from D_1 to D_2 the relative wage rate rises rapidly from W_1 to W_2 since the short-run supply to occupation a will be inelastic. Just how inelastic it will be depends on the availability of persons qualified to work in occupation a, but who are not now in occupation a. The major sources of this potential supply will be (1) persons trained in occupation a or whose training is suitable for occupation a, but who had chosen to work in alternative occupations at the relative wage W_1; and (2) persons not now in the labor force, principally married women working in the home, who are qualified and would be willing to enter or reenter occupation a at a high enough relative wage. The short-run supply to some occupations, particularly high-paying high-skill occupations, will be extremely inelastic, whereas occupations requiring either low skills or very general skills may have occupational supply curves considerably more elastic. Persons in occupation a are then receiving a relative wage rate perhaps well in excess of the wage rate that would balance supply and demand in the long run. The income resulting from

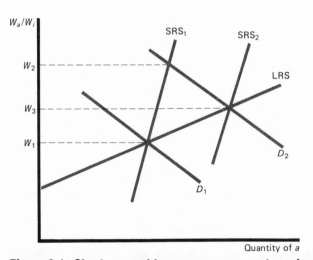

Quantity of a

Figure 9.1. Short-run and long-run responses to an increase in the demand for an occupation. As the demand for occupation a increases from D_1 to D_2, the relative wage of occupation a increases along the initial short-run supply curve SRS_1 to W_2. In the long run, the higher wage will induce an increase in the supply of labor. The short-run supply curve shifts outward until the wage rate falls to W_3, the long-run equilibrium relative wage.

the "excess" wage is in turn the result of the short-run supply blockage to occupation a. The incomes thus received are referred to as *quasi-rents*. A rent is any return to a factor in excess of the return necessary to induce the long-run quantity of that factor that is demanded. We would label these incomes as pure rents if they were permanent rather than transitional in nature. The concepts of rent and quasi-rent in the labor market are important in the discussions of union effects and public employment which we develop in later chapters.

As in the long run more and more people choose to make the investment necessary to enter occupation a, the short-run supply curve shifts outward until the labor market reaches a long-run equilibrium at the relative wage W_3. If the occupation is such that, say, 4 years of training are required in order to enter the occupation, then virtually complete achivement of long-run equilibrium will take at least 4 years even under our assumption of perfect conditions in the market. We say "virtually complete" because even with perfect and costless mobility there will be many workers who will not regard the return to entering occupation a at relative wage W_3 to be a worthwhile investment even though they would have been willing to do so if W_3 had prevailed earlier in their careers. The time path of the wage adjustment process might then look something like the one depicted in Fig. 9.2.

Once we approach the real world by relaxing our assumptions of perfect and costless information and mobility, the adjustment process takes on a different time path. The difference is due to a number of factors all of which are related to the costs and imperfections of

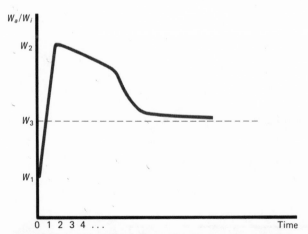

Figure 9.2. The time path of adjustment to a new long-run equilibrium relative wage: perfect and costless information and mobility. As demand for occupation a increases in the fashion described in Fig. 9.1, the relative wage rate may move rather quickly from W_1 to W_2. Over the next several years, the relative wage will fall slowly. Only after the effect of the higher wage has had time to produce new graduates prepared for occupation a will the relative wage begin to approach its long-run equilibrium level of W_3.

knowledge and/or to the lack of costless movement between jobs. When there occurs a rise in demand for an occupation, as in Fig. 9.1, the relative wage will not immediately rise to W_2; this is because of a sluggishness in the response of employers. The occupational market will be characterized as much by reported shortages as by a rising relative wage. Even after information about wages and jobs spreads among workers and employers, people will be uncertain as to what information present wage and employment levels convey about future conditions. Because of this uncertainty workers may not respond to a wage increase that has occurred very recently, since it may be temporary. Only after they observe a persistently higher wage will they respond. Further, the fact that for workers, information is costly and time-consuming to obtain will slow down the eventual adjustment to long-run equilibrium beyond the length of time that would be required if information were perfect and costless.

The fact that mobility is not costless also impedes movement toward long-run equilibrium. The institution of seniority provides a good illustration of this. The longer a worker is with a particular employer, the less likely it is that the worker will give up his job in order to obtain a more favorable wage in another occupation. And the longer an individual has been on a specific job, the greater will be that individual's accumulated experience and specific on-the-job training. Our analysis in Chap. 7 suggested that specific on-the-job training would result in somewhat higher wages being paid to a worker as a deterrent to job turnover. To such a worker, changes in relative *beginning* wages will be less effective as an inducement to job switching. The largest part of adjustment of equilibrium quantities in the various occupations is the result of the decisions of relatively young workers who have little or no experience or on-the-job training. It should be stressed that on-the-job training, experience, and seniority systems reduce the incentive of workers to change jobs, not their ability to do so.

9.3a
Cobweb adjustments in labor markets

The existence of information costs and reduced incentives to mobility do present impediments to instantaneous elimination of transitional wage differences. The existence of these impediments in some sense does slow down adjustment to long-run equilibrium, but the process of adjustment may not be a smooth one. Just as lack of perfect information may initially retard the supply response to a change in demand, it may also eventually result in too great a response. For example, consider what might happen in response to an increase in the demand for occupation a as in Fig. 9.1. Once the wage rises to W_2 in the short run, some individuals will respond to the now higher wage by entering or switching to occupation a. It is quite possible that many people will regard the increase in occupation a's relative wage from W_1 to W_2 as a permanent increase. If a long period of training is required in order to enter occupation a, then the wage will remain in the neighborhood of W_2 for a considerable length of time, thereby reinforcing the tendency to regard it as permanent even as increasingly large numbers of persons enter the training "pipeline" (for example, the 5 years of college training usually required to enter the pharmacy profession). The supply to occupation a may eventually become larger than is required for long-run equilibrium. As a result, the wage rate will actually go below the long-run equilibrium wage W_3. The lower-than-equilibrium wage eventually results in too few people entering the occupation, with a consequent rise in the wage above the long-run equilibrium wage of W_3. The market approaches long-run equilibrium with the wage rate bounding above and below the long-run equilibrium of W_3. Figure 9.3 illustrates the time path of adjustment. If there are no further disturbances to long-run demand and supply, the market will eventually settle down to W_3, the long-run equilibrium wage. In real life it is unlikely that long-run supply and demand conditions will remain stable for a long enough period of time to make possible the complete achievement of long-run equilibrium. The important point to remember here is that there is always *some* long-run equilibrium wage toward which the market is moving.

When a market approaches equilibrium in the fashion illustrated in Fig. 9.3, economists label that market as a "cobweb" type. The path of adjustment is markedly different from that of a smoothly adjusting market such as the one illustrated in Fig. 9.2. Economists have long recognized that most labor markets are characterized by cobweb rather than smooth

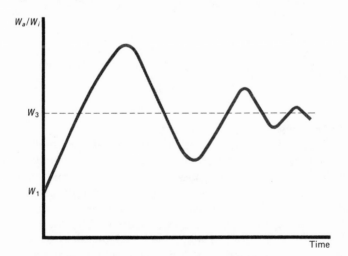

Figure 9.3. The time path of adjustment to a new long-run equilibrium relative wage: imperfect and costly information and mobility. Because of impediments to perfect mobility and the effect of information costs, the wage rate will not move smoothly from W_1 to W_2 to W_3 as in the previous graph. Rather, the market may approach the long-run equilibrium wage by bounding above and below W_3 in diminishing cycles.

adjustments. According to Robert F. Hebert, the earliest such recognition was by Emile Cheysson in 1887.[3] In a series of recent studies, Richard Freeman has estimated cobweb-type models for a number of occupations requiring college training. All his studies confirm the existence of both a strong but lagged responsiveness of supply to changing relative wage rates and a responsiveness of wage rates to changes in supply. For example, Freeman found that law school enrollment rates have changed by more than 3 percent for every 1 percent change in relative wages of lawyers. Further, every 1 percent change in relative wages has resulted in more than a 0.1 percent change in the percentage of entering students who eventually complete their studies. At the same time, a 1 percent increase in the total supply of law school graduates tends to reduce the relative wage of new lawyers by about 0.9 percent.[4] Similar responses were found for psychologists, physicists, and engineers.[5] In short, Freeman's studies confirm the appropriateness of Fig. 9.3 as a description of the adjustment process in occupational labor markets where a substantial amount of time passes between the decision of an individual to enter an occupation and his actual entrance. For low-skill occupations, particularly if information is good and can be obtained cheaply, adjustment to long-run equilibrium will be smoother and more rapid.

Recognition of the cobweb nature of labor markets in occupations requiring college degrees should be helpful to students making career choices. For instance, in the mid-1970s the beginning salaries of accountants had risen dramatically, leading to a similarly dramatic rise in enrollments in accounting curricula. The increased enrollments will not heavily increase the supply of accountants until the late 1970s. By 1980 increases in the supply of accountants should depress their relative wage. Many who choose to study accounting on the basis of a wage that includes a high quasi-rent element (such as the wage W_2 in Fig. 9.1) will thus be disappointed.

9.3b
Business cycles and transitional wage differences
The preceding section provides a description of transitional occupational wage differences that occur in response to changing relative de-

---

[3]R. F. Hebert, "Wage Cobwebs and Cobweb-Type Phenomena: An Early French Formulation," *Western Economic Journal,* vol. 11, December 1973, pp. 394–403. Students interested in knowing why the term "cobweb" is used should see fig. 1, p. 396.

[4]R. Freeman, "Legal 'Cobwebs': A Recursive Model of the Market for New Lawyers," *Review of Economics and Statistics,* vol. 57, May 1975, pp. 171–179.

[5]R. Freeman, "Labor Market Adjustments in Psychology," *American Psychologist,* May 1972, pp. 384–392; "Supply and Salary Adjustments to the Changing Science Manpower Market: Physics, 1948–1973," *American Economic Review,* vol. 65, March 1975, pp. 27–39; "A Cobweb Model of the Supply and Starting Salary of New Engineers," *Industrial and Labor Relations Review,* vol. 29, January 1976, pp. 236–248.

mands for various occupations. Such changes may occur even if the overall demand for labor does not change. Even when the economy remains in a condition of comparatively full employment, demands for some occupations will fall or rise in relation to others. However, occupational differences also are affected by the business cycle, i.e., changes in the overall demand for labor. For instance, the ratio of skilled to unskilled occupational wages tends to become larger during a recession but compresses during a recovery period. There are several explanations for this phenomenon,[6] but the most important one involves the firm's investment in human capital. When firms have invested heavily in a worker, they will be reluctant to dismiss that worker during a downturn in business activity. Given our discussion of specific training in Chap. 7, the reason should be clear. If the firm expects the downturn to be temporary, it runs the risk of laying off the worker only to find out a short time later that the worker has taken another job and is no longer available. The firm thus loses its investment in the worker and must start the investment process all over again with a replacement. On the other hand, if the firm had held onto the worker it would not have lost its investment, even though the worker was not entirely needed during the slack period in business activity. The defensive retention of workers during periods of slack activity is known as *hoarding,* and it causes the demand for skilled labor to hold up well during a recession when compared to the demand for unskilled labor. Consequently the differential between skilled and unskilled workers will widen during a recession.

During a recovery period the opposite occurs. The demand for skilled labor does not increase as much as the demand for unskilled labor, since the firm already has a hoard of skilled labor. Thus the occupational skill differential narrows to a more normal level.

Frequently the decision to change occupations is a decision to change industries as well. For analytical purposes, however, it is desirable to separate these two types of changes. Accordingly, we now consider transitional industrial wage differences.

9.4

INDUSTRIAL WAGE DIFFERENCES

In the long run perfect competition should result in the existence of no differences in wages among industries except to the extent that different industries require different occupational mixes. Another way of stating this expectation is to say that in long-run equilibrium, perfect competition will result in equal wages across all industries for any given occupation. There is, however, one possible caveat to this expectation,

---

[6]For one frequently cited explanation, see M. Reder, "The Theory of Occupational Wage Differentials," *American Economic Review,* vol. 45, December 1955, pp. 833–852.

and that caveat is concerned with nonwage aspects of a job. We established in the previous chapter that nonwage aspects make some occupations more attractive than others and hence will generate equilibrium occupational wage differences, *ceteris paribus.* It is not inconceivable that, for a *given occupation,* nonwage aspects of the job will differ across industries. If such differences exist in nonwage aspects, they will generate equilibrium industrial wage differences for specific occupations. In this case perfect competition will bring about long-run differences in industrial wages attributable not only to (1) differences in occupational mix among industries, but also to (2) differences in the innate attractiveness of various industries. Intuitively it seems that differences attributable to (2) would generally be very small or negligible. It is unlikely that nonwage aspects of accountants' jobs will be materially different as between, say, the brewing industry and the automotive industry. We shall thus ignore nonwage aspects except as they are reflected in *occupational* wage differences, and therefore consider perfectly competitive forces as leading to equal pay across industries for each occupation. Recall that in Chap. 3, where we assumed all labor to be homogeneous, we predicted that in the long run perfect competition would result in equality of pay across industries. Our recognition of the heterogeneity of labor has not greatly altered this prediction—we still expect that for *any given occupation,* equal pay will be the long-run ·result. Under the assumptions of perfect and costless information as well as perfect and costless mobility, industrial labor markets will adjust instantaneously to long-run equilibrium. To illustrate, let us assume the economy to be made up of two industries, *A* and *B*. Let us further assume that consumers change their purchases so as to increase the demand for the product of industry *A,* and decrease the demand for that of *B*. For simplicity, let us further assume that the resulting decrease in the demand for a given occupation in industry *B* is exactly offset by the increase in the demand for that occupation in industry *A* so that the aggregate (*A* plus *B*) demand for labor in that occupation is unaffected. This situation is illustrated in Fig. 9.4. Employers in industry *B* decrease employment from L^B_1 to L^B_2. With knowledge and mobility being perfect and costless, discharged workers switch immediately to industry *A,* where employers willingly hire them.

Again, we should realize that in the real world information and mobility are neither perfect nor costless. How, then, is the simple analysis of Fig. 9.4 affected? Principally, the short-run labor supply curves to each industry become less than perfectly elastic. Figure 9.5 illustrates a likely situation for a typical industry experiencing an increased demand for its output. When the demand for labor in that industry increases from D_1 to D_2, the industry may be able to attract labor only by raising its wage. The incentive of employers in the expanding industry to bid up wages comes from the higher-than-normal rates of profit that these employers are earning at their existing employment

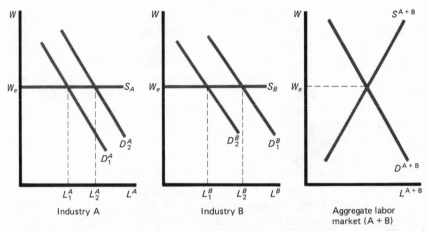

Figure 9.4. Labor market effects of shifts in the industrial composition of demand with perfect and costless information and mobility. If the demand for labor increases in industry A and decreases by the same amount in industry B, workers no longer demanded in industry B could shift to industry A with no effect on wages. Employment in that occupation increases from L_1^A to L_2^A in industry A and decreases from L_1^B to L_2^B in industry B.

levels. Profit maximization calls for an expansion of output and consequently employment. Only after all adjustments are worked out (i.e., only in the long run) will profit levels in the industry return to normal competitive levels. The higher wage (along with other types of informa-

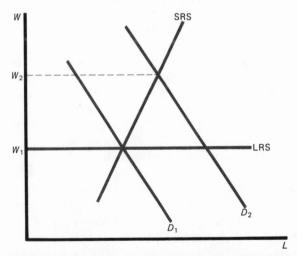

Figure 9.5. Effects of a change in the industrial composition of demand under conditions of imperfect information and mobility. Since information and mobility are neither perfect nor costless, short-run inelasticity is introduced into the supply curve of labor to an industry SRS. Consequently, in the industry experiencing increased demand, the wage rate will rise toward W_2 in the short run. In the long run, illustrated by the supply curve LRS, the wage rate will return to the market wage W_1.

tion) serves as a "signal" to the persons in the market that the industry is expanding. New entrants into the labor force would normally be the most important source of employees to the expanding industry. The mobility of employees out of other industries will normally be impeded by a number of factors similar to those that impeded occupational mobility: vested pension plans, the provision of specific training, etc. These factors will make the expanding industry less attractive to workers *relative to their present jobs* than would otherwise be the case.

The role of information and job search also affects industrial wages in much the same fashion as it affects occupational wages: it reinforces the short-run inelasticity of supply to the expanding industry. Nonetheless, in the long run information will spread and there will be a continual flow of new entrants into the labor force available to the expanding industry. Eventually the wage rate in the expanding industry of Fig. 9.5 will return to the normal, economywide level of W_1. Any wage above W_1 leads to a movement of workers to the expanding industry, however slow that movement may be. Thus, any wage above W_1, the economywide wage level for the given occupation, is transitional in nature.

Our analysis of the effect of changing product demand on industrial wages is similar to the analysis of the effects of changing productivity. In Chap. 6 we established that under perfect competition, industrial differences in productivity growth would not bring about differences in industrial pay levels.[7] However, our recognition in this chapter of information and mobility problems should bring forth the further recognition that differences in productivity growth will be irrelevant to industrial wage differences only in the long run. In the short run, an increase in productivity in an industry will result not only in employment growth but also in increased wages in that industry. The transitional wage differences that result from short-run supply inelasticity eventually will be overcome, and in the long run, differences across industries in productivity growth will be positively associated only with industrial differences in employment growth.

A number of attempts have been made to verify empirically the short-run and long-run predictions about industrial wage levels. Doing so is fraught with difficulties since we can never observe long-run equilibrium values that are entirely free of the effects of short-run factors. Nonetheless, available evidence does tend to support both the short-run and long-run predictions. For example, Melvin Reder cites the fact that there is not a significant correlation between productivity and hourly wages among 80 industry groups when productivity and wage rates are averaged over the 1899–1947 period. On the other hand, the correlation is usually high and significant when the correlations are for individual decade averages within the overall period of study. The nonsignificance

---

[7]It might prove helpful at this point to review our discussion of the effects of differential productivity growth in Chap. 6.

of the longer-term averages tends to confirm (or at least is consistent with) the long-run prediction of our theory, while the individual decade results tend to confirm that in the short run the supply of labor to an individual industry is less than perfectly elastic, so that industries where growth in the demand for labor is above average must in the short run pay above average wages.[8] Reder also reports that for averages calculated over the period 1899–1953, there is not a significant correlation between wage changes and employment growth among 33 industries studied. This finding is also consistent with the prediction that, in the long run, competition will eliminate industrial differences in wages despite vast differences among industries in the growth of labor demand. At the same time, there was a significant *negative* correlation between the long-term average growth of productivity for these industries and their trend in product prices. This finding further suggests that the benefits of growth in productivity have in the long run accrued to consumers in the form of lower prices rather than to employees in the form of rents. This is not to say that some rents (higher-than-competitive wages, even in the long run) will never accrue to any workers, only that such rents are not characteristic of the labor market. For instance, unions may attempt to secure for their members the rents that could potentially be obtained if competitive forces can be prevented from equalizing wages, but this possibility is the subject matter of Chap. 13.

9.5

REGIONAL WAGE DIFFERENCES

Under perfect competition with its assumptions of perfect and costless information and mobility, regional wages for the same type of labor should not differ across regions. Regional differences in demand and supply would not result in permanent regional wage differences, as we shall see. This does not imply that simple per capita wages or earnings should in the long run be equal across regions, as we also shall see. However, imperfect and costly information and mobility act as impediments to the equalizing of regional wage levels. The transitional regional wage differences that result from these impediments may be substantial and last for decades. The lack of information and the cost of movement are far more important in explaining the real world existence of regional wage differences than in explaining either occupational or industrial wage differences. This fact should be intuitive: One may be able to

---

[8]M. Reder, "Wage Differentials: Theory and Measurement," in *Aspects of Labor Economics,* National Bureau of Economic Research, New York, 1962, pp. 257–299. Reder's comments summarize data reported in S. Fabricant, *Basic Facts on Productivity Change,* National Bureau of Economic Research, Occasional Paper 63, New York, 1959; and J. Kendrick, *Productivity Trends in the United States,* Princeton University Press for National Bureau of Economic Research, Princeton, N.J., 1961.

change occupation and/or industry without changing residence. By definition, changing regions will involve substantial costs of movement, and information about job opportunities in other regions of the country will be particularly costly to obtain.

In this section we will explain the manner in which perfectly competitive forces would equalize the wages of comparable labor across regions. We will then discuss the importance of information and mobility problems which impede the elimination of regional wage differences. Since much of the concern of economists has been focused on the apparently sizable differential in wages between the North and the South of the United States, we will examine some of the evidence concerning this differential.

Even if the economy started with equal pay across all regions for each and every occupation, any number of factors might disturb this equality. For instance, productivity may increase more rapidly in one region than in others. An important natural resource may be discovered in one region of the country. Immigrants from abroad may all enter in one region and tend to settle there. In fact, any factor which shifts the demand for or supply of labor in a region relative to other regions can disturb the equality of wages across regions. Therefore, let us begin with an example in which the two regions of a country have different pay levels. For the sake of relevancy, let us say that the two regions are the South and the North of the United States, but the example is relevant to any regional wage differential. There are three market mechanisms which would bring about a movement toward equality of pay. They are (1) interregional trade in goods, (2) mobility of capital, and (3) mobility of labor.[9] We will consider each of these three equilibrating mechanisms one at a time, as if the other two were inoperative.

9.5a
Interregional trade

Let us assume for simplicity that labor is homogeneous and that both regions produce only one good. Let us further assume that technology and the relative endowments of natural resources are the same for both regions so that the production functions are the same for both regions, and that the only difference between the regions in the costs of production is because of their different wage rates. Let us also assume that the regions initially do not trade with each other, but that the cost of transporting goods is zero. Figure 9.6 depicts the situation, with D^N_1 and D^S_1 representing the original value of marginal product schedules for the North and South respectively. If the lower wage rate in the South

---

[9]For a sophisticated technical treatment of the topics we discuss here, see G. Borts, "Returns Equalization and Regional Growth," *American Economic Review,* vol. 50, June 1960, pp. 319–347.

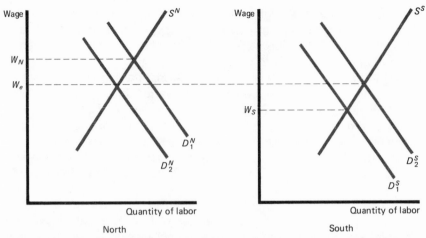

Figure 9.6. The elimination of a regional wage differential by interregional trade. Lower wages in the South would initially result in lower prices in the South. However, the lower prices in the South induce the North to purchase the output of Southern firms, raising the demand for labor in the South from D_1^S to D_2^S. Correspondingly, the demand for labor falls in the North from D_1^N to D_2^N. In both regions the wage rate moves to W_e.

results in lower production costs, competition within each region will have caused product price to be lower in the South. Now let us assume that Northerners find that they can buy the good under question more cheaply from Southern producers. This recognition results in an increased demand for the output of Southern firms and a corresponding decrease in the demand for Northern output. Consequently, output price will fall in the North and rise in the South. The changing product prices change the VMPP schedules of each region. The demand for labor in the North falls to D_2^N in Fig. 9.6 and rises to D_2^S in the South. Thus the effect of interregional trade is to equalize prices, and through this process to equalize wages.

We can generalize the price equalization effect of trade in goods to the real world situation wherein many goods are produced. It will be the case that within each region, competition will force wages to be equal across industries. It is still true, however, that a lower wage in the South would result in the North's "importing" goods from the South, causing real wages to rise in the South and fall in the North.

To further broaden our model, we should consider the case where the resources required for a particular industry are very abundant in one region and hence more cheaply obtained than in the other. In this case price competition will result in the relatively more efficient region specializing in the production of that good.

Now relax the assumption of zero transportation costs. Lack of information may impede achievement of regional price and wage equalization in a transitional fashion, but transportation costs will raise a permanent barrier to equalization of regional prices and wages through trade. Along related lines some goods and most services must be consumed where they are produced; in other words, some goods simply can't be traded across regions. Hence, in the real world, trade in goods can never completely equalize wages across regions without assistance from capital and labor mobility.

9.5b
The mobility of capital

The effect of capital mobility on regional wages is quite straightforward. If there is a difference between regional wages as exhibited in Fig. 9.6, then there is an incentive for firms to move to the South, or more likely, for newly-created capital to find its initial employment in the South. The incentive is in the lower cost of production, *ceteris paribus,* that results from using the lower-cost labor of the South.

We have established earlier that increases in the capital stock will tend to increase the marginal productivity of labor. The increased productivity will increase the demand for labor, although a falling product price will partially offset this increase. As we pointed out in Chap. 6, it is possible that in a few industries (specifically in agricultural products where the product demand curves are highly inelastic) the negative effect on labor demand of a falling product price will more than offset the positive effect of increased productivity so that an increase in capital may actually decrease the demand for labor. However, when we sum across all industries in a broad region, the effect of increased productivity should be to increase the demand for labor. We can then use Fig. 9.6 to depict the results of a flow of capital out of the North and into the South in response to a lower wage rate in the South. The demand for labor increases in the South from D^S_1 to D^S_2. At the same time, the demand for labor in the North decreases from D^N_1 to D^N_2. Both movements contribute to the convergence of Northern and Southern pay levels to the uniform wage rate W_e.

In Fig. 9.6 capital mobility results in a complete elimination of the regional wage difference. However, in the real multi-industry world where regions tend to specialize in the production of goods that require resources that are relatively abundant in that region, capital mobility cannot be sufficient to bring about regional equality of wages. It would be illogical, for example, for an industry to relocate in a region where labor costs are lower but where raw materials must be shipped in from the firm's former region at considerable expense.

9.5c
The mobility of labor

The migration of labor has received considerably more attention from labor economists than have the two other equilibrating mechanisms. To understand its effect we should once again assume that wages differ

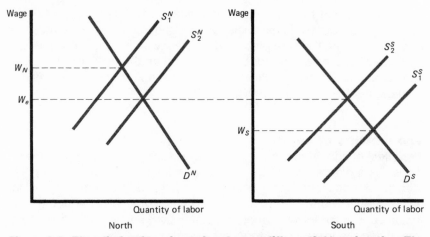

Figure 9.7. The elimination of a regional wage differential by migration. The higher wage in the North W_N than in the South W_S will induce migration of labor from the South to the North. Consequently the supply of labor in the South will be reduced from S_1^S to S_2^S, and the supply of labor in the North will be increased from S_1^N S_2^N. The supply shifts will cause wages in both regions to move toward equality at a wage rate of W_e.

between the North and the South as in Fig. 9.7. W_N and W_S are the original wage levels in the North and the South respectively. The original levels of supply in the two regions are S^N_1 and S^S_1. Under conditions of perfect and costless information and mobility, there will be a tendency for labor to migrate on balance out of the South and into the North, thereby decreasing the supply of labor in the South from S^S_1 to S^S_2 and increasing the supply of labor in the North from S^N_1 to S^N_2. The tendency results from the desire of individuals to seek the highest pay that they can obtain for their services. As a result of these shifts in the supply of labor the real wage will rise in the South and fall in the North. As long as there is a wage difference there is a tendency for labor to migrate out of the low-wage region and into the high-wage region.

Two forces impede the rapid adjustment toward regional wage equality that is suggested by Fig. 9.7. Again information is imperfect and costly to obtain. Hence there may be considerable delay in the spread of information and thus in diminution of the wage difference, although the presence of family and friends in other regions somewhat improves the flow of information.[10] Perhaps more important is the effect of movement

---

[10]For a measurement of the impact of "family and friends" on the decision to migrate, see J. A. Dunlevy and H. A. Gemery, "The Role of Migrant Stock and Lagged Migration in the Settlement Patterns of Nineteenth Century Immigrants," *Review of Economics and Statistics,* vol. 59, May 1977, pp. 137–144. See also P. Nelson, "Migration, Real Income and Information," *Journal of Regional Science,* vol. 1, spring 1959, pp. 43–74.

costs on the propensity to migrate. It should be apparent that the costs of moving one's physical belongings can be substantial, running into thousands of dollars. Less obvious may be the psychic costs of movement such as severing community ties and leaving behind one's friends and relatives. Both the monetary and psychic costs of movement are likely to be higher the older the potential migrant.

On the other hand, the benefits from migration are likely to be smaller the older the potential migrant. The older worker has fewer years of work left in which to take advantage of a higher wage in another region. Whether a particular worker decides to migrate or not is determined by that worker's view of the likely benefits from migration as compared to its costs. In fact migration may be regarded as a human capital investment and can be analyzed accordingly.[11] The potential monetary benefit to a migrant in any one year is the difference between what an individual can earn in his own region and what he could earn in the other region. The total benefit is the discounted sum of each year's benefit over the remaining worklife of the individual. For a Southern individual who is potentially attracted to the North by a higher wage rate, the individual would choose to migrate if the benefits exceed the costs, i.e., if

$$C < \sum_{t=0}^{n} \frac{(W_t^n - W_t^s)}{(1 + i)^t} \tag{9.1}$$

where W_t^N and W_t^S are annual real wages in the year t for the North and South respectively, n is the number of years of worklife remaining, i is the individual's internal rate of discount, and C is the cost of migration, including both direct monetary costs and the individual's dollar value equivalent of the psychic cost of migration.[12] Equation 9.1 is similar to the human capital equation that we developed earlier in Chaps. 7 and 8. From equation 9.1 we can deduce some hypotheses about the tendency to migrate. The tendency to migrate should be greater the larger the wage differential and the younger the worker. We have already hypothesized that migration would tend to mitigate any existing differential in wages. In the following section we examine the empirical evidence on these hypotheses, with particular reference to wage differences and migration between the Northern and Southern regions of the United States.

---

[11]The classic analysis of migration as a human capital decision is by L. A. Sjaastad, "The Costs and Returns of Human Migration," *Journal of Political Economy,* vol. 70, October 1962, pp. 580–593.

[12]The dollar value equivalent of the psychic cost of migration can be thought of as the dollar amount that the individual would willingly pay in order to avoid these costs.

9.6

THE NORTH-SOUTH WAGE DIFFERENTIAL IN THE UNITED STATES

Until quite recently economists have been persuaded of the existence of a substantial differential between the North and the South as a result of the findings of a number of studies. In these studies a variety of definitions of the South have been used; the term North has generally been used to designate all the states not included among the states of the South. Because of the different definitions of the South that have been used, the results of these studies are not strictly comparable. Nonetheless they all suggest that wages in the South are substantially below Northern wages. The long-term existence of a large differential seems markedly in contrast with the theory presented above which predicts that competition will eliminate or at least narrow over time a regional wage differential.

One reason for the apparent contradiction between theory and fact concerns the heterogeneity of labor. The theory presented above treats labor as homogeneous. Therefore it is strictly applicable to any one type of labor but not to the average of all types of labor. Those industries in which the North has specialized will use different combinations of the various types of labor than the industries located in the South. To pose the problem in another light, we can say that the pattern of industrial specialization in the South has made use of the abundance of relatively unskilled labor of that region and that Northern industries similarly make use of that region's relative abundance of skilled labor. As long as economic forces tend toward regional equalization of wages within each skill category, it does not matter that the North has a higher overall average wage. The higher overall average wage is the result of the higher degree of human capital required by Northern industries. Thus a higher average wage in the North does not necessarily imply a misallocation of labor between the regions.

A number of empirical studies covering the census South[13] have accounted for the heterogeneity of labor by controlling for industrial mix or human capital mix.[14] Yet even these studies report a differential of at least 10 percent for what are in essence like categories of labor. A differential of this magnitude seems to have persisted for some time, and has been accepted by many economists as reflecting a failure of market forces to bring about regional wage equality. The acceptance of this

---

[13] The census defines the South quite broadly. Included are Alabama, Arkansas, Delaware, District of Columbia, Florida, Georgia, Kentucky, Louisiana, Maryland, Mississippi, North Carolina, Oklahoma, South Carolina, Tennessee, Texas, Virginia, and West Virginia.

[14] The two approaches amount to the same thing since industrial mix is seen as important only insofar as it reflects regional differences in human capital requirements.

position has come under attack by Philip Coelho and Moheb Ghali.[15] All the theory concerning regional wage differentials has been with reference to *real* wages. Yet all the previous empirical studies had compared *money* wages despite the well-known fact that the level of prices tends to be lower in the South. Coelho and Ghali found that when the comparison is made in terms of real wages, there is no wage differential at all, as our theory predicts. A more recent study by Don Bellante reaches the same conclusion.[16] The 10 percent differential in money wages must then be reflecting the 10 percent differential in living costs between the North and the South.

Just as more recent evidence has tended to verify the results of competitive theory with regard to regional wage levels, so too has it tended to confirm the theory's predictions about migration flows. Economists and demographers have long considered migration to be unresponsive to wage differentials; hence migration could not bring about movement toward regionally equal wages.[17] More recent studies using more sophisticated methods and better data have tended to reach the opposite conclusion. Specifically, it has been found that the higher the regional wage difference, the greater the tendency of the population to migrate from low to high wage areas. Further, it has been found that, for any given wage differential, the tendency to migrate declines with increasing age. In other words, the movement of labor in such a way as to equalize wages takes place mostly on the part of young workers, just as the movement of younger workers provides the major impetus for equalization of industrial wages and the balancing of supply and demand in occupational labor markets. Age then can be seen as an impediment to the attainment of regional equality of wages. But the continual entrance of new people into the labor market does ensure that the impediment is transitional in nature, even though the transitional period may be quite prolonged. It has also been found that the tendency to respond to wage differences is greater for more highly educated persons, possibly reflecting the contribution of education to a person's ability to acquire information and act on it.[18]

---

[15]P. R. P. Coelho and M. A. Ghali, "The End of the North-South Wage Differential," *American Economic Review,* vol. 61, December 1971, pp. 932–937.

[16]D. Bellante, "The North-South Differential and the Migration of Heterogeneous Labor," *American Economic Review,* vol. 69, March 1979.

[17]For a review of the literature from which this consensus view emerged during the 1950s, see H. S. Parnes, *Research on Labor Mobility: An Appraisal of Research Findings in the United States,* Bull. 65, Social Science Research Council, New York, 1954.

[18]For a survey of the empirical literature on migration, see M. Greenwood, "Research on Internal Migration in the United States: A Survey," *Journal of Economic Literature,* vol. 13, June 1975, pp. 397–433.

In summary, we have attempted to explain in this and the preceding two chapters the manner in which economic forces reflecting individual choices allocate labor across occupations, industries, and geographical regions. We conclude that the real world evidence supports reasonably well the contentions of the theory. In a world of uncertain and costly information, where movement is costly, it is asking too much to expect market forces to produce perpetual long-run perfectly competitive equilibria in each labor market. It is quite reasonable to expect that economic forces constantly drive labor markets in the direction of such equilibria and consequently toward the most efficient allocation of labor consistent with a free market for labor. There is sufficient evidence to confirm that for the most part this latter expectation is met.[19]

Although in general the predictions of the competitive model are substantial, we do not argue that there are no imperfections in particular labor markets. Indeed, the existence and effects of such imperfections are the subject matter of Part III of this book.

QUESTIONS AND EXERCISES

1. Our analysis of migration implicitly assumes that individuals show no preference for the nonwage characteristics of one region over those of another. Thus, competitive forces tend to equalize real wages across regions. How would this conclusion change if all workers would prefer to live in the "Sunbelt" if wages were equal between the "Sunbelt" and the "Snowbelt"?

2. In general, the lack of perfect and costless information produces a dispersion of wages about the occupational mean, and the less perfect and more costly information is, the greater dispersion will exist. Are there circumstances where more nearly perfect information might create a greater dispersion? (Hint: If people *really* knew about quality differences among M.D.s, do you think the earnings of M.D.s would be more equal or less equal than they are at present?)

3. Migration should tend to equalize wages across regions by shifting regional labor supply curves. However, can we expect migration to equalize wages if birth rates are continually higher in the lower wage regions?

4. If a national "incomes policy" dictated that all wages must grow each year at a rate equivalent to the economywide rate of growth of productivity, how would the labor market be affected by changes in the occupational structure of labor demand? How would the labor

---

[19]Much of the evidence supporting the contention of efficiency in labor markets is contained in L. Gallaway, *Manpower Economics,* Irwin, Homewood, Illinois, 1971. The empirical work of Gallaway, as much as that of any other labor economist, has been instrumental in gradually bringing the economics profession around to the view that labor markets behave by and large in the manner predicted by competitive theory.

market be affected by shifts in the industrial or geographical composition of labor demand?

5. If government were to subsidize the relocation of workers changing jobs, how would such a program affect the tendency toward regional wage equalization? What economic arguments would justify such a program?

REFERENCES FOR FURTHER READING

For a critical examination of various theoretical explanations of the alleged North-South wage differential, see L. Gallaway, "The North-South Wage Differential," *Review of Economics and Statistics,* vol. 45, August 1963, pp. 264–272. See also the article by Coelho and Ghali cited in footnote 15 of this chapter.

A more sophisticated presentation concerning the industrial wage structure is given in R. Perlman, *Labor Theory,* Wiley, New York, 1969, chap. 5.

A view of occupational and industrial mobility that is in opposition to competitive theory is contained in P. B. Doeringer and M. J. Piore, *Internal Labor Markets and Manpower Analysis,* Heath Lexington Books, Lexington, Mass., 1971. A critique of the "dual labor market" theory of Doeringer and Piore is contained in G. Cain, "The Challenge of Dual and Radical Theories of the Labor Market to Orthodox Theory," *American Economic Review,* vol. 65, May 1975, pp. 16–22.

PART III

WAGE AND EMPLOYMENT DIFFERENCES ATTRIBUTABLE TO IMPERFECTIONS IN COMPETITION

e outlined in Part II the wage differences that occur even if product and labor markets were purely competitive. Besides the differences that would exist in purely competitive markets, there will be sources of wage differences which go beyond these and which are attributable to imperfections in competition. In the following chapters which constitute Part III, we present and discuss the sources of wage differences which are attributable to these imperfections in competition.

Whereas the differences discussed in Part II are consistent with an efficient allocation of labor across occupations, industries, and regions, the wage differences attributable to imperfections in competition result in a misallocation of labor with its adverse impact on output and employment. We will in some instances be able to present evidence concerning the magnitude of this impact.

In Chap. 10 we relax the assumption that employers are perfectly competitive in their product and labor markets. We find that by introducing monopoly into the analysis marketwide levels of wages and employment are reduced. Monopsony in the factor market reduces wages and employment as well.

In Chap. 11 we relax the assumption that employers regard all workers as perfect substitutes in production. The fact that employers do discriminate on grounds unrelated to workers' productivities leads to wage and employment differences by race and sex.

We consider in Chaps. 12 and 13 the consequences of unions on the allocation of labor and the determination of wages. Our presentation in Chap. 12 covers the important topics of union growth and collective bargaining. In Chap. 13 we discuss the effects of labor unions on wages and employment, not only in the unionized sectors of the labor market but in the nonunion sectors as well. In addition, we examine the impact of two governmental restrictions—state right-to-work laws in Chap. 12 and federal minimum wage laws in Chap. 13.

The existence of public goods and externalities prevents a free market from achieving the most efficient allocation of the labor resource. Consequently, the allocation of resources in an economy can be improved by governmental action. We describe in Chap. 14 the conditions for an *optimal* allocation of labor between the private and public sectors as well as outline the manner in which the political process affects the *actual* allocation of resources between the two sectors.

MONOPOLY AND MONOPSONY

In this chapter we relax the assumption we made in our basic model that employers are perfectly competitive in their product and labor markets. This will enable us to examine the independent effects of monopoly and monopsony on the allocation of labor and on the levels of wages and employment.

Both monopoly and monopsony can exist in product markets and in factor markets. A monopolist in the product market is a sole seller of a product or service which has no close substitutes; a monopolist in the factor market is a sole seller of a factor of production (e.g., a powerful labor union) which has no close substitutes. A monopsonist in the product market is the sole buyer of a product or service; a monopsonist in the factor market is the sole buyer of a factor of production.

Both monopoly and monopsony represent imperfections in competition. Thus, their existence causes an impact on wages, employment, and economic welfare. Our interest in this chapter is in outlining how product markets characterized by monopoly and factor markets characterized by monopsony cause wages, employment, and economic welfare to deviate from what they would be in competitive markets. It is not our intention to argue that monopoly and monopsony best characterize product markets and labor markets in general in the United States either today or in the past, although instances of both monopoly and monopsony have been documented in particular markets. Our purpose, rather, is to spell out as clearly as we can the causes and consequences of these market imperfections, partly because they help us understand the world, but partly because they describe what should be avoided.

We begin by examining monopoly in the product market. We see that the monopolist produces less output than does the purely competitive firm, given identical costs of production, and sets a product price which exceeds marginal cost. The monopolist also hires less labor at every wage than does the purely competitive firm. As long as there are competitive sectors in the economy, the output loss due to monopoly can be partially offset; nonetheless, on balance there remains a loss in economic welfare. We present some evidence which has attempted to establish the loss in economic welfare due to monopoly.

In the model of monopsony in the labor market we see that wages and employment are not as high as they would be under purely competitive conditions. We present here as well some evidence which supports the existence of monopsony in various markets in the United States.

We defer until Chap. 13 our discussion of monopolistic sellers of labor in labor markets, because such a discussion is best developed in a general presentation of unions and their economic effects.

10.1

MONOPOLY

Because a monopolist in a product market is the one seller of a product or service which has no close substitutes, there is no distinction between the monopolistic firm and the industry: the monopolist is the industry. Thus, the demand curve for the monopolist's output is the demand curve for the industry's output and is downward-sloping like all industry demand curves.

10.1a
Price and marginal revenue of the monopolist

We illustrate in Fig. 10.1 the demand curve for the monopolist's output. The downward-sloping demand curve means that additional output can be sold only by lowering product price. For example, if the price were $10, then the monopolist could sell, say, 100 units, and total revenue would be $1,000. If the price were lower, say $9.95, then the monopolist could sell more units, say 101, and total revenue would increase to $1,004.95. How does the monopolist's total revenue change as additional output is sold? It does not change by an amount equal to product price, as is the case for the purely competitive firm, but by an amount less than product price. For output $0Q'$, marginal revenue is less than price. Further, marginal revenue is less than price for all quantities of output sold. In our example marginal revenue of the 101st unit is $4.95, the amount by which the firm's total revenue changes by selling 101 units instead of 100 units. This amount is less than the price required to sell 101 units, $9.95. Further, the schedule of marginal revenue declines as the firm sells additional output. Indeed, there is some product price reduction which will cause the firm's total revenue to fall. This is

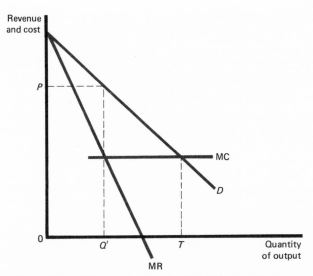

Figure 10.1. The monopoly model. The demand curve for the monopolist's product, D, is downward-sloping. Because the monopolist must lower product-selling price in order to sell additional output, the change in total revenue from selling additional output MR is less than the price of the output sold. The monopolist produces the quantity 0Q', the output for which MC = MR. Had this firm been a purely competitive producer with identical costs, the quantity 0T would have been produced, the output for which MC = price (which is identical to MR for the purely competitive firm).

illustrated in those price-quantity combinations for which marginal revenue is negative.

If the monopolist's marginal cost curve is MC in Fig. 10.1, then the quantity of output which maximizes the monopolist's profits is $0Q'$, the quantity for which marginal revenue is equal to marginal cost. For this output the monopolist charges price $0P$, the maximum price that consumers are willing to pay for this quantity, but a price which exceeds the marginal cost of that output. Given identical marginal costs, a purely competitive firm would have produced a larger quantity of output $0T$, that quantity for which marginal cost also equals marginal revenue (but marginal revenue is equal to price in the model of pure competition). The fact that price exceeds marginal cost for all quantities $0Q'$ to $0T$ means that society values this extra output more than it values those other goods which have to be given up to have the extra output from the monopolist. But the monopolist has no incentive to expand output beyond $0Q'$, for this is the quantity for which profits are at a maximum.

10.1b
The schedule of marginal revenue product

In Chap. 2 we established that the purely competitive firm's demand for labor is the schedule of VMPP, defined as the marginal physical product of labor MPP multiplied by marginal revenue MR, the change in the firm's total revenue from selling additional output. Because in pure competition marginal revenue is equal to price, the purely competitive firm's demand for labor is VMPP = MPP · MR (= P). The monopolist's demand for labor is also a schedule of the MPP of labor multiplied by MR. The only difference is that, for the monopolist, the change in total revenue from selling additional output is not equal to product selling price; MR is less than price.

Any firm's demand for labor in the short run is negatively sloped because of diminishing returns in production. The monopolist's demand for labor is negatively sloped for a second reason, however. The monopolist must lower product selling price to sell the additional output which is produced by additional inputs of labor, and MR is less than price for all quantities of output sold. Thus, the monopolist's demand for labor is MRP, where MRP = MPP · MR, and MR is less than P. As always, the demand for labor indicates the maximum price that the firm will pay various inputs of labor.

10.1c
The profit-maximizing quantity of employment: The monopolist and the purely competitive firm contrasted

We have illustrated in Fig. 10.2 the monopolist's and the purely competitive firm's demand for labor. Let us assume that both firms are purely competitive in the labor market. (This is not as confusing as it may

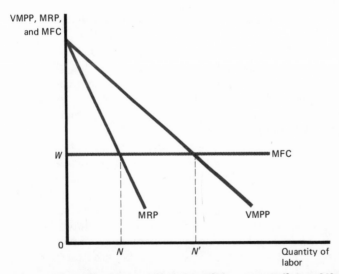

Figure 10.2. The demand for labor of the monopolist and the purely competitive firm contrasted. The monopolist's demand for labor is MRP; the purely competitive firm's demand for labor is VMPP. If both firms are purely competitive in the labor market, the monopolist employs ON labor, the quantity for which MFC = MRP. The purely competitive firm employs a larger quantity of labor ON', the quantity for which MFC = VMPP.

sound. Think of the public utility which may be the only seller of electricity in a market, but nonetheless is one of many firms in the labor market hiring typists.) If a firm is purely competitive in the labor market, then it can hire all the labor it chooses at the prevailing wage, a wage over which it has no control. Thus, the supply of labor *to each firm* is perfectly elastic at the market wage, and as we established in Chap. 2, the wage is marginal factor cost. At the wage $0W$, the profit-maximizing quantity of employment for the purely competitive firm is $0N'$, the quantity for which the change in its total revenues just equals the change in its total costs. At wage $0W$, the best quantity of labor for the monopolist is $0N$, again the quantity for which the change in its total revenues just equals the change in its total costs. But because of the differences between VMPP and MRP, the monopolist hires a smaller quantity of labor at each and every wage than does the purely competitive firm.

Notice that the existence of monopoly does not create a divergence in wages; workers hired by the purely competitive firm and by the monopolist receive the market wage $0W$. This conclusion may seem counterintuitive to some who envision monopolies "sharing their monopoly profits" with their workers in the form of higher wages. The effect of monopoly on wages has been examined by economists, and we present this evidence in the following section.

Note also that each firm pays each worker a wage equal to the maximum price that it would pay, i.e., the amount by which its total revenue changes from hiring the last worker. For the purely competitive firm this is the worker's VMPP; for the monopolist this is the worker's MRP.

Thus, the existence of monopoly makes itself felt not in wage differences but in other ways. First, the monopolist hires less labor at every wage than does the purely competitive firm. Consequently, one potential impact of monopoly on the economy is the reduced employment and output in the monopolistic sectors, although as we shall see, this impact can be offset partially by increased employment in the competitive sectors. A second effect is to redistribute income from consumers to monopolists. This effect has been the subject of substantial attention in recent years; its potential impact appears to be quite substantial. A final effect of monopoly is to misallocate labor. By this we mean that as a consequence of monopoly, some workers are forced out of higher-valued productivity jobs into lower-valued productivity jobs. We examine each of these effects in turn. However, we first examine the evidence concerning the effects of monopoly on wages.

10.2

THE EFFECT OF MONOPOLY ON WAGES

We argued in the preceding section and illustrated in Fig. 10.2 that the existence of monopoly creates no divergence in wages between the monopolist and the purely competitive firm; in Fig. 10.2 both firms pay the wage $0W$. Studies which have examined this question have found no evidence that the existence of monopoly per se causes wages to be higher than they otherwise would be. Leonard Weiss concluded that whereas monopolistic firms do tend to pay high wages for given occupations, these wages are not more than can be accounted for by the personal characteristics of workers; had these workers been employed in the competitive sectors of the economy, *ceteris paribus,* they would have earned the same wage.[1] Thus, monopoly exerts no independent effect on wages, and workers in monopolistic industries tend to receive no "monopoly rents." John H. Landon has investigated the influence of monopoly on wages within the newspaper industry.[2] Using a sample of 68 cities in 1966, he examined whether the number of newspapers in a city (a measure of the degree of monopoly)[3] was in any significant way related to wages of newspaper workers in those cities, holding constant other influences on newspaper wages such as degree of unionization, average citywide wage levels, and other variables. He found no relation between higher degrees of monopoly power and higher wages. Whereas it is always the case that no one statistical study is conclusive, it is noteworthy that no study has found monopoly per se to exert a positive and significant effect on wages. Thus, the conclusion that monopoly does not result in wage differences appears to be supported by the statistical evidence.

10.3

THE EFFECTS OF MONOPOLY ON OUTPUT, EMPLOYMENT, AND ECONOMIC WELFARE

It has become common to investigate the adverse effects of monopoly by analyzing its direct impact on output, which then enables one to infer its impact on employment. For example, consider Fig. 10.3. The purely competitive firm would produce output $0Q_c$ at price $0P_c$; for this quantity $MC = MR$ (= price). The monopolist also produces that output for which $MC = MR,$ but because MR is less than price for all quantities of output, the monopolist's output will be sold at a price which exceeds

[1]L. W. Weiss, "Concentration and Labor Earnings," *American Economic Review,* vol. 56, March 1966, pp. 96–117.

[2]J. H. Landon, "The Effect of Product-Market Concentration on Wage Levels: An Intra-Industry Approach," *Industrial and Labor Relations Review,* vol. 23, January 1970, pp. 237–247.

[3]Although the monopoly model describes the output and pricing decisions made by "one seller," in statistical studies it is common to use measures of the "degree of monopoly." A common measure is a concentration ratio, defined as the percentage of total industry sales accounted for by some (small) given number of producers.

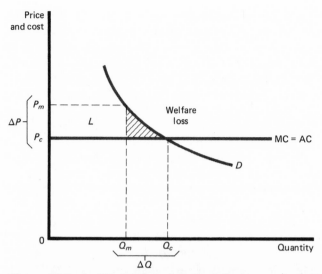

Figure 10.3. An illustration of the loss in economic welfare due to monopoly. A firm which is purely competitive in the product market would produce $0Q_c$ at price $0P_c$. For the quantity $0Q_c$, MC = MR (= price). The monopolist would produce less output, say $0Q_m$, and set a higher price, $0P_m$. Thus, the loss attributable to monopoly is the reduced output (the "welfare loss") indicated by the hatched area. An additional effect of monopoly is the redistribution of income from consumers to monopolistic producers. The amount of the redistribution is the rectangle L.

MC. The monopolist will produce less output, say $0Q_m$, and sell it at a higher price, say $0P_m$.[4]

As price rises above its competitive level, there are two economic effects. First, those consumers who cease buying the product at the higher price suffer a loss, illustrated by the hatched triangle in Fig. 10.3. This is a loss in output (or "welfare loss") due to monopoly.

It is important to note that the hatched area is a *net* welfare loss to the entire economy. The gross loss in output *in the monopolized industry* is the entire area under the demand curve which lies between output levels Q_m and Q_c. But because the resources which would have produced $Q_c - Q_m$ units of output are released to the competitive sectors, thereby increasing output there by the amount of the rectangle lying below the hatched triangle, this incremental gain in output in the competitive sectors must be subtracted from the gross output loss in the monopolized industry in order to arrive at net output (or welfare) loss

---

[4]Figure 10.3 is similar to graphs in the literature which illustrate the welfare loss due to monopoly. This particular graph, however, is from R. A. Posner, "The Social Costs of Monopoly and Regulation," *Journal of Political Economy,* vol. 83, August 1975, p. 808.

represented by the hatched triangle. (For a fuller explanation of the points we make here, see the article by D. Kamerschen cited in footnote 5 of this chapter.) But there is another effect as well. Consumers who continue to purchase the product suffer a loss (the rectangle L) which is exactly equal to the gain in revenue that the monopolist receives. Consequently, part of the economic effect of monopoly is to redistribute income from consumers to monopolistic producers. If a firm can shift the distribution of income in its favor by becoming or remaining a monopolist, this ability has a clear economic value and firms will expend resources to do so. Thus, the social costs of monopoly consist not only of the lost output resulting from higher-than-competitive price, but also the opportunity cost of the resources necessary to gain and/or protect the monopoly power.

Most estimates of the welfare loss due to monopoly have been attempts to approximate the value of lost output (the area of the hatched triangle in Fig. 10.3) in various sectors of the economy. This is a particularly complicated procedure; nonetheless, many such estimates have been made.[5] Arnold Harberger's results published in 1954 showed this loss due to monopoly in manufacturing to be about one-tenth of one percent (0.10 percent) of national income calculated for the late 1920s.[6] (If this estimate is correct, then monopoly costs each individual in the economy $1.50 in 1953 prices, and "economists might serve a more useful purpose if they fought fires or termites instead of monopoly," noted George Stigler.[7])

A more recent estimate of this loss is by John J. Siegfried and Thomas K. Tiemann.[8] They calculated the loss due to monopoly in manufacturing and mining in 1963 to be roughly comparable to the estimates of Harberger, about 0.07 percent of national income. (This amounts to $1.90 for every individual in the United States in 1963.) Thus, their results show not only that the welfare loss due to monopoly is relatively small but also that it has remained small since Harberger's original estimates based on data of the late 1920s.

More recently it has been argued that such estimates of the welfare loss due to monopoly, while they may well be accurate as far as they go,

---

[5]D. R. Kamerschen lists thirteen of the "more important and/or stringent assumptions" required to estimate this loss. See D. R. Kamerschen, "An Estimation of the 'Welfare Losses' from Monopoly in the American Economy," *Western Economic Journal,* vol. 4, summer 1966, pp. 221–236.

[6]A. Harberger, "Monopoly and Resource Allocation," in *Taxation and Welfare,* Little, Brown, Boston, 1974, pp. 91–101.

[7]G. J. Stigler, "The Statistics of Monopoly and Merger," *Journal of Political Economy,* vol. 64, February 1956, p. 34.

[8]J. J. Siegfried and T. K. Tiemann, "The Welfare Cost of Monopoly: An Inter-Industry Analysis," *Economic Inquiry,* vol. 12, June 1974, pp. 190–202.

seriously underestimate the total cost of monopoly to society because they neglect the fact that monopoly power has an economic value, that firms compete for monopoly power, and thus the opportunity cost of resources which flow into the acquisition and/or maintenance of monopoly represents a major cost (perhaps the major cost) to society of monopoly.[9] Let us examine this argument in some detail.

Assume that all firms are purely competitive in the product market. For a variety of reasons such as shifts in the pattern of product demand and/or technological change, purely competitive firms may well make economic profits in the short run. Yet, whereas economic profits may exist in the short run, they will tend to erode over time. This is because the existence of profits attracts new firms into the industry, and the entry of new firms tends to increase supply, depress product price, and thus erode profits. Consequently, in a regime of pure competition, there are always tendencies for price to equal average total costs of production over time due to the entry of new firms. If, on the other hand, new firms can be prevented from entering various industries, then economic profits can be perpetuated over time.

Many economists note that the only method of preventing profit-seeking entrepreneurs from entering profitable industries is to forbid them to do so or carefully regulate the numbers allowed to do so, and the only agency in society with the power to do this is government. Thus, their attention shifts to those sectors of the economy which are regulated by government.

The Civil Aeronautics Board regulates the route structure and the conditions of entry into the airline industry, the Federal Communications Commission limits the number of licenses in the broadcasting industry, and so forth. Further, price competition among the firms is severely curtailed. (Everyone is familiar with various forms of nonprice competition, from movies, meals, and champagne in the airline industry, to china, silver, and electric knives in the banking industry.) The cost to society from regulation is likely to be extremely high. Posner suggests that it is very high "given that about 17 percent of GNP originates in industries—such as agriculture, transportation, communications, power, banking, insurance, and medical services—that contain the sort of controls over competition that might be expected to lead to supracompetitive pricing. Indeed, the costs of regulation probably exceed the costs of private monopoly."[10]

Whereas it is common procedure to examine the impact of monopoly by estimating the value of lost output due to monopolistic product

---

[9]See the article by Posner cited in footnote 4 as well as G. Tullock, "The Welfare Costs of Tariffs, Monopolies, and Theft," *Western Economic Journal,* vol. 5, June 1967, pp. 224–232.

[10]Posner, op. cit., pp. 818–819.

pricing, output losses imply a loss in employment as well. The employment effect, however, has only been inferred. Before we leave this topic let us examine in a more direct manner the effects of monopoly on employment.

Consider Fig. 10.4, panels a, b, and c. Assume that pure competition prevails in both product markets and factor markets. The economywide demand for labor and the economywide supply of labor establish an equilibrium wage $0W$ and an equilibrium level of employment $0N$. This is represented in panel c. The representative firms in panels a and b hire $0n_a$ and $0n_b$ quantities of labor respectively at the market wage $0W$. Now let firm a become a monopolist. The introduction of monopoly into one or more sectors of the economy reduces the economywide demand for labor to D^*, the economywide wage level falls to W^*, and the monopolistic firm in panel a reduces employment to $0n^*_m$. Notice, however, that the competitive firm in panel b increases employment to $0n^*_c$. Thus, some of the workers who become unemployed from the introduction of monopoly spill over into the competitive sector.

The shaded area in panel a represents the lost value of output due to monopoly and is the consequence of reduced employment by the monopolist. The shaded area in panel b represents the increase in the total value of output attributable to the increased employment in the competitive sectors at the lower wage $0W^*$. Thus, the welfare loss represented in panel a is partially offset by the gain in output and employment in panel b—only partially offset, however, because total economywide employment, $0N^*$, is now less than total employment in

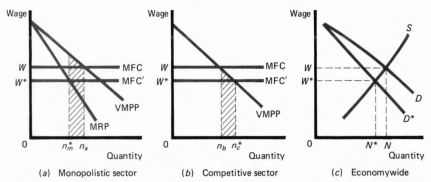

Figure 10.4. The employment loss due to monopoly. If all firms were purely competitive in the product market, the market demand for and supply of labor would establish an equilibrium wage OW and an equilibrium level of employment ON. At wage OW, the firm in panel a would hire $0n_a$; the firm in panel b would hire $0n_b$. Now let the firm in panel a become a monopolist so that its demand for labor changes to MRP instead of VMPP. The market demand for labor falls to D*; the equilibrium wage falls to OW*, and the equilibrium level of employment falls to ON*. The monopolist reduces employment to $0n_m^*$; some of the unemployed workers spill over into the competitive sector, however, and the purely competitive firm expands employment at wage OW* to $0n_c^*$.

pure competition, $0N$. Note also, however, that a misallocation of labor necessarily results; even those workers who do find employment in the competitive sectors are forced into lower-valued jobs as a result of monopoly.

10.4

THE EFFECTS OF MONOPOLY SUMMARIZED

If a firm is the one seller of a product or service that has no close substitutes, then the demand for its output is the industry demand. In order to sell additional output, the firm must lower product price, and marginal revenue is less than price for all quantities of output. The profit-maximizing monopolist produces that quantity of output for which marginal revenue is equal to marginal cost. The price charged by the monopolist is the maximum price that consumers are willing to pay, reflected in the monopolist's demand curve. This price will necessarily be in excess of the marginal cost of the output produced.

Monopoly clearly results in a reduced demand for all inputs. The demand for labor becomes MRP instead of VMPP. The monopolist hires less labor at every wage than would the firm which is purely competitive in the product market. This is but one more instance where a change in one part of the economic system makes itself felt in the markets for labor.

Thus the monopoly model clearly predicts a loss in economic welfare. When compared to the firm which is purely competitive in the product market, the monopolist produces less output at every structure of costs, sets a price which exceeds marginal cost so that labor is misallocated among the various industries in the economy, and hires less labor and other inputs at every wage. It does not, however, pay a wage any different from the purely competitive firm: both types of firms pay the same (albeit lower) wage.

These consequences are indeed potentially serious, and economists have demonstrated considerable ingenuity in attempting to discover to what degree the effects of monopoly are present in the U.S. economy. There are unusual complications which one encounters in any measure of the impact of monopoly on the economy. For this reason these measures have been presented typically as "range of magnitude" estimates. The estimates we have discussed show the loss in output from monopoly in manufacturing and mining to be in the neighborhood of $2.00 per person.

More recently it has been argued that estimates of this type seriously understate the impact of monopoly on the economy because they neglect another potentially serious effect. When a monopolist raises price above cost, not only is there lost output but there is a redistribution of income from consumers to monopolists as well. The potential which exists for a monopolist to become better off at the expense of consumers has an economic value, and firms will devote considerable resources to acquiring and/or maintaining this potential.[11] This can only be achieved by appealing to governmental agencies to limit entry into the various industries. Consequently, some of the highest-quality labor hired by the railroad industry, to cite but one of many possible examples, is in Washington and the various state capitals wooing politicians and bureaucrats instead of managing the railroads, a fact which to some degree accounts for the condition of the railroads.

It does not necessarily follow that regulated industries will be profitable; firms in those industries may be inefficient producers. It does mean, however, that the restriction of entry into a regulated industry prevents product price from falling as a result of the entry of new firms and the resulting increase in industry supply.

Posner has concluded that the welfare loss due to regulation is likely to be quite substantial, exceeding the loss in the nonregulated sectors. It is not known whether the relatively trivial welfare losses in the nonregulated sectors are due to competitive pressures in those sectors or to the existence of antimonopoly laws such as the Sherman Act. We can conclude, however, that the reduced output, employment, and welfare in the regulated sectors are attributable to some degree to the stifling of competition there.

10.5

MONOPSONY

A monopsonist in the labor market is the sole buyer of a factor of production. Because there is only one demander, there is no distinction between the monopsonist's demand for labor and the market demand for labor.

10.5a
The schedule of marginal factor cost

If the firm is a monopsonist, then the market supply of labor is also the supply of labor to the firm. In Fig. 10.5 we illustrate the supply of labor to the monopsonist. It is an upward-sloping schedule indicating that additional workers are available for employment, but only at higher wages. But whereas in pure competition in the labor market the wage was marginal factor cost, this will no longer be true if the firm is a monopsonist. To attract additional workers, the monopsonist must offer a higher wage, and the higher wage necessary to attract additional workers is a wage which must be paid all workers. Assume for purposes

---

[11]Using this approach, Anne Krueger has estimated the social costs to India and Turkey of their policy of licensing imports. See A. O. Krueger, "The Political Economy of the Rent-Seeking Society," *American Economic Review,* vol. 64, June 1974, pp. 291–303.

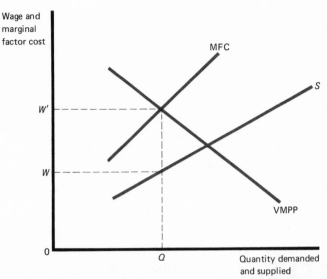

Figure 10.5. Monopsony in the labor market. If the firm is a monopsonist in the labor market, then the market supply of labor S is the supply of labor to the firm. If the firm must raise the wage to attract additional workers, then the change in the firm's total costs from increasing employment, MFC, exceeds the wage necessary to attract additional workers. The profit-maximizing monopsonist employs OQ workers; for the last worker employed, MFC = VMPP. The monopsonist pays the wage OW equal to the supply price of OQ labor, but less than the VMPP attributable to the last worker employed.

of illustration that the wage is $4.00. At this wage the firm can attract, say, 10 workers. If the wage were $4.25, the firm could attract more workers, say 11. Marginal factor cost of the eleventh worker is not $4.25, an amount equal to that worker's wage; it is a larger amount. It is $4.25 plus the $.25 which must be paid each of the ten workers. Thus, marginal factor cost of the eleventh worker is $6.75, an amount greater than the wage. In monopsony marginal factor cost exceeds the wage for every quantity of labor. We illustrate this idea in Fig. 10.5. Notice that the schedule which shows how total costs change from hiring additional workers (MFC) lies above the schedule which shows the wage necessary to attract additional workers (S).

10.5b
The employment and wage decision by the monopsonist
Let us assume that the firm is purely competitive in the product market (even though it is a monopsonist in the labor market), so that its demand for labor is VMPP. This combination of circumstances could be approximated by a coal-mining firm which is perhaps the only employer in some remote labor market, but nonetheless is one of many producers of coal. The monopsonist will chose that quantity of labor which maximizes

profits. This choice requires hiring all workers who are expected to add more to the firm's total revenues than to its total costs, and hiring no workers who are expected to add more to the firm's total costs than to its total revenues. Thus, the profit-maximizing quantity of employment for the monopsonist is $0Q$ in Fig. 10.5; for the last worker employed, VMPP = MFC.

But the monopsonist (unlike the firm which is purely competitive in the labor market) also makes a decision about what wage to pay. Because there is no market-determined wage to which the monopsonist must adhere, what wage is paid? A wage equal to the maximum price that the monopsonist is willing to pay, $0W'$, or a wage at which $0Q$ workers are willing to work, $0W$? The monopsonist pays the wage $0W$, equal to the supply price of labor.

10.6
THE ECONOMIC EFFECTS OF MONOPSONY

The effects of monopsony can be outlined with reference to Fig. 10.5. If the labor market were purely competitive, the wage would be determined by the intersection of the market supply of labor S and the market demand for labor. At that wage (not shown), the equilibrium volume of employment would be greater than $0Q$. Thus, the existence of monopsony results in employment and wage levels which are less than they would be in pure competition.

The volume of employment $0Q$ and the wage $0W$ are equilibrium values: there is no net tendency for either to change. There are, nonetheless, equilibrium unfilled job vacancies in the sense that the firm would choose to increase employment beyond $0Q$ if it could do so at wage $0W$. Thus, labor markets characterized by monopsony tend to evidence chronic unfilled job vacancies.[12]

Note lastly that the wage paid by the monopsonist is less than the maximum price that it would pay—the VMPP of the last worker hired. We might ask why it is that in purely competitive labor markets the firm pays a wage equal to the maximum price that it would pay—the worker's VMPP—while the monopsonist pays a wage less than the maximum it would pay. What are the real forces that bring about this conclusion? Recall the two assumptions of pure competition: (1) there are enough firms in the market as demanders of labor that the decisions of any one firm to hire more workers (or to go out of business) do not affect the wage rate; (2) the firm views labor inputs as homogeneous, i.e., the firm has no reason to prefer one input over another input. These assumptions, when

---

[12]R. W. Hurd, "Equilibrium Vacancies in a Labor Market Dominated by Non-Profit Firms: The 'Shortage' of Nurses," *Review of Economics and Statistics,* vol. 55, May 1973, pp. 234–240.

examined from the perspective of the worker, are sufficient to assure the maximum conceivable number of alternatives in employment. It is the existence of these alternatives which assures that all workers employed in each firm which is purely competitive in the labor market receive a wage equal to the amount by which the firm's total revenue changes by hiring the last input—the VMPP of the last worker hired. The worker facing a monopsonist has no such alternatives, however. He or she works at the wage offered by the monopsonist or doesn't work at all, at least not in that labor market.

C. R. Link and J. H. Landon have found evidence of monopsony in the markets for nurses.[13] They showed that a 100 percent increase in the concentration of hospitals in a city was associated with $400 less in annual beginning salaries for B.S. and diploma nurses. The market for nurses does exhibit most of the characteristics described by the monopsony model: there are a limited number of potential employers (hospitals), and nurses possess highly specialized skills which are not likely to be transferable to alternative employments.[14]

There are other areas of the economy as well where one might predict monopsony power. J. H. Landon's study of the newspaper industry (cited in footnote 2 above) found monopsony to be significant in that industry. In cities with smaller numbers of newspapers, wages tend to be lower, controlling for other wage-determining influences. Landon attributed this result to monopsony power by newspapers. The two factors of monopoly and monopsony coexist in many instances: the one newspaper in town may have not only some degree of monopoly power but also a considerable amount of monopsony power in that it may be the only employer in the labor market for certain occupational categories such as typesetters. Thus, Landon concluded in his study that the potential positive effect on wages due to monopoly in the newspaper industry was more than offset by the potential negative effect due to monopsony, so that on balance newspaper wages tended to be lower, *ceteris paribus,* the smaller the number of newspapers in a city.

Professional sports is another highly visible area where employers exercise considerable monopsony power, in this case because of legally binding agreements which limit the employment opportunities available to players. Roger G. Noll has argued that "a professional sports league is essentially a cartel, with the purpose of restricting competition and dividing markets among firms in the industry." The device known as the player reservation system "includes rules governing the signing of new players, the promotion of players from minor to major leagues (of primary importance only in hockey and baseball), and

---

[13]C. R. Link and J. H. Landon, "Monopsony and Union Power in the Market for Nurses," *Southern Economic Journal,* vol. 41, April 1975, pp. 649–659.

[14]The study by R. W. Hurd which we cite in footnote 12 examines the shortage of nurses.

the transfer of players from one major-league roster to another. These rules differ in detail from sport to sport, but their intention is everywhere the same—to limit, if not prevent, the competitive bidding among teams on the services of players."[15] Professional sports is one area of the economy where the reduction of monopsony power is sometimes strikingly visible. When the American Football League was established, many players on NFL teams quickly joined the new AFL teams, improving their salaries dramatically in the process. To an economist this represents nothing more than the predictable consequences of increasing the degree of competition in markets. Most sportswriters missed the point, however. To them it represented greed pure and simple; the players were trying to wreck professional football by their exorbitant salaries and, indeed, were corrupting the youth of America by their example.

The monopsony model, then, is the model of reduced alternatives in the labor market. If workers face a limited number of employers (in the limit, one employer) in labor markets, certain conclusions follow. We have presented evidence of monopsony in the markets for nurses, certain newspaper occupations, and professional athletes. Many economists argue that monopsony power by firms is likely to be greatly exaggerated given the occupational, industrial, and geographical mobility that characterizes American labor markets. Nonetheless, monopsony power can be perpetuated in certain occupational labor markets if employers are able to divide markets and restrict competition.

QUESTIONS AND EXERCISES

1. Assume that a firm is purely competitive both in the product market and in the labor market. Now assume that the firm becomes a monopolist. Explain as you would to someone with no training in economic analysis why the introduction of monopoly into the product market reduces the quantity of labor demanded by the firm at each and every wage.

2. In the mid- to late 1970s the Civil Aeronautics Board began to allow airlines to service routes from which they had been excluded because of governmental regulations. (*a*) What has happened to the price of airline tickets? Why? (*b*) What has happened to airline profits? Why?

3. What consumer interests are protected by regulatory agencies whose purpose is to regulate entry into industries?

---

[15]These two quotations are from R. G. Noll, "The U.S. Team Sports Industry: An Introduction," in R. G. Noll (ed.), *Government and the Sports Business,* Brookings, Washington, D.C., 1974, pp. 2–3.

4. What consumer interests are protected by regulatory agencies whose purpose is to regulate entry into occupations?

5. In your view, is monopsony a serious social problem? Why?

REFERENCES FOR FURTHER READING

For an alternative treatment of the analytics of monopoly and monopsony, see C. E. Ferguson and S. C. Maurice, *Economic Analysis,* rev. ed., Irwin, Homewood, Ill., 1974, chaps. 9 and 11, secs. 11.2b and 11.8.

A good discussion of monopsony in the baseball players' market is in S. Rottenberg, "The Baseball Players' Labor Market," *Journal of Political Economy,* vol. 64, June 1956, pp. 242–258. See also R. L. Bunting, *Employer Concentration in Local Labor Markets,* The University of North Carolina Press, Chapel Hill, N.C., 1962.

The classic treatment of the demand for and supply of governmental regulation is G. J. Stigler, "The Theory of Economic Regulation," *Bell Journal of Economics and Management Science,* vol. 2, spring 1971, pp. 3–21.

For an advanced treatment of the regulated monopoly's choice of technology, see A. Link, "A Comment on the 'Efficient Allocation of Resources in a Regulated and Unionized Monopoly,'" *Southern Economic Journal,* vol. 44, October 1977, pp. 383–384.

RACE AND SEX DISCRIMINATION

In Chap. 8 we presented an explanation of occupational choice and supply. We concluded there that market wages will differ across occupations even when comparing occupations requiring the same amount of human capital. We also concluded that the differences in wages would be optimal in terms of economic welfare provided that everyone had access to those occupations for which he or she might be qualified or could become qualified. This condition will prevail only if employers regard persons of equal skills to be homogeneous, or in other words, perfect substitutes for one another. This assumption has been basic to our analysis up to this point. The assumption is quite useful in the analysis of such matters as the effect of capital growth or unions on wage levels, as well as the other topics that we have previously covered. The usefulness of the assumption for some analyses is not significantly affected by the realism of this or other simplifying assumptions, while other analyses are materially affected. In this chapter we shall relax the assumption that employers regard workers of equal skill as perfect substitutes. In other words, we will recognize the fact that in our society many employers will discriminate against blacks and other minorities, as well as against women. In relaxing the assumption of nondiscriminatory behavior, we will examine the sources and forms of discrimination. More importantly, we will analyze the impact of discrimination on the wages and employment of both the victims and the beneficiaries of race and sex discrimination.

11.1

THE ECONOMIC ANALYSIS OF DISCRIMINATION

Discrimination against blacks has long been a subject of concern among social scientists, journalists, and public figures. Interest has become particularly intense since the civil rights movement of the early 1960s. During the 1970s, discrimination against females likewise became an issue of considerable discussion and activity. Although the origins of the economic analysis of discrimination can be traced to the English economist Francis Edgeworth in 1922,[1] the current interest is most directly related to the pioneering work of Gary S. Becker, which only slightly precedes the beginning stages of the civil rights movement.[2] By Becker's account, practically no articles on discrimination appeared in the economics literature during the 5 years following the publication of his work. After that a constantly increasing stream of articles has been written, and the subject continues to be one of the most researched areas of economics.

11.1a
Types of discrimination

Discrimination in the labor market against minorities can be classified into two types: *wage discrimination* and *occupational discrimination.* Wage discrimination can be said to exist when two groups of workers (e.g., whites and blacks) working in the same occupation receive different average wages. This could come about if a single employer hired whites and blacks (or men and women) for the same job but paid a lower wage to the blacks (or women). While such a practice is now illegal, it had not explicitly been prohibited by federal law before the 1964 Civil Rights Act. There is evidence, however, that this form of wage discrimination has never been a significant problem. A far more likely form of wage discrimination occurs when, within a given occupation, some employers hire whites exclusively, or virtually exclusively, while other employers exclusively hire nonwhites at a lower wage than that paid by the employers hiring whites. Becker's analysis has focused on this latter form of wage discrimination.

A more consequential type of discrimination is occupational discrimination. This occurs when minorities or women are excluded in one way or another from certain desirable occupations, and are thus crowded into less desirable occupations where their presence depresses wages. Wages are higher than they otherwise would be in those occupations from which minorities and/or women have been excluded.

---

[1]F. Y. Edgeworth, "Equal Pay for Men and Women for Equal Work," *Economic Journal,* vol. 32, December 1922, pp. 431–457.

[2]G. S. Becker, *The Economics of Discrimination,* The University of Chicago Press, Chicago, 1957; rev. ed., 1971.

Labor market discrimination, although the primary concern of this chapter, is not the only area of discrimination against minorities and women. Discrimination in the provision of government services has had a tremendous effect on the earnings of blacks, for example. The institution of slavery had the sanction of government; it allowed whites to have "property rights" over blacks (or, stated otherwise, did not provide to blacks the protection from coercion provided to whites). After the abolition of slavery in the United States, state governments denied blacks access to educational institutions and to other forms of human capital investments. The collective will of the majority sometimes took legal form, as in the so-called "Jim Crow" laws. In other instances, collective discrimination took the form of strong societal pressures so as to coerce all whites into acting in the discriminatory fashion favored by the majority. Females have similarly faced unequal treatment under law. However, the distinction between labor market discrimination and collective segregation is not clear, as the two have in the past reinforced each other. We will nonetheless endeavor to distinguish between the two and focus our analytical effort on labor market discrimination.

11.1b
Sources of labor market discrimination
Given the existing attitudes toward race and sex that are prevalent in society, there are essentially four sources of discriminatory behavior on the part of private employers: employer prejudice, employer's imperfect information, employee prejudice, and customer prejudice. First, the employer may be personally prejudiced against women or a minority. For example, an employer may dislike blacks to the extent that he or she will refuse to hire them even if profits must be sacrificed in order to do so. Unlike employer prejudice, the other three sources of discrimination result partly from profit-maximizing behavior. For example, employers may not have perfect information about *individual* blacks, but may have found through past experience that the average black has been a less productive worker than the average white, perhaps due to the lesser average quality of schooling that has been available to blacks. Such a recognition will result in the employer's discriminating against *all* blacks, even those whose productivity is higher than the white average. For that matter, even as average productivity of blacks becomes equal to the average of whites, employers will have imperfect information about the present and will continue to discriminate on the basis of their past experiences.

The employer may also discriminate because of employee prejudice. For example, the employees of a firm may refuse to work side by side with blacks, in which case serious labor relations problems would present themselves to the employer who would hire blacks. More likely, white workers would not go so far as to refuse to work with blacks, but racial friction might result in lower group productivity for a racially mixed work force than for a completely white work force. Similarly, customer prejudice may make it unprofitable for employers to hire minorities or women. This source of discrimination is most likely to be of importance in service industries.

All four sources of discrimination may result in either wage discrimination or occupational discrimination. We shall first consider the effects of wage discrimination on the wages of minorities and women.

11.2

WAGE DISCRIMINATION

Because much of the interest in discrimination concerns discrimination against blacks, we will present our analysis in terms of racial earnings differentials. Most of the analysis is equally applicable to other minorities and to women. We begin by limiting the analysis to a single occupation. We assume that there are no innate differences in productivity between blacks and whites. Regardless of the source of discrimination, we will regard an employer as a discriminator if he would hire blacks only if they could be hired at less cost than comparable whites. Following Becker, we say that an employer's discrimination coefficient is DC_i if the employer would be indifferent between employing blacks or whites if the black/white wage ratio W_b/W_w were equal to $1/(1 + DC_i)$. For example, if an employer's discrimination coefficient DC_i is .25, he in effect treats blacks *as though* their wage were 25 percent higher than it actually is. Although he prefers whites, he is willing to pay them no more than 25 percent above what he must pay blacks. If the market wage rate is \$3.20 for blacks and \$4.00 for whites, the ratio W_b/W_w is .80. The employer in our example would be indifferent between hiring blacks or whites, since $1/(1 + DC_i)$ is also equal to .80. But at a black/white ratio above .80, he would not hire any blacks. Conversely, at a black/white wage ratio below .80, he would hire blacks exclusively despite the preference for whites. Thus, DC_i represents the intensity of the ith employer's preference for hiring whites over blacks: it measures the highest wage premium that he would willingly pay in order to avoid hiring blacks. Employers differ in their discrimination coefficients. Some will be nondiscriminating, in which case their values of DC_i will be zero—they will regard blacks and whites as perfect substitutes. The market demand for blacks can be thought of as a schedule which arrays employers from lowest to highest discrimination coefficients, as in Fig. 11.1. The horizontal axis measures the number of blacks (holding constant the number of whites). The horizontal segment of the demand curve at a wage ratio of 1.00 represents the demand for blacks by the nondiscriminating employers. Beyond these employers, the quantity of black workers demanded will increase only if the black/white wage ratio is reduced below 1.00. Because the value of DC_i is greater than zero for many employers, the market for blacks becomes segmented from the

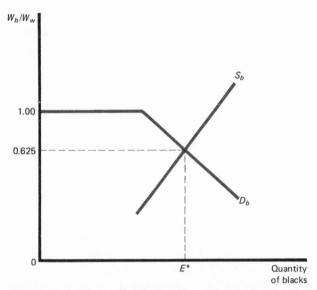

Figure 11.1. Wage discrimination and the market for black labor. D_b is the demand for black labor and is a function of the black/white wage ratio W_b/W_w. The supply curve is a positive function of the wage ratio. The equilibrium W_b/W_w ratio is determined by the interaction of demand and supply, as is black employment E^*.

general market for whites. Given the supply of blacks to the market, an equilibrium black/white wage ratio is established as that value of W_b/W_w at which the quantities of black workers demanded and supplied are equal. In our example in Fig. 11.1, the equilibrium wage ratio is .625, and E^* is the number of blacks who will find employment in this market. The segment of the demand curve to the left of the intersection of the demand and supply schedules represents employers whose DC_i are less than .6, since the wage ratio of .625 is equal to $1/(1 + .6)$. The employers whose DC_i are greater than .6 will hire no blacks.

If the supply of blacks in a particular region were to increase, there would be an excess supply at the existing wage ratio. Competition among blacks for the existing jobs would, over time, drive the wage ratio downward to a new equilibrium. The effect of changes in the relative supply of blacks has some relevance to regional differences in the black/white wage ratio. Empirical studies of discrimination invariably find a lower black/white wage ratio in the South than in the North. Yet even if the distribution of employers' discrimination coefficients were identical as between the North and the South, this analysis suggests that the black/white wage ratio would be lower in the South because the supply of black workers is relatively greater in the South.

The Becker approach to wage discrimination has been criticized on several grounds. Critics contend that nondiscriminating employers, who would have lower labor costs as a result of their behavior, could sell their products at lower prices. In highly competitive product markets, this advantage for nondiscriminators will force the discriminating firms out of business. Such a criticism would be correct if the only source of discrimination were employer prejudice. Then, only employers who would otherwise be receiving monopoly rents could afford to pay a premium in order to avoid the employment of blacks. Employers in competitive markets could not afford to do so.[3] On the other hand, what if the source of discrimination is based on customer prejudice? In this case, it is competition itself that forces the employer to discriminate. Blacks within the affected occupation will be limited to employers whose markets are such that customer prejudice is not a problem, such as in manufacturing. The effect of competition with regard to employee prejudice is not so clear. An employer who considers hiring blacks in a certain occupation may receive strong resistance from white employees who may be in other occupations but who must nonetheless work alongside the black employees. For example, a crew of white bricklayers may have to work alongside a crew of black hodcarriers. Whether or not such resistance is forthcoming depends on whether or not the job into which the employer wishes to place blacks is considered by whites as a job in which it is "acceptable" for blacks to be employed. If such pressure is forthcoming, the employer may find it less costly to discriminate. In some situations, he may be able to avoid such pressure altogether by hiring blacks exclusively in all occupations within his employ. Given that blacks have been blocked from receiving training in many occupations, it is unlikely that such an option will exist. Even if this option did exist, the employer might be subject to very heavy community resentment of such a practice.

Another possible criticism of the Becker approach is that it appears to suggest that in a discriminatory society, blacks are paid less than their marginal products. Yet such a behavior by an entrepreneur would not maximize profits. Rather, we should expect that if blacks are available at lower wages than whites, nondiscriminating employers will take advantage of their lower cost and maximize profits by employing labor-intensive means of production. The employment of blacks will be at the profit-maximizing level. But this means that blacks will be employed in jobs that are essentially different from the jobs done by the whites who ostensibly are in the same occupation. In effect, the occupations are now different and require different training and skills. What started out as wage discrimination evolves into occupational discrimination—the most prevalent form of discrimination, as we have stated. We turn our attention now to that form of discrimination.

---

[3]The fact that monopolists can and do pay a premium in order to discriminate is discussed in A. A. Alchian and R. A. Kessel, "Competition, Monopoly, and the Pursuit of Pecuniary Gain," in *Aspects of Labor Economics,* Princeton University Press, Princeton, N.J., 1962.

11.3

OCCUPATIONAL DISCRIMINATION

Occupational segregation has existed because it has been possible for society at large to prevent blacks and other minorities as well as women from having access to certain occupations. Until recently, the custom of designating certain jobs as "men's work" or "women's work" has not been successfully resisted. Indeed, the victims of such segregation—women—have in the past been as accepting of this institutional arrangement as if it were part of a natural order. In many countries it continues unabated to the present. For much of our history blacks and other minorities have been relegated to certain occupations in such a pervasive manner that the practice of occupational segregation, until recent decades, has not been a primary focus of the civil rights movement. Rather, efforts have been focused upon school segregation, upon discrimination in the provision of both public and private services, and upon wage discrimination.

Barbara Bergmann has developed a model of discrimination which, while not substantially in conflict with the Becker model, lends itself more readily to an analysis of occupational discrimination.[4] By tradition, women or minorities are excluded from certain positions. As a consequence women and minorities are crowded into a limited number of occupations, thereby lowering the wage in those occupations below what it would be in the absence of occupational discrimination. At the same time, the supply of labor is less than it otherwise would be in the "white only" or "male only" occupations, with the result that wages will be higher in these occupations than they would be in the absence of segregation. It should be noted that segregating occupations does not alone cause wages to be lower for women or minorities—it is necessary that the number of occupations available to women and minorities be limited.

In Fig. 11.2 we take as an example two occupations, W and B, where occupation W is limited by tradition to whites, while B is a traditionally black occupation. Let us assume that the occupations are alike in all important respects. Then, in the absence of segregation, the wages of occupations W and B will be equal to each other at the wage rate w_e. As we learned in Chap. 8, if the wages of the two occupations were to diverge, the supply of labor to the higher wage occupation would increase and the supply to the other occupation would decrease, causing the wage rates of the two occupations to move back to equality. Now if the effect of segregation is to reduce the supply of labor available to occupation W, the equilibrium wage will be w_w. Similarly, the crowding of blacks into B will result in an equilibrium wage of w_b. Note

---

[4]B. Bergmann, "The Effect on White Incomes of Discrimination in Employment," *Journal of Political Economy,* vol. 79, March/April 1971, pp. 294–313.

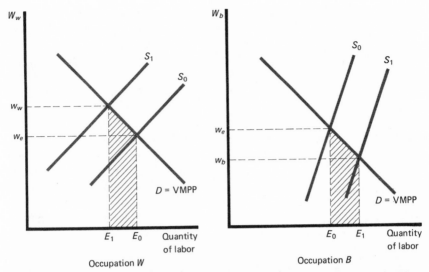

Figure 11.2. Occupational discrimination. Occupation W is limited to whites; occupation B is open to blacks. In the absence of such limitations, the wage in both occupations would be w_e, given supply curves S_0 in both occupations. However, the exclusion of blacks from occupation W results in a supply curve of S_1, thereby resulting in a wage rate of w_w in that occupation. At the same time, the crowding of blacks into occupation B results in a supply curve of S_1 to that occupation, with the further result that the wage rate will be w_b.

that in both the white and black occupations, labor is paid the value of its marginal product. The lower wages of blacks are not the result of payment below marginal productivity; rather, the crowding of blacks into occupation B forces their marginal productivity to be lower than it would be in a regime of free labor markets. It is the divergence between blacks and whites in their marginal products that causes their wages to differ. But because the marginal products of blacks and whites are unequal, a loss in output is imposed upon the society. The loss comes from the fact that if a black could leave B to enter W, the value of his output would be higher in W than in B. Hence, the output lost in occupation B when the worker leaves is less than the increase in value produced in occupation W as a result of his working in that occupation. In net terms, then, output increases if he can leave B for W. Conversely stated, since he cannot leave B to enter W, there is a net loss in potential output attributable to that worker as compared to what would result if there were no racial barriers in the market.

The total net welfare loss from occupational segregation can be analyzed in a manner similar to that used in Chap. 10 for analyzing the welfare loss attributable to monopoly. The shaded area under the portion of the occupation B demand curve between E_0 and E_1 represents the amount by which output in occupation B will be increased by crowding blacks into B. The shaded area under the demand curve of occupation W measures the amount by which output is lower in W as a result of the exclusion of blacks. Since the marginal products of each of the excessive number of blacks ($E_1 - E_0$) crowded into occupation B are lower than they would be if those workers could enter occupation W, then the shaded area (increased output) in occupation B must be less than the shaded area (decreased output) in occupation W. Hence, there is a net welfare loss attributable to occupational discrimination.

Little has been done to measure empirically the welfare loss attributable to occupational discrimination. Since the income distributional aspects of occupational discrimination are of much more crucial consequence, economists have devoted considerable effort toward measuring the effects of wage and occupational discrimination on the incomes of whites and blacks, and on the incomes of males and females.

11.4

MEASURING DIFFERENCES IN EARNINGS BY RACE AND SEX

Despite the considerable empirical literature that exists in the area of discrimination, there exists no consensus as to what constitutes the best measure of the effects of race and sex discrimination in the labor market. When one sees or hears statements to the effect that the mean income of females 18 years of age or older in the United States in 1969 was 60 percent of the mean for corresponding males, or that the mean income of blacks was 66 percent of the mean for whites,[5] one cannot infer from these numbers that labor market discrimination caused the earnings of women to be 40 percent below the income of men, or that it caused the income of blacks to be 34 percent below that of whites. The reason we cannot reach these conclusions is that *current labor market* discrimination is not the only cause of a black/white or female/male ratio less than 1.00.

11.4a

Black/white earnings differences

In the case of the black/white ratio, past discrimination by government in the provision of education lessens income opportunities for blacks. Governmental discrimination of this type has taken two forms. First, the quantity of institutions of secondary and higher education to which blacks have had access has been considerably below the quantity accessible to whites. As a consequence the attainment of high school and college diplomas has been more costly to blacks. However, the

---

[5]Both the female/male and black/white percentages are derived from the 1970 Census of Population data.

second form of governmental discrimination—school segregation—has been considerably more consequential. The racial segregation of schools by law in the South had resulted in the provision of a much inferior quality of schooling to blacks. The de facto segregation of schools in the North had also resulted in an inferior quality of education offered to blacks, although probably to a lesser extent than did the de jure segregation of the South. Hence part of the black/white differential can be attributed to the lower educational attainment of blacks relative to whites, and not to labor market discrimination. Of course, some of the lower educational attainment of blacks *is* the result of labor market discrimination. However, the relation is not as straightforward as it might seem at first glance. The fact that blacks earn less than whites at all education levels will not necessarily reduce the rate of return to, and hence the incentive to invest in, education by blacks. Let us take for example the incentive of a black to invest in a B.S. degree. The lower earnings of black college graduates as compared with white college graduates lowers the dollar *return* to blacks from acquiring a college degree. On the other hand, the fact that black high school graduates receive lower earnings than comparable whites means that the opportunity *cost* of acquiring a college degree is lower for blacks than for whites. Hence, labor market discrimination may have no effect on black investment in human capital. For labor market discrimination to be the cause of lower human capital investment of blacks, it is necessary that discrimination be more intense at higher education levels than at lower levels.

Typically, discrimination has been more intense at higher education levels, but this situation has reversed itself in the 1970s, as we will see below. However, if educational attainment of blacks is lower for this reason, it is due to *past* labor market discrimination. What is desired is a measure of the effects of *current* labor market discrimination. In order to construct such a measure, it is necessary to compare blacks and whites of equal human capital. Joan Haworth, James Gwartney, and Charles Haworth have in effect done this in a study of the black/white earnings ratio. They have done so by developing the black/white earnings ratio that would exist if blacks had the same productivity-related characteristics, such as education, age, etc., as do whites.[6] They find that for 1959 the black/white earnings ratio was approximately .709. This figure

---

[6]J. Haworth, J. Gwartney, and C. Haworth, "Earnings, Productivity, and Changes in Employment Discrimination during the 1960's," *American Economic Review,* vol. 65, March 1975, pp. 158–168. Technically, their earnings ratio is a nonwhite/white ratio, as some non-Negro nonwhite races are included in the numerator. However, their nonwhite sample is overwhelmingly made up of blacks so that the inclusion of non-Negroes will not significantly distort the ratio. See also J. Long, "Earnings, Productivity, and Changes in Employment Discrimination during the 1960's: Additional Evidence," *American Economic Review,* vol. 67, March 1977, pp. 225–227.

suggests that the income of blacks was lower than that of whites by as much as 29.1 percent as a result of then current labor market discrimination.[7] By any standard this differential is substantial. Of considerable interest is whether this differential has narrowed since 1959. Haworth, Gwartney, and Haworth also examined the black/white ratio for 1969 and found it to have risen to .790. Further, James Smith and Finis Welch found that within each age-education category, the black/white earnings ratio was higher in 1969 than in 1959, although the rise was most pronounced for younger, more highly educated categories.[8] While the progress toward parity might seem to be substantial, it should be remembered that the 1960s produced a very considerable and widespread public effort toward racial equality. Yet blacks were still earning about 21 percent less on average than whites of comparable productivity. Between 1970 and 1975, however, the situation improved dramatically. Richard Freeman found that by 1975 the earnings of young male black college graduates were roughly equal to those of comparable whites. For males with less education, equality was not achieved, although blacks had gained substantially relative to whites during the early 1970s. The rate of return to investment in higher education became greater for blacks than for whites. For black women, their income by 1975 was at least equal to that of comparably educated white women; among women college graduates, earnings were actually higher for blacks.[9]

It would appear that black college graduates have achieved equality with whites as measured by wage ratios, while other groups of blacks are making substantial progress toward equality. As younger blacks continue to replace the older victims of discrimination in the labor force, the overall black/white earnings ratio should continue to move toward 1.00, particularly since educational attainment among young blacks is approaching that of whites. (Blacks in 1975 made up about 10.6 percent of the enrollment at colleges and universities, and about 11 percent of the total population of the United States.)

There is thus reason for optimism that one of America's historically most serious problems is steadily approaching solution. In the study cited in footnote 4, Barbara Bergmann estimated that the end of discrimination would reduce the wages of whites with an elementary education by 10 percent. For other whites, the loss would be very much

---

[7] This number indicates only the effect of current labor market discrimination, and not previous governmental or labor market discrimination. Further, labor market discrimination not only lowers black earnings but also raises the earnings of whites whose earnings form the denominator of the black/white earnings ratio of .709.

[8] J. Smith and F. Welch, "Black-White Male Wage Ratios: 1960–70," *American Economic Review,* vol. 67, June 1977, pp. 323–338.

[9] R. Freeman, *Black Elite,* McGraw-Hill, New York, 1976.

smaller. However, these estimates are based on the degree of discrimination that existed in 1959. It stands to reason that much of this effect on white wage levels has already taken place. What discrimination is left could be eliminated with a negligible effect on white wages.

11.4b
Female/male earnings differences

As with black/white comparisons, any comparison of female/male pay differences must necessarily compare females and males of equal productivity if the purpose is to measure the effects on women's wages of current labor market discrimination. The simple female/male earnings ratio reflects not only current labor market discrimination but also the disincentive effects of past labor market discrimination on the educational attainment of women. Also entangled in simple female/male earnings ratios is the effect of the division of labor that takes place within the typical household in our society, wherein wives specialize in household work and husbands specialize in market work.

The traditional division of labor between husbands and wives in western society is a complex institution. The division of labor partly reflects biological facts of life: only women can bear children, and for most of human history, could nurture infants. The division also reflects the domination of society by men, quite apart from any biological considerations, and is thus counterpart to the subjugation of racial or religious minorities. Whatever the reasons for this division of labor, one of its effects has been to limit the opportunities for women in the labor market. The distinction between "acceptable" and "unacceptable" occupations has been more sharply drawn for women than for racial minorities. Because of this division of labor and occupational segregation, women have not reached a level of educational attainment equal to that of men.

Given that society has imposed these limitations upon women, married couples who would choose not to subscribe to these traditions have until recently had little choice but to observe the traditions. As the work of Solomon Polachek implies, even where a husband and wife have equal educational attainment and no noneconomic inclination toward the traditional division of labor, the existing labor market status of women means that the couple would maximize its utility by observing the traditional division of labor.[10] Further, it is rational for the couple to concentrate postschooling investments which raise earning power in the male. Again, employers with imperfect information respond to average

---

[10]S. Polachek, "Potential Biases in Measuring Male-Female Discrimination," *Journal of Human Resources,* vol. 10, spring 1975, pp. 205–229. See also J. Mincer and S. Polachek, "Family Investments in Human Capital: Earnings of Women," *Journal of Political Economy,* vol. 82, pt. II, March/April 1974, pp. S76–108.

or typical experience, being unable to forecast easily what an individual woman's work history will be. When employers make decisions about the provision of on-the-job training, they tend to discriminate against women because of the interruptions of the women's work histories that result from childbearing. Thus, productivity will not be equal, even between males and females of equal age and educational attainment.

Nonetheless, it is worthwhile to examine the relative earnings that women would receive if they had the same educational and age distribution as men. Such a number indicates the combined effect of wage and occupational discrimination, and of the inferior on-the-job training and experience of women. Victor Fuchs has done this for both 1959 and 1969.[11] He finds that the average ratio of female to male hourly earnings for employed whites was .61 in 1959 and .64 in 1969.

If this magnitude of improvement seems paltry, one should remember that what improvement did occur during the 1960s occurred without strong prodding from government and in the absence of any substantial change in attitudes toward women's roles and status;[12] the women's movement is a phenomenon more of the 1970s than of the 1960s. Further, there was a substantial increase during the 1960s in the labor force participation rates of women. Given the validity of the "crowding" hypothesis explained above in this chapter, the increased participation of women, *ceteris paribus,* would tend to lower the female/male wage ratio. In fact, the female/male earnings ratio increased by 20 percent between 1959 and 1969. As might be expected, the female/male earnings ratio did not increase to the same degree across all groups. For women who were never married, the ratio of their earnings to those of never married men was .86 in 1969. Never married women are most likely to have had continuous work histories and so their earnings suffered least. The wage ratio also was higher in both years for women under 35 than for older women. Similarly, the wage ratio was higher for those with more than 12 years of education than for others. The pattern of the youngest, better-educated women suffering the least effect is similar to the pattern exhibited for black/white comparisons.

The female/male earnings ratios thus far presented are for whites. Blacks were excluded in order to separate the effects of sex discrimination from those of racial discrimination. However, Fuchs also compiled some data for blacks. He found that by 1959, earnings of black females were 15 percent less than those of comparable white females. However,

---

[11]V. Fuchs, "Recent Trends and Long Run Prospects for Female Earnings," *American Economic Review,* vol. 64, May 1974, pp. 236–242.

[12]The Federal Equal Pay Act of 1963 and Title VII of the Civil Rights Act of 1964 were aimed at sex discrimination, but did not receive strong enforcement emphasis and were rather ineffectual during the 1960s. On this point see R. Oaxaca, "Sex Discrimination in Wages," in O. Ashenfelter and A. Rees (eds.), *Discrimination in Labor Markets,* Princeton University Press, Princeton, N.J., 1973, p. 149.

for those black women with more than 12 years of education, the difference between black and white female earnings was virtually zero.

Time will tell if the women's movement and society's increasing consciousness of the goal of sex equality during the 1970s will have significantly raised the female/male earnings ratio. While conclusive results are not yet in, it does not appear that the 1970s will have produced nearly as much progress in terms of the female/male differential as in terms of the black/white differential. In fact, there is strong reason to believe that little progress will have been made during the 1970s, since the increase in the female labor force participation rate occurring during the 1970s was even greater than that of the 1960s. Unless occupational barriers to women drop rapidly enough to offset the effect on women's wages of rising women's participation rates, the crowding of yet more women into their traditional occupations will dampen any prospects for rapid improvement.

11.5

DISCRIMINATION AND THE ROLE OF GOVERNMENT

It is common to regard government policy in a democratic society as reflecting the will of the majority of the voters of that government's constituency. Perhaps it is more proper to view government policy as reflecting the will of a coalition of interest groups strong enough to hold sway over a majority of legislators or over holders of top administrative offices. In any event, government policy will reflect, within fairly wide bounds, the goals of the collective society or the portion of that society that is allowed to vote, regardless of the fact that equal weight is not given to all members of society. Consequently, when racism and sexism were more in vogue in the United States, government actions were the primary instruments of discrimination. Similarly, government actions became the primary instruments against racism and sexism when movement toward equality became a common objective. We have already pointed out the role of government in the segregation of public services, particularly education. And as Thomas Sowell has pointed out, government as an employer has been more discriminatory than private industry until this became politically infeasible in recent years.[13] However, the changing political climate of the late 1950s and 1960s led to a rapid reversal of the government's position. By 1970, significantly less employment discrimination was observed in the government sector than in the private sector.[14]

One issue of considerable interest is the extent to which the

---

[13]See chap. 7 of T. Sowell, *Race and Economics,* McKay, New York, 1975.

[14]J. Long, "Public-Private Sectoral Differences in Employment Discrimination," *Southern Economic Journal,* vol. 42, July 1975, pp. 89–96.

improvement during the 1960s and 1970s in the black/white earnings ratio can be attributed to government action against private employers. The question is very difficult to answer empirically, because there is no way of knowing with certainty what would have happened in the absence of the government intervention that has taken place. One of the more influential attempts to answer this question is that of Richard Freeman.[15] Freeman has regressed the black/white wage ratio for both men and women on a number of time series, among others a variable measuring cumulative Equal Employment Opportunity Commission (EEOC) expenditures up to the date of the observation, and a black/white relative education variable. Freeman found the relative education variable to be significant, indicating that much of the increase in the black/white wage ratio can be attributed to the increased educational level of blacks relative to whites, a finding consistent with those of Haworth, Gwartney and Haworth, and of Smith and Welch, cited previously in this chapter. More importantly, the EEOC expenditure variable is positive and highly significant, thereby giving some support to the argument that federal government programs have improved the labor market status of blacks by in effect shifting outward the relative demand for blacks.[16]

Richard Butler and James Heckman have criticized Freeman's findings.[17] They agree with Freeman that activities of the federal government have raised the relative wages of blacks, but argue that it was the government's expansion of welfare programs during and after the mid-1960s, not federal antidiscrimination policy, that accounts for the rise in the black/white wage ratio. Butler and Heckman contend that these welfare programs have caused low-skilled, low-income persons (who are disproportionately black) to withdraw from the labor force. The reduction in the relative supply of blacks would raise the relative earnings of blacks, as Figs. 11.1 and 11.2 both show. Indeed, when Butler and Heckman replicated the Freeman study but added a relative labor force participation variable, they found no impact on the black/white wage ratio, for either men or women, of federal antidiscrimination

---

[15]R. Freeman, "Changes in the Labor Market for Black Americans, 1948–72," *Brookings Papers on Economic Activity,* 1973, no. 1, pp. 67–120.

[16]There are currently two large-scale federal antidiscriminatory programs: the Equal Employment Opportunity Program, which Freeman considered, and the Federal Contract Compliance Program. The Office of Federal Contract Compliance deals with firms having or seeking contracts with the federal government for $10,000 or more. The enforcement authority of this office began in 1970 and thus its impact could not be measured in Freeman's study. For an analysis of the impact of the Federal Contract Compliance Program, see the symposium on the topic published in *Industrial and Labor Relations Review,* vol. 29, July 1976.

[17]R. Butler and J. J. Heckman, "The Government's Impact on the Labor Market Status of Black Americans: A Critical Review," in L. J. Hausman et al. (eds.), *Equal Rights and Industrial Relations,* Industrial Relations Research Association, Madison, Wis., 1977.

policy as measured by Freeman. They further point out that if government antidiscrimination policy had shifted outward the relative demand for blacks as Freeman contends, then the labor force participation rates of blacks relative to whites should have increased. In fact, the opposite has been observed.[18]

Because the studies cited above as well as others can only provide support—not proof—for one or another argument, the question of government impact is difficult to answer precisely. A question of at least equal importance is whether improvements in the income and job opportunities available to minorities and women can be maintained and advanced if government intervention in the form of affirmative action programs and racial quotas does not become a permanent fixture of the labor market. The answer to this question depends in part upon whether or not the civil rights and women's movements have succeeded in pervasively promoting fundamental changes in society's attitudes toward minorities and women. For this question also, the answer is not apparent.

QUESTIONS AND EXERCISES

1. The analysis of occupational discrimination assumes that both occupations are equally attractive. How does the analysis of wage rates change if, in the absence of discrimination, occupation W would pay a higher wage? Which occupation is more likely to exclude blacks?

2. Researchers have often found that the relative wage of blacks moves procyclically. Why might this happen?

3. Between 1960 and 1970 the black/white wage ratio increased more in the South than in the North, although in both years the ratio was higher in the North. How might this result be partially explained by net migration of blacks out of the South?

4. Investment in specific training by firms seems to be continually growing in importance. *Ceteris paribus,* would this factor lead to less or more discrimination against women over time?

5. Why might employers who have in the past discriminated against minorities nonetheless have also favored antidiscrimination legislation?

---

[18]See Fig. 11.1. A government-induced increase in the relative demand for blacks would shift the demand curve for blacks to the right. Since there would be a movement up the supply curve in response to the higher relative wage for blacks, the labor force participation rate of blacks would have increased. On the other hand, if the higher relative wage for blacks had been induced by a leftward shift of the supply of black labor, as Butler and Heckman contend, then by definition we should observe a decline in the black labor force participation rate.

REFERENCES FOR FURTHER READING

An excellent nontechnical book on racial discrimination and its economic impact is that by Thomas Sowell, cited in footnote 13 of this chapter. On the status of women in the labor market, see J. M. Kreps, *Sex in the Marketplace: American Women at Work,* Johns Hopkins Press, Baltimore, 1971.

For an analysis of the impact of the Contract Compliance Program, see the symposium cited in footnote 16 of this chapter. See also the entire volume *Equal Rights and Industrial Relations* cited in footnote 17, but particularly chap. 1 by R. Oaxaca. For a discussion of some policy issues, see P. A. Wallace, "Employment Discrimination: Some Policy Considerations," in O. Ashenfelter and A. Rees (eds.), *Discrimination in Labor Markets,* Princeton University Press, Princeton, N.J., 1973.

UNION GROWTH
AND COLLECTIVE BARGAINING

In the unionized sectors of the economy particular wages are determined through collective bargaining between firms and labor unions, the representatives of workers. Thus in these sectors economic agents are not price takers; they do not view the wage as given by market forces beyond their control. Thus, economists view unions and collective bargaining as imperfections in competition.

Through collective bargaining, unions attempt to improve wages, hours, and working conditions of their members. There is ample evidence that in many instances some unions succeed in doing this. But others do not, and not all successful unions achieve these results in all circumstances. Nonetheless, it is the prospect of improved conditions of employment that constitute the major economic benefit to individual workers from joining unions. The costs of union membership vary widely today and have varied even more widely in the past. One of the most important costs of union membership in the past was the possibility of being fired by employers hostile to union activity. A major impact of federal legislation enacted in this century has been to reduce this cost dramatically. The monetary costs—dues and initiation fees—can be substantial for certain unions of skilled workers, although for most unions of lesser skilled workers these costs are nominal.[1] According to the

---

[1]Some information on the magnitude of dues and fees is in M. Estey, *The Unions,* Harcourt, Brace & World, New York, 1967, pp. 70–71.

neoclassical model an individual would choose to join a union if the expected benefits from joining were greater than the expected costs. The costs and benefits of union membership to individuals have changed over time in the United States and individuals have adjusted to such changes in costs and benefits. Thus, in this chapter we examine union growth in the United States. Evidence strongly supports the hypothesis that changes in union membership throughout the twentieth century can be explained by a model in which the movement of relative benefits and costs of union membership to individual workers over time plays a major role. This model of union growth is that developed by Orley Ashenfelter and John Pencavel.[2]

Our second major topic is the behavior of the union and the firm in collective bargaining. The union attempts through collective bargaining to make the terms of employment of its members better than they would be in the absence of the union. Of course, any improvements in the terms of employment raise the costs of production to the firm, and any profit-maximizing firm will attempt to negotiate the smallest increases in costs that it can. Because collective bargaining consists of a series of proposals and counterproposals, we see that typically the union's initial demands are more than it expects to receive and the firm's initial offer is less than it expects to pay. Thus the *process* of collective bargaining is one in which the union lowers its demands and the firm raises its offers. From the many models of the process of collective bargaining, we present that of Nobel laureate Sir John Hicks[3] as well as outline the statistical evidence in its support. It is, of course, possible that the union and the firm may not reach agreement over the terms of employment. The union's ultimate weapon in getting the firm to agree to its terms is the strike. The successful strike is one that persuades the firm to accede to the union's terms, and this is usually accomplished by withholding labor from the firm and thus stopping its production, sales, and profits. The firm's ultimate weapon is the lockout; a lockout denies employment to labor. Both the strike and the lockout are examples of work stoppages and represent breakdowns in collective bargaining. Work stoppages are not random events in the economy. Statistical studies show that work stoppages both in the United States and in Great Britain are related in a predictable way to a limited number of labor market variables such as the level of unemployment and the movement of real wages. We present these studies and explain how changes in labor market variables can be expected to change the outcome of collective bargaining.

Our discussion of unionism is spread primarily over two chapters. In

---

[2]O. Ashenfelter and J. Pencavel, "American Trade Union Growth: 1900–1960," *Quarterly Journal of Economics,* vol. 83, August 1969, pp. 434–448.

[3]J. R. Hicks, *The Theory of Wages,* 2d ed., St. Martin's, New York, 1963, chap. 7 and pp. 350–354.

this chapter we examine the two topics we have mentioned—the growth of unions in the United States as well as certain aspects of collective bargaining. In the following chapter we examine the economic impact of unions. There is substantial evidence that in many instances unions do have an impact on relative earnings; i.e., unions can establish a wage for their workers which is greater than that of nonunion workers with comparable skills. We examine the circumstances in which this is possible, present recent estimates of this union-nonunion differential, and see what factors affect the size of the differential. We also outline the effect of unionization on the size of GNP. We defer until Chap. 17 our discussion of the effects of unionism on the distribution of income.

Our presentation of these various union topics over a number of chapters still leaves untouched a number of interesting aspects of unions. For example, we say nothing about their internal organization or their political and social roles. Thus, one with a deep interest in unions and union-related topics will no doubt want to search out other courses and texts in the industrial relations area. Our omission of these topics in no way depreciates the value of such knowledge, but there are numerous courses where the topics we choose to omit are covered in great detail.

George E. Johnson has noted that "the study of the behavior and effects of trade unions is not currently one of the major growth industries of the economics profession."[4] Nonetheless, in our view there are many interesting and important issues which we present in this and the following chapter: the determinants of trade union growth, models of collective bargaining and its outcome, and the economic effects of unions. These are all topics which can be analyzed within the framework of the neoclassical model.

12.1

THE ASHENFELTER-PENCAVEL MODEL OF UNION GROWTH

In Table 12.1 we show union membership in the United States over the period 1930–1972 both in absolute numbers and as a percentage of the total labor force. An economist's attempt to explain such changes in union membership proceeds from the hypothesis that individuals join unions if the expected benefits from joining are greater than the expected costs. This hypothesis, when fully spelled out, predicts that union membership should vary directly with the level of economic activity. Ross Robertson has described the cyclical changes in union membership during the nineteenth century in this way:

---

[4]G. E. Johnson, "Economic Analysis of Trade Unionism," *American Economic Review,* vol. 65, May 1975, p. 23.

Table 12.1
Union membership in the United States, 1930–1972

Year	Total Membership (in thousands)	Total Membership as a Percentage of the Total Labor Force
1930	3,401	6.8
1931	3,310	6.5
1932	3,050	6.0
1933	2,689	5.2
1934	3,088	5.9
1935	3,584	6.7
1936	3,989	7.4
1937	7,001	12.9
1938	8,034	14.6
1939	8,763	15.8
1940	8,717	15.5
1941	10,201	17.7
1942	10,380	17.2
1943	13,213	20.5
1944	14,146	21.4
1945	14,322	21.9
1946	14,395	23.6
1947	14,787	23.9
1948	14,319	23.1
1949	14,282	22.7
1950	14,267	22.3
1951	15,946	24.5
1952	15,982	24.2
1953	16,948	25.5
1954	17,022	25.4
1955	16,802	24.7
1956	17,490	25.2
1957	17,369	24.9
1958	17,029	24.2
1959	17,117	24.1
1960	17,049	23.6
1961	16,303	22.3
1962	16,586	22.6
1963	16,524	22.2
1964	16,841	22.2
1965	17,299	22.4
1966	17,940	22.7
1967	18,367	22.7
1968	18,916	23.0
1969	19,036	22.6
1970	19,381	22.6
1971	19,211	22.1
1972	19,435	21.8

SOURCE: *Handbook of Labor Statistics, 1975—Reference Edition*, U.S. Department of Labor, Bureau of Labor Statistics Bulletin 1865, 1975, table 158, p. 389.

Membership of the unions always rose rapidly during prosperous periods and fell just as rapidly with the onset of depression. On the economic upswing everything was favorable to organizing endeavors. Price rises in commodities, both retail and wholesale, preceded increases in rents and wages, and real incomes fell at a rate that frightened workers into collective action. Nor did they fear the wrath of employers because of union activity, for jobs were plentiful. Furthermore, employers were less likely to resist efforts to form societies, for they could always pass on to their customers such wage-rate increases as might be extracted from them. On the downswing labor's advantage was undone. As general unemployment came on, those fortunate enough to have jobs accepted wage cuts rather than go hungry. Attempts by unions to resist wage reductions were met by countereffforts of belligerent employers, themselves frequently banded together. Union members, when called upon to strike rather than take lower wages, withdrew from the society, for they knew the employer could hire nonunion labor to break the strike.[5]

Robertson intends this description of the cyclical nature of union activity to apply to unions in the nineteenth century. Even though some portions of his description are not valid in the twentieth century, it is still the case that a cyclical pattern of union membership has been discovered for this century as well. Joseph Krislov and Virgil Christian have established that during the period 1949–1966 the number of new union organizing elections rose during economic recoveries and fell (or else did not rise) during contractions, and that unions were relatively more successful during recoveries.[6] The most complete test of the economic hypothesis, however, is the model developed by Ashenfelter and Pencavel.

Beginning with the premise that costs and benefits of union membership to individuals do change over time, and that individuals do adjust to such changes in costs and benefits, Ashenfelter and Pencavel have set out first to identify, then quantify, the changes in costs and benefits of union membership. Their arguments are similar to those above by Robertson. During periods of economic expansion, price level changes typically outpace money wage increases such that real wages decline. If one of the major appeals of unions is their promise to raise wages, then the expected benefits from joining a union should increase with price level increases. Similarly, employment expands during periods of economic expansion. The increased availability of jobs reduces the costs of employer retaliation and improves the union's prospects for successful organizing. Thus, union membership should vary directly with price level changes and with employment changes.

---

[5]R. M. Robertson, *History of the American Economy,* 3d ed., Harcourt Brace Jovanovich, New York, 1973, pp. 229–230.

[6]J. Krislov and V. L. Christian, Jr., "Union Organizing and the Business Cycle," *Southern Economic Journal,* vol. 36, October 1969, pp. 185–188.

In addition to these two variables, Ashenfelter and Pencavel complete their model by incorporating into it three other explanatory variables which are designed to capture the impact of various social and political forces. One such social force is labor's stock of grievances. Although this is a difficult concept to quantify, it does seem plausible that the greater the number of grievances that workers have, the greater will be union membership gains, given the price level and employment changes that occur. The variable that they choose to measure the degree of labor discontent and unrest at any time is the level of the unemployment rate in the trough of the previous recession. The greater that value, the greater union membership gains, *ceteris paribus.*

They include a political variable which is designed to take account of the general climate of political opinion. Because the Democratic party has usually contained within it a high degree of pro-labor sentiment, Ashenfelter and Pencavel argue that union membership gains should be greater, the greater the percentage of Democrats in the House of Representatives, *ceteris paribus.*

Their last argument is one that we might describe as a "diminishing marginal returns to organizing" argument. In their view the greater the percentage of workers in the union sectors that have already joined unions, the smaller the membership gains to any further organizing effort of a given intensity. Thus, they argue that the higher the ratio of trade union membership T to employment in the unionized sectors (defined as manufacturing, mining, construction, and transport and utilities), $E,$ the smaller the growth in union membership, *ceteris paribus.*

Summarizing their model briefly before we turn to their statistical tests, Ashenfelter and Pencavel argue that changes in trade union membership should be positively related to (1) changes in the price level $P,$ (2) changes in employment $E,$ (3) the unemployment rate at the trough of the previous recession, $U,$ and (4) the percentage of membership in the U.S. House of Representatives which is associated with the Democratic party, $D,$ but negatively related to (5) union membership as a percentage of employment in the unionized sectors of the economy, $T/E.$

Using data for the period 1900–1960, Ashenfelter and Pencavel establish that 75 percent of the change in trade union membership over this period was associated with changes in their five explanatory variables. Further, each of the five variables was found to be a statistically significant determinant of changes in union membership. The authors do not claim that their model provides an exact description of the record of union growth during this 60-year period. Indeed, they point out that some determinants of union growth (e.g., the quality of union leadership) virtually defy quantification. Nonetheless, their model does provide a compact description of a historical process. Further, their results support explanations of union growth which have been widely held for many years.

The success of their model has prompted further research into the determinants of union growth. Arvil Adams and Joseph Krislov have tested the model's ability to explain new union organizing during the period 1949–1970, where new organizing is defined as the annual number of workers who vote to join unions. Again, they find that about 75 percent of the variation in new union membership over this period is explained by the model.[7] Adams and Krislov did find one result which conflicted with an original finding by Ashenfelter and Pencavel. We mentioned above that the latter had found the ratio T/E to be negatively related to union growth. Thus, the conclusion was inescapable that current union successes in organizing workers would make future successes less likely. By contrast, Adams and Krislov did not find the variable T/E to have been a significant determinant of new organizing during 1949–1970. Thus, they conclude that there need be no "concern regarding the possible stagnation of union growth because of the movement's size."[8]

Nonetheless, there continues to be debate regarding the prospects for union growth. The reasons for the debate can be readily identified. We see in Table 12.1 that union membership as a percentage of the total labor force reached a peak of 25.5 in 1953 and has been declining slowly ever since. Even if one agrees that Ashenfelter and Pencavel have correctly identified and measured the major historical determinants of union growth, they found that about 25 percent of the actual growth over 1900–1960 was associated with "other factors" and thus remains unexplained. Further, no one argues that because a set of explanatory variables is successful in explaining past events, those same variables will be equally successful in predicting future events; over time there may be considerable changes in the structure of relationships.

William J. Moore and Robert J. Newman have examined a number of structural factors which they argue should account for differences in union membership across the states.[9] Using data for each of the years 1950, 1960, and 1970, their purpose was to identify those factors which accounted for differences across the states in union membership U as a percentage of employment in nonagriculture E. One can see from Table 12.2 that the ratio U/E varies dramatically across the states—in 1972 from 7.5 percent in North Carolina to 41.3 percent in West Virginia. If the reasons for these differences can be established, the implications for

[7] A. V. Adams and J. Krislov, "New Union Organizing: A Test of the Ashenfelter-Pencavel Model of Trade Union Growth," *Quarterly Journal of Economics,* vol. 88, May 1974, pp. 304–311.

[8] Ibid., p. 305.

[9] W. J. Moore and R. J. Newman, "On the Prospects for American Trade Union Growth: A Cross-Section Analysis," *Review of Economics and Statistics,* vol. 57, November 1975, pp. 435–445.

Table 12.2
Union membership as a percentage of employment in nonagricultural establishments, ranking by states, 1972

State	U/E
1. West Virginia	41.3
2. Michigan	38.4
3. Washington	38.3
4. Pennsylvania	38.2
5. Hawaii	37.0
6. New York	36.2
7. Illinois	35.6
8. Ohio	34.8
9. Indiana	33.9
10. Nevada	33.6
11. Missouri	32.9
12. Montana	30.7
13. Wisconsin	29.7
14. New Jersey	29.1
15. California	28.9
16. Minnesota	28.3
17. Oregon	27.9
18. Alaska	27.6
19. Rhode Island	27.3
20. Connecticut	26.1
21. Massachusetts	26.0
22. Kentucky	24.9
23. Maryland–District of Columbia	21.7
24. Delaware	20.3
25. Iowa	20.0

union organizing strategies as well as the potential benefits and costs to unions of various organizing strategies can be estimated.

Moore and Newman found differences in the ratio U/E across the states to be systematically related to seven variables. They found that (1) the percentage of employment in blue-collar occupations, (2) the degree of urbanization, (3) the percentage of the labor force represented by nonwhites, and (4) the percentage of the labor force represented by older workers were all factors favorable to union membership. They interpreted these results as suggesting that blue-collar workers are less costly to organize than their white-collar counterparts, and that large towns and large firms are less costly to organize. Their results for nonwhites and older workers suggest that nonwhites view unions as protecting their minority interests and that older workers have a concern for job security and seniority which they view unions as protecting.

They found (5) the percentage of the labor force represented by

26.	Utah	19.4
27.	Alabama	19.2
28.	Maine	19.1
29.	Colorado	18.9
30.	Wyoming	18.5
31.	Tennessee	18.4
32.	Vermont	17.7
33.	New Hampshire	17.2
34.	Nebraska	17.0
35.	Idaho	17.0
36.	Louisiana	16.9
37.	Arizona	16.6
38.	Arkansas	16.4
39.	North Dakota	16.1
40.	Oklahoma	16.0
41.	Virginia	15.5
42.	Kansas	15.4
43.	Florida	14.7
44.	Georgia	13.9
45.	Texas	13.5
46.	New Mexico	13.2
47.	Mississippi	12.6
48.	South Dakota	11.8
49.	South Carolina	9.0
50.	North Carolina	7.5
	All States	27.2

SOURCE: *Directory of National and International Unions of the United States.* U.S. Department of Labor, Bureau of Labor Statistics, 1973.

women, (6) the existence of a state "right-to-work" law,[10] and (7) a southern state variable to be impediments to union membership. Many women expect fewer benefits from union membership because their labor market attachment is not as strong as males. A right-to-work law adversely affects union membership because it outlaws within states which adopt it the union security arrangement known as the union shop. (We discuss in more detail below the possible effects of public policy on the prospects for union growth.) The "southern" variable captures all those forces which tend to make southern workers, *ceteris paribus,* less willing to join unions than workers in the non-South.

Their statistical results show that these seven variables explain about 60 percent of the variation in U/E across the states in each of the years 1950, 1960, and 1970. Moore and Newman use their results to

---

[10]State right-to-work laws are defined and discussed in some detail below.

conclude that in some states unions are doing less well than their model predicts they should, although such interpretations should be drawn cautiously given that their model leaves unexplained about 40 percent of the actual variation in U/E across the states.

Nonetheless, their results support widely held assessments of the prospects for union growth. Industries such as manufacturing and mining which include a high proportion of blue-collar occupations are not typically high-growth industries. Industries such as government and services which have shown greater growth in employment include a high proportion of white-collar occupations. Further, even within manufacturing the proportion of white-collar to blue-collar workers has risen. Neither of these developments bodes well for union growth. Similarly, the rising number of females in the labor force (particularly married females) is not a factor that encourages union growth. The South does continue to be a fertile field for unionization even though Moore and Newman found public attitudes in the South regarding unions to be significantly different from those in the non-South.

Their finding that right-to-work laws exert an independent effect in discouraging unionism is novel.[11] Most students of this question wonder why the existence of this law should affect union membership. Their argument follows this general line of reasoning: The Taft-Hartley Act, a federal law enacted in 1947, allows the union shop. The union shop is a union security arrangement whereby workers employed by a firm which has a contract with a union must join the union within some specified period of time, typically 30 days. But the Taft-Hartley Act also includes a section, Section 14-b, which permits an individual state to outlaw within that state the union shop provisions which federal law allows. The states which have outlawed the union shop within their own boundaries are known as right-to-work law states.[12] There are a substantial number of these states, primarily (but not exclusively) in the South. Thus, within each of these states a union shop is against state law; a union shop provision cannot be bargained about in collective bargaining. But in states which do not outlaw the union shop, such a provision can appear on the agenda for collective bargaining.

Every student of this issue knows that *in fact* there are union shops in right-to-work law states; further, many labor-management contracts in states which do not outlaw the union shop do *not* contain a union shop provision. In short, if unions are strong enough to get a union shop, they appear to do so regardless of what state law allows. Similarly, if they are

---

[11]See K. Lumsden and C. Petersen, "The Effect of Right-to-Work Laws on Unionization in the United States," *Journal of Political Economy,* vol. 83, December 1975, pp. 1237–1248, and the references cited there.

[12]Agency shops may be allowed, however. This is an arrangement where nonunion workers pay union dues but do not join the union.

not strong enough to get a union shop, they don't, even if state law allows a union shop. The existence of a state right-to-work law appears to have little if anything to do with it. Consequently, they view the struggle over the union shop as one of symbol rather than substance. Organized labor has fought very hard and long to have Section 14-b of the Taft-Hartley Act repealed. One must thus conclude either that they view this provision as hampering their organizing activities or that any victory—symbolic or not—is worth a considerable sacrifice of their resources.

12.2

COLLECTIVE BARGAINING

Collective bargaining can take place in a variety of circumstances. In a newly organized plant, bargaining may be over the terms of the initial contract. Or, given an existing contract, bargaining may take place during the weeks preceding the expiration of the existing contract. Bargaining may also be taking place while a strike is in progress. In any event the parties are attempting to arrive at the terms of a contract which is a legally binding agreement and which will normally be in force during a number of years.[13]

Consider what facts each party brings to collective bargaining. The firm knows its costs of production, the prevailing wage levels in its industry and local labor market, and general labor market conditions. It has only expectations about its future sales and profits during the next few years. The union knows the terms of employment covered by the existing contract as well as general labor market conditions. Like the firm, it has only expectations about the firm's future sales and profits during the lifetime of the new contract. The firm wants to keep increases in costs of production to a minimum; the union wants the best package possible for its members. Neither the union nor the firm knows what the terms of the new contract will be; each knows only the terms of the existing contract. Let us begin our analysis of the process of collective bargaining by examining the costs and benefits to each party of accepting the other's initial proposal. We see that the costs to each party of accepting the other's initial proposal typically exceed the benefits. Thus our interest focuses on the process of adjustment during subsequent bargaining sessions. If the union lowers its demands and the firm raises its offers during subsequent sessions, it is likely that the parties will arrive at a new contract without a work stoppage. There are benefits as well as costs to a work stoppage. We examine these benefits and

---

[13]Some labor-management contracts contain a provision by which negotiations can be reopened during the lifetime of the contract. Alternatively, some "evergreen" contracts contain a provision which continues the existing contract for an indefinite period of time until a renegotiation is requested by either party.

costs in some detail so as to understand better why strikes might occur, as well as how the number of strikes in the economy is influenced by labor market conditions.

12.2a
The benefits and costs of accepting the union's initial demands

Consider the alternatives available to the firm in response to the union's opening proposal. One possibility is for the firm to agree to the union's opening demands. The benefits of such a strategy are to prevent the possibility of a strike (or to end the strike if bargaining is taking place during the course of a strike) with its interruption of production, sales, and profits. The costs of this action are to increase the firm's costs of production by an amount which typically even the union regards as unrealistic, and these increased costs will prevail during the lifetime of the new contract, usually 2 or 3 years. The degree to which increases in the costs of production increase product selling price will of course adversely affect the firm's competitive position in the product market. One might argue that other firms in the same industry would encourage the firm to accept a proposal such as this because it would make them relatively better off in the product market. However, they are more likely to realize that yielding to a high-cost proposal by the union also puts them under considerable pressure to do the same when their contracts come up for renewal. Thus the firm generally receives moral support from the other firms in the industry.

The benefits to the union if its initial proposal is accepted can be dramatic and substantial. They might be wages or fringe benefits that up to now had only been dreamed about. Dramatic union success strengthens the political position of the elected union officials with their members, may result in increased membership in the union, and can tilt the scales in their favor in future bargaining with other firms in the industry. The potential costs of making unrealistic initial demands are in reality quite small. There is always the possibility that the firm will break off negotiations or refuse to bargain seriously until the union adopts a more realistic stance, but these costs are minimal.

Thus, for the firm, the costs of accepting the union's initial offer are likely to be well in excess of the benefits. For the union, the benefits of making unrealistically high initial demands will normally exceed the costs. The rejection by the firm of a union's opening demands in no way should be interpreted as a failure of collective bargaining; the process does serve a useful purpose. For example, it may provide useful information to the firm. The union may be using opening demands only as a signal to the firm of what it intends to bargain for seriously a few years down the road. It may also be the case that union officials are threatened politically by a faction of the union membership which views recent wage gains as unacceptable. If this is the case, then initial demands are really to quench the fires within the union rank and file and are not directed at the firm. Keep in mind, however, that it is always possible for the firm to accept the union's opening demands. This could occur as a result of inexperienced bargainers for the firm, or as a result of the fact that the firm has information which the union does not have about future events which could affect the firm's revenues or costs. The union never wants to find itself in a position of not having demanded as much as it could have received. The costs of such an error to union officials in the form of rank and file unrest could be tremendous.

12.2b
The benefits and costs of accepting the firm's initial offer

We can analyze in a similar fashion the benefits and costs to the union of accepting the firm's first offer, keeping in mind that the union has already at this point made its initial demands. The initial proposal of the firm will of necessity be less attractive than the initial union demands; otherwise the firm would have accepted the initial union proposal.

The benefits to the union of accepting the firm's first offer are likely to be minimal. If the firm's offer is less than the union was led to anticipate, then the union typically views the offer as an insult. Even if the firm's initial offer is more attractive than the union had anticipated, the union could well conclude that the settlement which lies down the road might be even more attractive than they had reason to believe. Thus, there would again be minor benefits from accepting this higher than anticipated first offer.

The costs of accepting the firm's first offer are likely to be high. One can imagine how long union officials would keep their jobs if they accepted an insultingly low initial offer by the firm. Similarly, even if the first offer by the firm were higher than anticipated, the costs of acceptance are high because of the potentially even higher package that now seems possible.

For the firm, the major benefit of the union's accepting its initial offer is a signed contract which will remain in force a number of years, a contract which might give the firm a competitive advantage in the product market as well as a period of peace with its workers. For the firm, the existing contract terms normally provide the starting point for its first offer. Whether the first offer exceeds the existing contract terms by minimal or substantial amounts provides a great deal of information to the union, and management may well expect to benefit from this if it results in the union's adjusting its demands. The firm's initial (say low) offer may be accompanied by a lengthy presentation of economic conditions in the industry and/or in the total economy, the purpose of which is to make the union's demands appear unreasonable. An initial (say higher than expected) offer indicates to the union that the firm recognizes that wage gains may be healthy. (As we see below, however, this can be costly.) The firm can also in its initial offer signal a willingness to compromise on some issues but not others, for example by offering some unexpected improvements in working conditions but lower than expected increases in wages or fringe benefits. In short, there are a variety of benefits to be gained by the firm in both the level and the composition of its initial offer.

The costs to the firm of making an initial offer which all know will be unacceptable are minimal. The union is unlikely to overreact by breaking off negotiations because they know that there will be other better offers. The costs of making higher than anticipated concessions early in collective bargaining may be quite costly to the firm, however. It does not want the union to begin revising upward its ideas of the final agreement. So even if it has concessions in mind, it is likely to hold these until bargaining has proceeded past the first round.

Thus, for the union, the costs of accepting the firm's initial offer tend to exceed the benefits; for the firm, the benefits of making a low offer exceed the costs. As before, it is always conceivable that the union could accept the firm's first offer, and the firm doesn't want to find itself offering a contract which includes terms more generous than it could have achieved.

12.2c
The movement toward a strike or settlement

If a new contract is reached through collective bargaining, the terms of the contract will typically be less than the union's initial demands and more than the firm's initial offer. Thus the process of collective bargaining is one in which the union adjusts its demands downward and the firm adjusts its initial offers upward.

This entire process of adjustment has been formalized in a model of collective bargaining developed by Sir John Hicks. In Fig. 12.1 we present a graphical representation of Hicks's model; we also present below some empirical evidence concerning the curves depicted there. Both the *employer's concession curve* and the *union resistance curve* are time-paths between possible wage rates and the expected duration of a strike.[14] The firm would prefer its initial wage offer 0Z and no strike. Higher wages commit the firm to increased costs over the lifetime of the new contract. But incurring a strike because of a breakdown in collective bargaining also imposes costs on the firm in the form of lost production, sales, and profits. Further, the longer the expected duration of a strike, the greater the expected costs will be. The

---

[14]More precisely, the term *wage rate* is simply a shorthand expression meaning the dollar amount of all the benefits under consideration, whether the particular benefits are wages, working conditions, fringe benefits, or hours. Because the analysis is not affected at all by the particular benefit being considered, we adopt the conventional shorthand phrase wage rate, but refer always to the dollar value of benefits (or costs in the case of the firm).

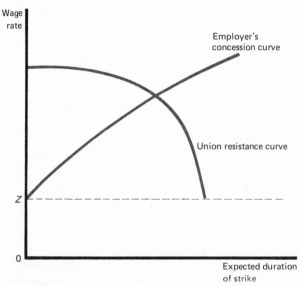

Figure 12.1. Hick's model of collective bargaining. The employer's concession curve is positively sloped, representing the firm's willingness to agree to a wage higher than its initial offer 0Z rather than incur the costs of a strike of increasingly long duration. The union resistance curve is negatively sloped, representing the union's willingness to accept a wage lower than its initial demand rather than incur the costs of a strike of increasingly long duration.

employer's concession curve represents the wage (measured on the vertical axis) that the firm will agree to rather than accept a strike of some given duration (measured on the horizontal axis). The curve is upward-sloping, illustrating the fact that the longer the expected duration of a strike, the higher the wage the firm will pay to prevent it.

Union members would of course prefer their initial wage demand with no strike. But in most cases they are required to make a choice. Calling a strike presents the cost of unemployment and interrupted income. Settling for a low wage without a strike imposes costs on union members for the duration of the contract. The union resistance curve represents the wage that union members would accept rather than undergo a strike of some given duration. This curve is downward-sloping, representing the fact that the longer the expected duration of a strike, the lower the wage the union will accept to avoid it.

Hicks's model has been tested by Yochanan Comay, Arie Melnik, and Abraham Subotnik.[15] These authors examined eight cases of collec-

---

[15]Y. Comay, A. Melnik, and A. Subotnik, "Bargaining, Yield Curves, and Wage Settlements: An Empirical Analysis," *Journal of Political Economy,* vol. 82, pt. I, March/April 1974, pp. 303–313.

tive bargaining which took place during strikes in New York City during 1966–1967. Each of the cases examined involved at least five rounds of offers and counteroffers. The authors' purpose was to translate each offer and counteroffer into monetary terms so as to create employers' concession curves and union resistance curves. They found that in these eight cases the union tended to maintain its wage demands for the early periods of a strike, then rapidly reduce them to achieve a settlement. By contrast, management's concession curve rose rather steadily during the entire length of a strike. They found that this simple model was quite accurate in predicting the dollar amount of the final settlements.

But this model says little about the prospects of a strike; it says only that the process of collective bargaining typically involves the union's lowering its demands and the firm's raising its offers. What accounts for the strikes that do occur in the economy? In 1973 there were 5,393 work stoppages in the United States; the average duration of these strikes was 24 calendar days; 2,251,000 workers were involved in these strikes, 2.9 percent of all workers in the economy.[16] It has to be the case that in these instances the firm and the union did not adjust their offers and counteroffers so as to arrive at a settlement without a strike. This observation leads us, then, to an examination of why they did not.

A fruitful approach to this question requires us to keep in mind that choices made by individuals in collective bargaining are like all other choices that individuals make in that they have consequences in the future; choices made today cannot alter the past. Thus decisions by the union or by the firm to accept the other's last proposal have consequences which cannot be known with certainty. Both the firm and the union can only form expectations about what the future holds. Consider the case in which collective bargaining takes place in a stable economic environment. Specifically, assume that recent movements in real wages of union members have been proceeding at a steady, known rate, that employment levels have been high and stable, and, further, that union members, union officials, and the firm all expect these circumstances to continue in the future. This situation is one in which we would expect the parties involved in collective bargaining to form similar expectations about the future, and these similar expectations cause there to be some probability of a new contract being agreed to without a work stoppage. Now introduce some instability into this environment. For example, let the price level rise unexpectedly so that real wages decline. Or let the level of employment (or unemployment) change unexpectedly. Will the price level continue to rise over the lifetime of the new contract? At the same rate? Will the unemployment rate continue to rise in the future? The parties to collective bargaining are not likely to form their expectations of

---

[16]These data are from *Handbook of Labor Statistics, 1975—Reference Edition* (cited above in Table 12.1), table 159.

future movements in these variables in an identical manner. The unexpected movements in real wages and employment will be interpreted differently and will result in a divergence in expectations as between the union and the firm. Thus these differences in the union's and the firm's expectations will clearly reduce the probability of a new contract being agreed to without a stoppage. Orley Ashenfelter and George Johnson have found both the unemployment rate and movements in real wages to be significantly related to the number of strikes in the United States.[17] John Pencavel has found the same results to be true for Great Britain.[18] These results are consistent with the analysis we have presented; movements in the unemployment rate and in real wages do give rise to differences in expectations among the parties to collective bargaining and increase the probability of strikes.

Both of the studies found higher unemployment rates and higher recent rises in real wages to be associated with lower numbers of strikes. These results suggest that high rates of unemployment raise the cost of a strike relative to the benefits. It is true that declining job vacancies and the associated increases in the number of unemployed diminish the opportunity to moonlight and supplement strike benefits, and thus increase the likelihood of a new contract being signed without a work stoppage. Similarly, if real wages have not been rising (due perhaps to unanticipated inflation), the union rank and file will bring increasing pressure on union officials to hold out for higher money wages, increasing the likelihood of a strike. Indeed, Ashenfelter and Johnson view union officials as serving as an intermediary between the union rank and file and the firm. In periods of rapidly rising price levels, the wage demands of the union rank and file may increase appreciably more than the firm's willingness to grant wage increases. Thus the best strategy for union officials may be to allow a strike if for no other reason than to bring the wage expectations of the rank and file into line with what the firm is willing to pay. Thus whether or not a new contract is arrived at without a strike is seen to be strongly influenced by a limited number of labor market variables; any public policies that result in stability of employment and the price level will also tend to diminish the number of work stoppages in the economy.

What relationship does the union wage arrived at through collective bargaining bear to the market wage for nonunion workers with equivalent skills? We know that in many instances unions do negotiate wages for their members which exceed those of similar workers in the nonunion sectors of the economy. How can unions bring this about? Are there

---

[17]O. Ashenfelter and G. E. Johnson, "Bargaining Theory, Trade Unions, and Industrial Strike Activity," *American Economic Review,* vol. 59, March 1969, pp. 35–49.

[18]J. H. Pencavel, "An Investigation into Industrial Strike Activity in Britain," *Economica,* vol. 37, August 1970, pp. 239–256.

limits to their ability to achieve these higher than competitive wages? We turn now to an examination of the impact of unions on wages, employment, and economic welfare.

QUESTIONS AND EXERCISES

1. In Fig. 12.1, what meaning would you attach to the intersection of the employer's concession curve and the union's resistance curve?

2. Given the steady decline in union membership as a percentage of the labor force, what union strategy would you advocate if your objective were to bring about a rise in this ratio?

3. If it is true that Southern workers are, *ceteris paribus,* less willing to join unions than workers in the non-South, what might account for this difference?

4. If you were responsible for collective bargaining for a union, how much investment in information about the economic circumstances facing the firm and the industry would you recommend making? Why?

5. Increases in benefits to workers arrived at through collective bargaining can take two general forms—increases in wages and increases in nonwage benefits such as fringe benefits and working conditions. How might the existence of a progressive personal income tax affect the union membership's preferences as between these two general forms of benefits?

REFERENCES FOR FURTHER READING

One of the very best presentations of the many aspects of unionism is A. Rees, *The Economics of Trade Unions,* The University of Chicago Press, Chicago, 1962. Other very fine general presentations are M. Estey, *The Unions,* Harcourt, Brace & World, New York, 1967; P. Taft, *Organized Labor in American History,* Harper & Row, New York, 1964; J. G. Rayback, *A History of American Labor,* Free Press, New York, 1966; I. Bernstein, *The Lean Years,* Penguin, Baltimore, 1966.

For an advanced presentation and discussion of formal theories of collective bargaining, see W. N. Atherton, *Theory of Union Bargaining Goals,* Princeton University Press, Princeton, N.J., 1973.

Unions in some cases have negotiated dramatic revisions in existing contracts in order to save jobs. For an examination of some of these cases, see P. Henle, "Reverse Collective Bargaining? A Look at Some Union Concession Situations," *Industrial and Labor Relations Review,* vol. 26, April 1973, pp. 956–968.

THE UNION IMPACT
ON WAGES, EMPLOYMENT,
AND ECONOMIC WELFARE

Neoclassical economic theory assumes that all workers are alike in that each prefers more goods to less goods. Thus, each worker would become better off with increased consumption of market goods (no fewer nonmarket goods), increased consumption of nonmarket goods (no fewer market goods), or increased consumption of both goods. In short, each worker would become better off with higher earnings and better fringe benefits, and shorter hours worked (per week, year, or lifetime). As we saw in the previous chapter, an individual would choose to join a union if the expected benefits to union membership were greater than the expected costs. The expected benefits are those that we have mentioned—better "terms of employment" than would exist in the absence of the union. The costs to union membership will be some monetary costs in the form of membership fees, normally inconsequential for industrial unions, but quite substantial for some craft unions.

If higher benefits to union members result in higher costs to firms, firms will predictably choose to reduce employment of union labor and increase employment of nonunionized resources. But how much lost employment will occur if unions negotiate real wage increases for their members of, say, 15 percent? The economic concept that is crucial to understanding this question is the elasticity of demand for union labor, for it measures the loss in employment of union workers (in percentage terms) which results from a rise in union wages (also in percentage terms). The more elastic the demand for union labor, the greater will be the percentage loss in union employment given any percentage rise in the union wage. Thus, the more elastic the demand for union labor, the greater the costs associated with union attempts to raise benefits for their members. By contrast, if the demand for union labor is inelastic, then any given percentage rise in the union wage will have a smaller percentage impact on employment of union workers. Consequently, the more inelastic (or the less elastic) the demand for union labor, the lower the costs associated with union attempts to raise benefits for their members. Clearly, we would predict unions to be more successful in raising wages of their members the more inelastic (or less elastic) the demand for union labor.

Suppose that unions are able to raise wages of their members higher than they would be in the absence of the union. We would say then that unions have an *impact on relative wages.* If the average wage for union workers with given skills is U and the average wage for nonunion workers with identical skills is $N,$ then the union impact on relative wages is measured by the ratio $(U - N)/N$. Thus, if U is $5.00 and N is $4.00, the union impact on relative wages is ($5.00 − $4.00)/$4.00, or 25 percent.

If the demand for union labor is highly inelastic so that union wage gains result in minimal employment losses of union members, can we therefore conclude that there are no costs to society (or trivial costs) of union wage policies? No, for the costs of union wage gains may be borne by *nonunion workers* and by other nonunion individuals. These costs will be in the form of a misallocation of labor among the various sectors of the economy with the corresponding loss in national output, as well as a redistribution of income away from the nonunion sectors toward the union sectors.

In the following section we begin our discussion of the union impact on wages, employment, and economic welfare by examining the determinants of the elasticity of demand for union labor. This will enable us to outline those circumstances in which unions can achieve an impact on relative wages.

13.1

THE ELASTICITY OF DEMAND FOR UNION LABOR

In Chap. 6 we presented the determinants of the elasticity of demand for labor. Because we are concerned here with the determinants of the elasticity of demand for union labor, we modify our earlier discussion accordingly to take account of this emphasis.

The demand for union labor will be more inelastic:

1. The less the elasticity of substitution of other inputs for union labor
2. The more inelastic the demand for the product produced by union labor
3. The less the ratio of union labor costs to total costs of production
4. The less elastic the supply of other substitute factors of production

Each of these factors tends to make the loss in union employment given any rise in the union wage less than it otherwise would be, and makes possible a union impact on relative wages.

13.1a
The elasticity of substitution of other inputs for union labor

The elasticity of substitution of other inputs for union labor is a measure of the responsiveness in factor combinations to changes in relative factor prices. To illustrate this concept, consider a purely competitive labor market divided into two groups of workers. Assume that all workers in both groups are alike in their skills, education, and other productivity-related respects, and that a firm can and does employ individuals from both groups. Now assume that one of the two groups chooses to form a union and that the union attempts to raise members' wages relative to those of identical nonunion workers employed by the firm. The firm will predictably choose to cease its employment of union workers whose wage has risen and to employ only nonunion workers. In this case the elasticity of substitution is infinitely high. Given this predictable response by employers, the potential costs of lost employment (and income) to union workers would prevent their gaining relative to nonunion workers. Thus, there would be no union impact on relative wages.

It would clearly be in any union's interest to block nonunion labor substitutes and any other substitutes, e.g., physical capital, for union labor. Unions can and have been able to do this in a variety of ways. They have favored the closed shop, a legal arrangement whereby the union is the sole supplier of labor to firms. Although the closed shop is outlawed in interstate commerce as a result of the Taft-Hartley Act of 1947, innumerable ways have developed since then to ensure that in many types of employment the union remains the sole supplier of labor to many firms. The union shop achieves much the same result as the closed shop in that whereas new employees may be recruited by the firm in the union shop rather than being supplied by the union, employees must agree to join the union within some short period of time. Even in the open shop, the legal requirement that wage increases negotiated for the firm's union members apply to the firm's nonunion members as well guarantees that no union-nonunion wage discrepancy will develop within the firm which would induce the firm to substitute nonunion labor for union labor.

Does it follow that union success in blocking identical nonunion substitutes assures a low elasticity of substitution of other inputs for union labor? Not necessarily. There may be capital inputs which are readily substitutable for union labor. The degree to which such substitutions are possible depends on unique characteristics of particular production processes. For example, the substitution of capital for a union airline pilot in the production of a flight from New York to San Francisco is difficult if not impossible. Thus, the elasticity of substitution between the two inputs is low. On the other hand, the substitution of capital for union window washers in the production of "clean windows" is not difficult at all. Thus, the elasticity of substitution between the two is high. The lower the elasticity of substitution between capital and union labor, the smaller the loss in union employment given any increase in the union wage relative to the price of capital. We know that, as a general proposition, skilled labor, unskilled labor, and capital are substitutes as well as complements in any production process. However, the elasticity of substitution between skilled labor and capital is lower than that between unskilled labor and capital.[1] Thus, the fact that unions historically have had their greatest successes in organizing skilled workers follows in part from the low elasticity of substitution of capital for unionized skilled workers. Our generalization about the effect of differences in the elasticity of substitution between other inputs and union labor is this: The lower the elasticity of substitution, the more inelastic the demand for union labor, and the greater the union impact on relative wages.

13.1b
The elasticity of demand for the product

The elasticity of demand for union labor is influenced as well by substitutions consumers can make in product markets. Assume that union wage increases raise the firm's costs of production, and that the firm raises product price. How will the firm's sales be affected? This depends on the elasticity of demand for the firm's product. The more elastic the demand for the product, the greater the percentage loss in sales (and thus employment) given any percentage rise in product price. If only one firm in an industry is unionized, a rise in its product price will reduce its sales dramatically as consumers shift to the close substitutes produced by other firms in the same industry. By contrast, if all firms in an industry are unionized, then a product price rise will have less impact on each firm's sales, although total industry sales will fall to the extent that consumers make substitutions in consumption across industries. A union's success in achieving an impact on relative wages will thus vary directly with the extent of unionization of an industry.[2] Our generalization is: The more inelastic the demand for the product, the more inelastic the demand for union labor, and the greater the union impact on relative wages.

---

[1]S. Rosen, "Short-Run Employment Variation on Class-I Railroads in the U.S., 1947–1963," *Econometrica,* vol. 36, July/October 1968, pp. 511–529. See also Z. Griliches, "Capital-Skill Complementarity," *Review of Economics and Statistics,* vol. 51, November 1969, pp. 465–470.

[2]S. Rosen, "Trade Union Power, Threat Effects and the Extent of Organization," *Review of Economic Studies,* vol. 36, April 1969, pp. 185–196.

13.1c
The ratio of union labor costs to total costs of production

The third determinant of the elasticity of demand for union labor concerns "the importance of being unimportant." Consider two firms, one in which union labor costs represent 10 percent of the firm's total costs of production, the other in which union labor costs represent 50 percent of the firm's total costs of production. A 10 percent rise in the union wage will raise costs of production by only 1 percent in the first firm, but by 5 percent in the second firm. Clearly the employment loss will be less in the first firm where costs of production increase less. Thus, the smaller the ratio of union labor costs to total costs, the more inelastic the demand for union labor, and the greater the union impact on relative wages.

13.1d
The elasticity of supply of other substitute inputs

The union impact on relative wages is influenced also by the elasticity of supply of other substitute inputs such as capital. Assume that the union bargains for a higher wage. As the firm attempts to substitute other inputs, say capital, it increases the demand for capital, raising the price of capital. What happens to the quantity of capital supplied as its price rises? Consider the case where the supply of capital is elastic. The increase in the demand for capital raises the price of capital, induces increased output from the capital goods industries (by a percentage amount greater than the percentage increase in the price of capital), and allows the firm the possibility of substituting capital for labor. The amount of substitution depends, of course, on the degree to which relative prices change. If the supply of capital is elastic, the price of capital will not rise appreciably, and this encourages increased substitution. By contrast, consider the case where the supply of capital is perfectly inelastic. In this case the increase in demand would raise the price of capital—thus tending to decrease capital's price advantage—and would not increase the output of capital. Thus, the firm would be effectively prohibited from substituting capital for labor, and the impact on employment would be inconsequential. Thus, the more inelastic the supply of capital and other substitute inputs, the more inelastic the demand for union labor, and the greater the union impact on relative wages.

13.1e
Elasticity of demand and union success

Pulling together the four determinants of the elasticity of demand for union labor, some of which reinforce each other and some of which do not, we can outline the circumstances favorable to union success. Both the closed shop and the union shop favor union success because both make impossible the use of the closest substitute for union labor—

identical nonunion labor. Unions will likely be successful in circumstances where the elasticity of substitution of capital for union labor is low (as in the case of skilled labor), and this is amplified if the supply of possible capital substitutes is inelastic. In numerous production processes such as contract construction, wages of particular skilled union occupations constitute a small portion of total costs of production; this favors union success. Finally, union power should vary directly with the extent to which firms in the industry are unionized.

Unions will be unsuccessful (or less successful) when open shops are allowed, among lower-skilled workers who can be more readily replaced by capital, in labor-intensive industries such as textiles where labor costs are a large portion of total costs of production, in industries which are not extensively organized, and in firms and industries where product demand is elastic.

We may cast this discussion of the circumstances favorable to union success in an alternative way. We presented in Chap. 10 the model of monopoly, defining a monopolist as a sole seller. Our discussion there was in terms of monopoly in the product market. A very powerful labor union may be the best example of monopoly in the labor market. If a union is the sole seller of a service for which there are no close substitutes, the demand for union labor may be highly inelastic, and as we have seen, there will be a substantial union impact on relative wages if this is the case. It is important to note that whereas a strong union may successfully block nonunion labor substitutes for its services, it is seldom in a position to block substitution of other inputs such as capital: the firm is normally in the position of being able to substitute inputs other than nonunion labor, and will be induced to do so if wages of union workers rise. Thus, the availability of substitutes in production other than nonunion labor will in many cases result in the demand for union labor being relatively elastic.

In the following section we survey recent evidence on the magnitude of the union-nonunion wage difference, discuss possible problems in the estimates, and show that the size of the wage difference varies systematically with market forces.

13.2

ESTIMATES OF THE UNION IMPACT ON RELATIVE WAGES

We stated earlier that if the union wage U is \$5.00 and the nonunion wage N is \$4.00, then the union impact on relative wages is (\$5.00 − \$4.00)/\$4.00, or 25 percent. A union impact on relative wages can arise (1) because unions raise union wages U *directly* and (2) because union wage policies *indirectly* cause nonunion wages N to be other than they would be in the absence of the union (that is, either higher or lower than the competitive wage). Nonunion wages will be higher than competitive wages if nonunion employers raise wages so as to escape being unionized. This effect on nonunion wages is known as the *threat effect.*

Alternatively, nonunion wages will be lower than competitive wages if increases in union wages cause unemployed union workers to spill over to the nonunion sectors, increasing supply to nonunion employers, and bidding down wages there below the competitive wage. This effect is known as the *spillover effect.* Because of both threat effects and spillover effects, the actual wages that nonunion workers receive are not those that would emerge in purely competitive markets. Thus, economists have measured a union wage–nonunion wage difference, not a union wage–competitive wage difference.[3]

In previous chapters we have seen that average wages between groups of workers may differ for numerous reasons. In Chap. 8 we discussed why, because of different human capital requirements associated with different jobs, there would be equilibrium differences in occupational wages even in the long run in purely competitive labor markets. In Chap. 9 we saw that transitional differences in average wages in purely competitive occupational, industrial, and regional labor markets exist because individuals do not possess perfect information and mobility. Further, differences in average wages exist because of imperfectly competitive markets: there are differences in wages by race and sex because of discrimination, as well as differences attributable to monopsony power by firms.

Statistical estimates of the union impact on relative wages are attempts to measure the difference in average wages between groups of workers alike in all respects except one: one group belongs to a union, the other does not. It is particularly difficult to find groups of workers which meet this criterion, and all estimates of union-nonunion wage differences run the risk of attributing to unionism wage differences which properly should be attributed to other factors such as skill, age, race, and other demographic and economic factors. Nonetheless, many such estimates have been made, and the estimates vary widely. It is not our purpose to present all the available evidence on this question. Rather, we are interested in seeing whether evidence does exist to support the numerous theoretical arguments we have developed in earlier sections of this chapter.

13.2a
Economywide estimates of the union impact on relative wages

Although economists for many years have measured union-nonunion wage differences, estimates of the union impact on relative wages stem in large part from the work of H. Gregg Lewis.[4] Lewis found the union

---

[3]A very clear discussion of these points is in R. L. Oaxaca, "Estimation of Union/Nonunion Wage Differentials within Occupational/Regional Subgroups," *Journal of Human Resources,* vol. 10, fall 1975, pp. 529–537.

[4]H. G. Lewis, *Unionism and Relative Wages in the United States,* University of Chicago Press, Chicago and London, 1963. Many of the earlier estimates are discussed in great detail in this work by Lewis.

impact on relative wages to have varied widely in the past. He estimated the *economywide* union impact on relative wages to have been 15 to 20 percent in 1923–1929, greater than 25 percent in 1931–1933, 10 to 20 percent in 1939–1941, 0 to 5 percent in 1945–1949, and 10 to 15 percent in 1957–1958.[5] Because the period 1957–1958 was one characterized by a reasonably stable price level and reasonably full employment, an economywide union impact on relative wages of 10 to 15 percent was viewed as a "normal" one given relatively stable economic conditions. Sherwin Rosen's study for virtually the same period produced estimates which reinforced those of Lewis, although Rosen's estimates ranged about five percentage points higher than those of Lewis.[6] Adrian Throop has estimated a union-nonunion wage difference for 1960 of 26 percent, an estimate substantially above that of Lewis.[7] A later study by Rosen estimates the relative effect of unionism in 1959 on all production workers to range from 25 to 35 percent.[8]

There is universal agreement, then, when speaking of the union impact across broad groups of workers, that unions can and do cause wages of their members to be greater than those of comparable nonunion workers. The estimates vary because the periods of study are not strictly comparable, because the data used do not always allow the same adjustments for "quality" differences across groups of workers, and because the groups of workers for whom estimates are derived vary across studies. One variation in the union impact on relative wages that has been investigated by economists is the cyclical variation which Lewis discovered in his estimates. We turn now to an examination of this question.

13.2b
Cyclical variations in economywide estimates

Lewis's finding that the economywide union impact on relative wages varied widely over time—from 0 to 5 percent in 1945–1949 to more than 25 percent in 1931–1933—led him and others to explain such variations in terms of relative wage rigidities. This hypothesis begins with the recognition that nonunion wages are much more responsive to changes in the demand for labor than are union wages which are negotiated for 1 to 3 years at a time. Given increases in the demand for labor and the corresponding increases in product demand (and perhaps the price level as well), nonunion wages tend to rise. If union wages rose at the same rate, there would be no narrowing of the union-nonunion wage

[5]Ibid., table 50, p. 193.

[6]S. Rosen, "Trade Union Power, Threat Effects and the Extent of Organization," op. cit., p. 192, fn. 2.

[7]A. Throop, "The Union-Nonunion Wage Differential and Cost-Push Inflation," *American Economic Review,* vol. 58, March 1968, p. 84.

[8]S. Rosen, "Unionism and the Occupational Wage Structure in the United States," *International Economic Review,* vol. 11, June 1970, p. 283.

differential. But union wages do not typically rise as fast. One reason is that they have been negotiated, and time elapses before they can be renegotiated. Further, wage increases granted to unions can be difficult if not impossible to retract if, in the future, declining demand for labor makes such a reduction desirable for the firm. Thus, union wage increases tend to lag behind those in the nonunion sector during economic upturns so that the ratio $(U - N)/N$ declines.

Similarly, in periods of declining demand for labor, union wages fall less (if at all) as compared with nonunion wages, so that the ratio $(U - N)/N$ increases. This hypothesis does seem to be an attractive explanation of the facts that, in Lewis's estimates, the greatest union impact on relative wages was in the depths of the depression in 1931–1933, while the impact was trivial in the inflation and recovery period 1945–1949 following World War II.

Attractive or not, not all economists agree that this hypothesis exhausts the possible reasons for the cyclical variation in the union-nonunion wage difference. Melvin Reder suggests, for example, that both the Norris-LaGuardia Act and the Wagner Act were manifestations of a change in the general political climate in the United States. As such, both these acts reduced the costs to unions of achieving relative wage effects, thereby decreasing the relative wage difference necessary to induce any given extent of unionism. As union membership spread to other formerly nonunion sectors, it produced a decline in the measured relative effect of unionism. This argument, says Reder, would also be consistent with some of Lewis's findings.[9] For this and other reasons, Reder concludes that an explanation which relies mainly on relative rigidity of wages to explain observed cyclical variation in union-nonunion wage differences is less than complete.

13.2c
Disaggregated estimates

The argument that unions achieve a greater impact on relative wages for skilled workers than for nonskilled workers does receive statistical support, although the evidence is not unchallenged. Using data from the 1960 Census of Population which allowed him to control for characteristics of individual workers associated with wages, Leonard Weiss estimated that unions in fully organized industries were able to raise annual earnings of skilled craft workers 8 to 15 percent and of unskilled operatives 6 to 8 percent as compared to poorly organized industries.[10]

---

[9]M. W. Reder, "Unions and Wages: The Problems of Measurement," *Journal of Political Economy,* vol. 73, April 1965, pp. 188–196.

[10]L. W. Weiss, "Concentration and Labor Earnings," *American Economic Review,* vol. 56, March 1966, pp. 96–117. Weiss's original estimate for craftsmen was 7 to 8 percent, but was subsequently revised to 8 to 15 percent. See F. P. Stafford, "Concentration and Labor Earnings: Comment," *American Economic Review,* vol. 58, March 1968, p. 174, fn. 1. Stafford also challenged Weiss's findings concerning the differential impact on the wages of craftsmen and operatives.

Sherwin Rosen found the union-nonunion wage difference of craft workers relative to all other production workers to be about 30 to 40 percent.[11] Recent studies by Paul Ryscavage and by Orley Ashenfelter have extended measurements of union relative wage effects to differences attributable to sex, race, and geographic region. To avoid what we feel could be a blur of statistics, we simply refer the interested reader to the studies.[12]

Rosen has shown that union power to achieve wage gains does increase with the extent of organization of an industry. He attributes this to the lower elasticity of demand for union labor which results from reduced product substitution between union and nonunion sectors of the economy. Further, Rosen has found strong evidence of a threat effect: nonunion wages do respond to union wage gains. Interestingly, Rosen shows that threats of further unionization fall at high levels of organization: "When overall organization of industry is high, remaining nonunion firms were the original holdouts and the hardest to organize to begin with."[13]

13.3

THE UNION IMPACT ON EMPLOYMENT AND ECONOMIC WELFARE

It is possible to make the case that union success in achieving an impact on relative wages need not lead to unemployment. If higher wages in the union sectors reduce employment there, and if the displaced workers spill over into the nonunion sectors, reducing wage levels there, then employment growth in the nonunion sectors can offset employment losses in the union sectors so that aggregate employment remains constant. In this case higher wages in the union sectors are at the expense of lower wages in the nonunion sectors. Such shifts in employment represent misallocations of labor nonetheless. As a result of this misallocation, economic welfare will be less than it otherwise would be.

Within a dynamic framework where the various demands for labor shift over time, union wage policies may be such as to result in no employment growth in the union sectors. Given certain not unrealistic considerations, union wage policies may cause unemployment to be

---

[11]S. Rosen, "Unionism and the Occupational Wage Structure in the United States," op. cit., p. 283.

[12]P. M. Ryscavage, "Measuring Union-Nonunion Earnings Differences," *Monthly Labor Review,* vol. 97, December 1974, pp. 3–9; O. Ashenfelter, "Discrimination and Trade Unions," in O. Ashenfelter and A. Rees (eds.), *Discrimination in Labor Markets,* Princeton University Press, Princeton, N.J., 1973, as well as "Racial Discrimination and Trade Unionism," *Journal of Political Economy,* vol. 80, pt. I, May/June 1972, pp. 435–464.

[13]S. Rosen, "Trade Union Power, Threat Effects and the Extent of Organization," op. cit., p. 195.

higher than it otherwise would be. We discuss in turn the effect of these costs of union wage policies on employment and economic welfare.

13.3a
A static analysis

In Fig. 13.1 we illustrate an economy divided into two groups of workers, U and N. The economywide demand for labor $VMPP_{u+n}$ and the economywide supply of labor S determine a competitive wage W_c. At this wage, employment in sector U is E_u; employment in sector N is E_n. Now let sector U become unionized and let the wage there rise to W_u. Employment falls in the union sector to E^*_u. If workers displaced in sector U spill over to sector N, increasing labor supply there, then wages in sector N fall to W_n (a wage less than the competitive wage), and employment expands to E^*_n. There need be no unemployment so long as displaced workers do indeed spill over to sector N; economy-wide employment remains constant at E_{u+n}. Even if some firms in sector N feel threatened by unionism and raise wages, there still is no necessary unemployment; in this case the bulk of the employment expansion in sector N will occur in those firms and industries which do not feel threatened and do not raise wages.

Even if there is no unemployment from union wage policies, there is a clear misallocation of labor between the two sectors. Workers who were formerly employed in sector U at wage W_c are now employed in sector N at the lower wage W_n. The value of the economy's output is thus correspondingly lower. Using Lewis's estimates of the union impact on wages and employment, Albert Rees estimated the size of the welfare loss in 1957 to be approximately 0.14 percent of gross national prod-

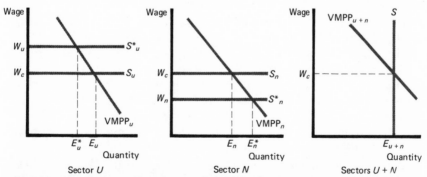

Figure 13.1. A union-nonunion wage difference and changes in the composition of employment. In an economy divided into two sectors, U and N, the economywide demand for labor $VMPP_{u+n}$ and the economywide supply of labor S, establish an equilibrium wage W_c and volume of employment E_{u+n}. At the wage W_c employment in sector U is E_u; employment in sector N is E_n. If sector U becomes unionized and wages rise there to W_u, employment falls to E_u^*. Workers displaced in sector U may spill over to sector N, increasing supply, and reducing the wage there to W_n. At W_n employment expands in sector N to E_n^*. Thus, in a static model there is no necessary unemployment as a result of union wage policies.

uct.[14] As we have seen, more recent studies of the union impact on relative wages have tended to arrive at estimates somewhat higher than those of Lewis. Approximations of the welfare loss which are based on these more recent studies would of course be correspondingly higher.

By introducing more realistic considerations into the static analysis, one can conclude that unemployment is a likely cost of union wage policies. For example, to the extent that some displaced workers in sector U remain there searching for reemployment, unemployment will appear in sector U. Further, if the rents received by union workers result in some nonunion workers flowing into the union sectors searching (unsuccessfully) for jobs there, then unemployment will be correspondingly higher in the union sector. To the extent that workers displaced in the union sectors are separated geographically from the nonunion sectors where employment is expanding for individuals with their skills and work experience, then costs of migration and higher costs of information increase the duration of unemployment.

13.3b
A dynamic analysis

To analyze the effect of union-nonunion wage differences on the rate of growth of union and nonunion employment, consider the sequence of events illustrated in Fig. 13.2.

We begin from an equilibrium in which a union impact on relative earnings exists. Wages and employment in the union sector are W_u and E^*_u; wages and employment in the nonunion sector are W_n and E^*_n. Economywide employment is $E^*_u + E^*_n$. The economywide demand for labor is growing at a rate determined by the rate of capital formation and the rate of technological change. Let the economywide demand for labor increase, and assume initially that the demand for labor increases equally in both sector U and sector N. In the union sector, the increase in the VMPP of union labor allows a wage increase to W^*_u with no adverse effect on union employment. If unions limit their wage increases to W^*_u, there will be no spillover of displaced workers into the nonunion sectors. The increase in labor demand in the nonunion sector raises wages there to W'_n and increases employment there to E'_n as well. In this case employment growth is exclusively in the nonunion sectors.

Contrary to the assumption we made that the demand for labor grows equally in both sectors, this will not likely continue to be the case. The widening of the union-nonunion wage difference to $(W^*_u - W'_n)/W'_n$ raises the relative price of union labor and increases the demand for nonunion labor. The increased demand for labor in the nonunion sectors increases employment there while also tending to raise the nonunion

[14]A. Rees, "The Effects of Unions on Resource Allocation," *Journal of Law and Economics,* vol. 6, October 1963, pp. 69–78.

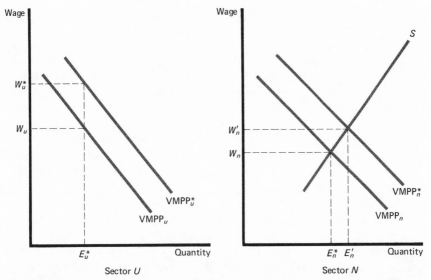

Figure 13.2. A union-nonunion wage difference and changes in the growth of employment. A union-nonunion wage difference $W_u - W_n$ exists. At wage W_u employment in the union sector is E_u^*. At wage W_n employment in the nonunion sector is E_n^*. Assume the demand for labor to increase equally in both sectors. In the union sector the union wage may rise to W_u^* with no employment loss there. The increase in demand in the nonunion sector raises wages there to W'_n, and employment increases in the nonunion sector to E'_n. Thus, the increase in the demand for labor results in employment growth only in the nonunion sector.

wage level. The slower rate of growth of labor demand in the union sectors slows the wage gains possible there without creating unemployment of union workers.

The data on union membership that we presented in the previous chapter in Table 12.1 can be interpreted within this framework, although we are unaware of any study which has done so. Although union membership has risen from 16,948,000 in 1953 to 19,435,000 in 1972, union membership as a percentage of the total labor force has declined steadily during the same period from 25.5 percent to 21.8 percent. These movements are consistent with our analysis: whereas the demand for union labor continues to grow, demand for and employment of workers in the nonunion sectors grows more rapidly.

13.3c
A summary of union effects
We have attempted to outline in the two prior sections the costs of union wage policies. If union wage policies do not cause (much) unemployment of their members, the costs are shifted to the nonunion sectors. In particular, the costs of union wage gains are lower average wages for comparable nonunion workers with the attendant redistribution of in-

come and misallocation of labor. However, employment growth is greater in the nonunion sectors than it otherwise would be.

There may be other costs as well that are implied by the neoclassical model. For example, if unionism is concentrated in certain geographic labor markets, the slow growth in employment in the labor markets may result in higher average unemployment rates for these areas as labor force entrants search unsuccessfully for jobs. Labor force participation may also be lower in these labor markets as new entrants become discouraged about finding a job and withdraw from the labor force (or never enter to begin with). Some workers will of course migrate, and such workers will tend to be younger and better educated than their counterparts who remain.

All our discussion in this chapter has focused on the union impact on relative wages and on the employment and welfare consequences of such policies. We have had nothing to say about the economic consequences of union work rules. It may be that these consequences dwarf those of union wage policies. But as yet, economists have not devoted the same attention to this question.

13.3d
Federal minimum wage laws and employment

The Fair Labor Standards Act of 1938 established a legal minimum wage and specified the sectors of the economy in which employers were bound by the provisions of the law to pay the minimum wage. Since 1938 the law has been amended numerous times in two directions: the minimum wage itself has been successively raised, and the extent of the law's coverage has been broadened to include more workers. Proponents of the minimum wage tend to favor it as an antipoverty measure; its opponents view it as a law with particularly perverse consequences for the employment of lower-skilled workers. We have chosen to discuss the impact of the minimum wage law on wages and employment in this section following our discussion of the union impact on the same variables chiefly because of the similarities in the analysis.

The effects of the minimum wage can be discussed with reference to Fig. 13.3. Assume that the supply and demand curves are for a lower-skilled occupation, and that the market wage W_e is an equilibrium wage; the equilibrium volume of employment is E. Now assume that government mandates that a minimum wage W_m be paid all workers currently receiving a lower wage. We can observe at the onset that the minimum wage will have its principal effect only in those labor markets in which the market wage is currently below or marginally above the new minimum wage; workers who are currently earning a wage appreciably above the new minimum will be largely unaffected. What are the consequences of raising the minimum wage to W_m? As we have seen, profit-maximizing firms will react to a rise in the relative price of an input in a predictable way, irrespective of the reason for the price rise. The

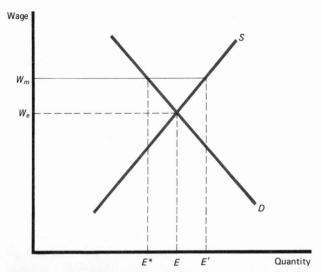

***Figure 13.3. An illustration of the employment effects of a minimum wage.
At an equilibrium wage W_e employment is E. If a minimum wage W_m is
established, employment falls to E*. If the quantity of labor supplied
increases to E' at the higher wage, E*E' is the appropriate measure of
excess supply (unemployment) brought about by the rise in the minimum
wage.***

predictable effect is to reduce the employment of the input, *ceteris
paribus.* Thus, all firms affected by the higher minimum wage will
reduce employment until the VMPP of the last worker employed is equal
to the new, higher minimum wage W_m. Consequently, the marketwide
volume of employment falls to E^*. Further, it is possible to make rather
reasonable a priori judgments about the elasticity of demand for
lower-skilled labor. We have seen (see footnote 1 above) that the
elasticity of substitution between unskilled labor and capital is higher
than that between skilled labor and capital, so that the demand for
lower-skilled labor is likely to be elastic. Consequently, the impact on
employment of lower-skilled workers could be quite substantial.

If the quantity supplied of labor increases to E' at the higher
minimum wage, E^*E' would be the appropriate theoretical measure of
the excess supply (unemployment) induced by the rise in the minimum
wage. This conclusion should be approached cautiously, however,
because although the higher minimum wage would, by itself, induce an
increase in the quantity supplied of labor, the reduced probability of
finding a job at the higher minimum wage may not result in a rise in the
expected wage (the actual wage adjusted by the probability of finding a
job at the actual wage). Thus, individuals who cease to be employed
(E^*E) as a result of the rise in the minimum wage may leave the labor
force, and individuals who would normally be induced to enter the labor
force at the higher minimum wage may refrain from doing so. For these

reasons, economists have chosen to examine the relation between minimum wages and employment rather than the relation between minimum wages and unemployment.

The theoretical prediction that employment of lower-skilled workers will be adversely affected by rising minimum wages has received extremely strong statistical support. Because it is the case that virtually every statistical test of this hypothesis has found an adverse effect on employment, we present only two of the more recent studies and direct the reader interested in other studies of this question to the references cited there. Marvin Kosters and Finis Welch have examined the employment effects of higher minimum wages which occurred over the period 1954 to 1968.[15] They found the most severe employment effects to be concentrated among teenagers, and among teenagers, nonwhite teenagers were disproportionately affected. In another study, Welch found that rises in the minimum wage from 1954 to 1968 together with increased minimum wage coverage had reduced the teenage/adult employment ratio appreciably, had heightened the vulnerability of teenage employment to cyclical changes in the level of economic activity, and had resulted in substantial shifts in teenage employment toward those industries which remained exempt from the provisions of the law.[16]

Assuming the validity of these and other comparable results, how can one explain organized labor's very strong and vocal support of increases in the minimum wage? We might note first that it is seldom the case that teenagers are union members; thus the costs of lost employment are not likely to affect union membership. Further, unions may benefit from increases in the minimum wage. This would be the case in partially unionized industries if rises in the minimum wage adversely affected the costs of production of similar products by nonunion firms, resulting in reduced *intraindustry* substitution in consumption. Perhaps more importantly, *interindustry* substitution in consumption could be reduced as well. This would be the case if rises in the minimum wage affecting nonunionized industries increased the costs of production in those industries. The degree to which unions would benefit from such a policy would depend, of course, on the elasticity of product demand in the various product markets. Thus, we see that the costs to unions from higher minimum wages are likely to be insubstantial, and the benefits to unions could be quite substantial. Union support of government-mandated minimum wage increases can be viewed as

---

[15]M. Kosters and F. Welch, "The Effects of Minimum Wages on the Distribution of Changes in Aggregate Employment," *American Economic Review,* vol. 62, June 1972, pp. 323–332.

[16]F. Welch, "Minimum Wage Legislation in the United States," *Economic Inquiry,* vol. 12, September 1974, pp. 285–318.

analogous to industry support of protective tariffs: in both cases the demand for government action is prompted by the desire to maintain employment in their own union or industry.

Although there are similarities in the analysis between the employment effects of collectively bargained wages and government-mandated wages, there is as well a major dissimilarity which is worthy of note. As we have seen, the employment loss attributable to union wage policies is partially offset if affected workers spill over to the nonunion sectors and find employment there. Workers who cease to be employed by increases in the minimum wage, however, face a bleaker future. As the number of industries exempted from the provisions of the minimum wage law continues to diminish over time, the chances for the reemployment of displaced workers similarly declines.

QUESTIONS AND EXERCISES

1. If the effects of the minimum wage on employment are adverse, what accounts for the support for the minimum wage?

2. How might unions bring about a union impact on relative wages in the absence of some degree of monopoly power?

3. Lewis's finding that the economywide union impact on relative earnings is 10 to 15 percent, assuming reasonably stable prices and reasonably full employment, prompts two questions: (*a*) Why not higher than 10 to 15 percent? (*b*) Why as high as 10 to 15 percent?

4. It has become increasingly common for union-management contracts to include provisions whereby wages adjust automatically to changes in the cost of living. What effect might this have on the union-nonunion wage difference over the course of the business cycle? Why?

5. If one desired to minimize the welfare loss attributable to unionization, what changes in the legal environment would one advocate? What are the benefits and costs of such changes to (*a*) politicians and (*b*) union members?

REFERENCES FOR FURTHER READING

A good discussion of union policies and their effect on the union-nonunion wage difference is in A. Rees, *The Economics of Trade Unions,* The University of Chicago Press, Chicago, 1962, chaps. 3 and 4.

Proposals for limiting the monopoly power of unions are found in H. G. Lewis, "The Labor-Monopoly Problem: A Positive Program," *Journal of Political Economy,* vol. 59, August 1951, pp. 277–287.

A presentation of the myriad public policy questions surrounding unionism is in P. D. Bradley (ed.), *The Public Stake in Union Power,* The University of Virginia Press, Charlottesville, Va., 1959.

WAGES, AND EMPLOYMENT IN THE PUBLIC SECTOR

All our previous discussion has been concerned with the allocation of labor in the private sector of the economy. The attention of labor economists has been overwhelmingly concentrated on studies of wages and employment in private industry. Yet more than one out of five workers in the United States is employed by government. If the various levels of government were profit-making agencies whose decision makers were motivated by the same factors and faced the same constraints as decision makers in the private sector, then no special model of public sector behavior would be necessary. The various levels of government could be treated as employers within the framework of marginal productivity analysis that we have applied to the private sector. But, in fact, the various levels of government neither are nor were ever intended to be profit-making agents. And the constraints facing public decision makers are of a very different nature than those facing their counterparts in the private sector.

In this chapter we analyze the operations of the government sector as they affect wages and the allocation of labor. We begin by establishing the rationale for the existence of the public sector, and discuss the levels of pay and employment that would exist in the public sector under optimal conditions. We examine the manner in which the political process prevents the attainment of the optimal allocation of labor between the public and private sectors, as well as outline the effects of the political process on actual pay levels in government.

14.1

WHY IS THERE A PUBLIC SECTOR?

Under ideal conditions, free market competition maximizes the output of the economy that is consistent with voluntary exchange. Stated otherwise, free markets would ideally result in the maximization of welfare rather than output. For example, gross national product could be increased if all men and women were forced by law to work. However, welfare would be decreased because those being forced to work obviously must feel that, even if they are paid the full value of their work, they would place more value on the nonmarket goods or leisure that they gave up in order to work. By definition, then, the additional value created for the rest of society must be less than the value of the time involuntarily given up by those forced to work. In net terms, then, society has lost value: there would be a net reduction in social welfare.

If a free market could optimally allocate resources so as to maximize social welfare, then anything that the government would do to affect the allocation of resources would lessen social welfare. However, the existence of "public goods" and "externalities" prevents a free market from achieving the optimal allocation of resources.

14.1a
Public goods and externalities

While free market competition may *tend toward* an optimal (i.e., welfare maximizing) allocation of resources, certain conditions prevent the free market from ever attaining the optimal allocation. The first condition involves the existence of what are called *public goods.* Public goods possess the following characteristics. First and most importantly, once a given quantity of a good is provided, the costs of excluding nonpayers from using the good are greater than the costs (in terms of reductions in the amount of the good available) imposed on those paying for the good. This does not mean that public goods can be provided costlessly. It does imply that as more and more individuals use the given quantity of the public good, there is no reduction in the amount of the good available to be used by other individuals. Because the marginal costs of additional users are zero, it would be inefficient to exclude nonpayers from using the good.

Potential inefficiencies exist because of the zero marginal cost of additional individuals using the public good. If everyone realizes that they can enjoy the benefits of the public good without having to pay for it, then no one will voluntarily agree to pay for the good. Instead, everyone will attempt to be a "free rider" and let others pay for the good. Consequently, less of the good (if any) will be provided although many individuals demand the good.

The classic example of a public good is a lighthouse. Once the lighthouse has been built, all ships within the area can enjoy the benefits of the lighthouse. The benefits accrue equally to shipowners who paid to construct the lighthouse and to those who did not contribute. Furthermore, as more ships enter the area served by the lighthouse, they do not detract from the amount of lighthouse services provided to other ships. Hence, it would be inefficient to exclude additional ships from using the services of the lighthouse. When the shipowners realize that they can receive the benefits from the lighthouse without having to pay for it, their incentive to voluntarily pay for the lighthouse is greatly reduced, perhaps to the point where no lighthouses are constructed.

Collective action, i.e., government action, can potentially correct the inefficiencies arising from the existence of public goods. Individuals can voluntarily agree to be taxed (with penalties for the nonpayment of taxes) so that the public good will be provided. Thus, government action can, in theory, improve upon the allocation of resources that would occur under completely voluntary exchange.

Related to the public good problem is the "externality" problem. The competitive pricing mechanism results in the optimal production of a good only if the price of a product reflects all the benefits and all the costs of that product. If production of a product causes some air pollution, the free market price of that product will not reflect the cost of cleaning up the air or the costs imposed on others due to the air pollution. Consequently, the price is less than the full marginal cost of the product and will result in too much of the good being produced. Government intervention in the form of policing activities, pollution taxes, etc., may eliminate such externalities in production by making the producer pay the full marginal cost. There are also externalities in consumption. For instance, inoculations against polio benefit not only the person who has been inoculated but also other persons, because these other persons are now less likely to contract the disease. In this example, a free market will produce too few inoculations. Government can correct this externality by providing inoculations at less than full cost through public health facilities, although the same purpose could be served by subsidizing private inoculations.

Given the existence of public goods and externalities, the existence of government can be justified by efficiency criteria.[1] Some questions remain, however. How much government is justified? Stated otherwise, what is the optimal allocation of labor between the public and private sectors? Also related is the question: What pay levels in the public sector, relative to the private sector, will bring about the optimal allocation of labor between the two sectors? While it is the latter question

---

[1]Other rationalizations can of course be offered for government involvement, such as fraud or lack of competition in certain sectors of the economy. These involve the necessity of policing activities and thus require the use of part of the labor force. However, these rationalizations can be conceived of as special types of externalities. We postpone any discussion of equity considerations in government intervention until Chap. 17, when we discuss income distribution.

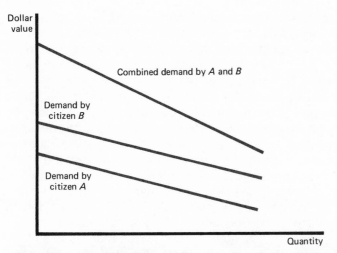

Figure 14.1. The total demand for a single public good. In a society made up of only two individuals, the total demand for a public good is the vertical sum of the demands of the two individuals. The individual demand curves show the dollar amount per unit that each of the two individuals, A and B, would willingly pay for each possible quantity of the public good.

that is the primary concern of this chapter, the two questions are highly interrelated.

14.1b
The public sector and the efficient allocation of labor

Presumably, all legitimate operations of government involve the creation of value. The value of the output of public goods is conceptually measured in a different manner than private goods, however. Imagine a citizen faced with a variety of possible quantities of a single public good such as interstate highways. If we knew the amount per mile that the individual would willingly pay in order to have access to the various quantities, we would know his demand schedule for the particular public good. The amount per mile that the citizen is willing to pay at each quantity represents the value of the public good for that citizen. If we take all such citizens and sum up, for each possible quantity measured in miles, the amount that all citizens are willing to pay for that quantity, we will have derived society's demand curve for interstate highways. The principle is illustrated in Fig. 14.1 for a hypothetical society made up of only two individuals. We have identified society's total demand for highways by vertically summing the individual demand curves.[2]

---

[2] This approach to the demand for public goods is related to that taken in P. A. Samuelson, "A Diagrammatic Exposition of a Theory of Public Expenditure," *Review of Economics and Statistics,* vol. 37, November 1955, pp. 350–356.

The law of diminishing marginal productivity applies to the production of public goods as it does to private goods. We can thus conceive of a schedule of the value of the marginal product for labor engaged in the production of a public good. For each possible quantity of labor employed, the value of the marginal product is equal to the marginal product of labor multiplied by the unit value of the output of the public good (as determined in Fig. 14.1) for the quantity of output produced by that quantity of labor. In other words, VMPP = MPP · V. If public decision makers employed labor up to the point where the value of the marginal product of labor is equal to the marginal cost of labor, then the VMPP schedule is a demand schedule for labor in the production of the public good. A similar demand for labor schedule can be derived for every other public good as well. The total demand for labor for producing public goods is found by horizontally summing the schedules for each public good. Figure 14.2 illustrates this summation process in a hypothetical government where two public goods, X and Y, are produced.

While the determination of the value of labor's output of public goods is straightforward, the value of policing activities or externality elimination requires some explanation. We can take the antitrust activities of the Department of Justice as a case in point. We explained in Chap. 10 that the existence of monopoly imposes a deadweight loss on society. If antitrust activities of the government eliminate, say, one million dollars of deadweight loss, then the activities can be thought of as having created a value of one million dollars. As with all other production activities, the use of human resources to create such value is subject to diminishing marginal productivity. Hence the schedule of the value of marginal product will be a negatively sloped function of the quantity of labor employed. We can horizontally sum up the demand for labor in policing

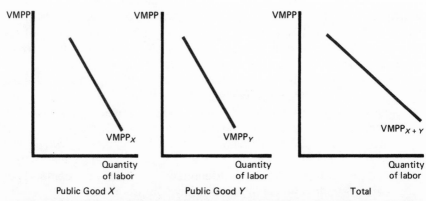

Figure 14.2. The demand for labor in the production of public goods. The total demand for labor for the production of public goods is the horizontal sum of the demand curves for labor in the production of each public good. In an economy of two public goods X and Y, the total quantity of labor demanded is the sum, at each possible VMPP, of the quantities of labor required to produce that level of VMPP of each of the public goods X and Y.

and externality elimination activities (as we did for public good production) to obtain the total demand for labor for these types of activity. Further, if we horizontally sum the demand for labor schedules in both public goods production and in policing and externality activities, we will have arrived at a schedule of the demand curve for labor for the total public sector.

Let us assume for the moment that public decision makers can know the value of marginal product schedules of labor in each government activity, and that decision makers in each activity wish to employ labor up to the point where the VMPP equals the marginal cost (i.e., the wage rate) of labor. Assuming for simplicity that labor is homogeneous, the wage rate would be determined by the combined demands for labor in the public and private sectors, as in Fig. 14.3. E_{pr} and E_{pu} are the levels of employment in the private and public sectors respectively. The illustrated division of labor between the public and private sectors would be welfare-maximizing because any shifting of labor between the two sectors would reduce the creation of value in the losing sector by more than the value of the increased activity in the receiving sector. The optimal division of labor would require equal pay between the public and private sectors. If we modify the above model to account for the heterogeneity of labor, the analysis would lead us to conclude that within each occupation pay should be equal between the public and private sectors, assuming no differences between public and private employment in the stability of employment and in working conditions. A secondary conclusion of the analysis is that the existence of an externality is not a sufficient justification for government activity to eliminate the externality. At the margin, the cost of the remedy should be no greater than its benefits. A similar statement can be made regarding the production of public goods.

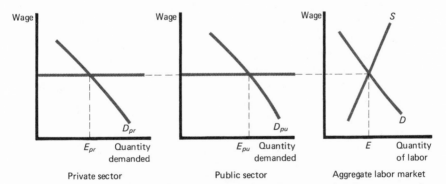

Figure 14.3. The optimal division of labor between the public and private sectors. The economywide demand for labor is the horizontal sum of demands for labor in the public and private sectors. Given a market-determined wage rate, employment of E_{pr} and E_{pu} workers in the private and public sectors respectively will maximize the value of the joint output of public and private goods.

We should now determine under what conditions the actual allocation of labor between the public and private sectors will be the optimal
allocation depicted in our model. These conditions are:

1. Marginal productivity is measurable or can be approximated in both
the private and public sectors.
2. Decision makers in the private sector attempt to maximize profits;
those in the public sector attempt to maximize the excess of total
benefits of government activity over total costs.
3. In both sectors, an excess supply of labor is rationed by a fall in
wages, and an excess demand by a rise in wages.
4. Nonwage aspects of employment are identical between the two
sectors, and workers are indifferent between the two sectors at equal
pay rates.

Condition 1 is in principle attainable, but with much more difficulty in the
public than in the private sector. In the private sector, product price is
the standard by which value can be measured. In the public sector, the
benefits of government programs cannot be determined by such a
readily available measuring rod. The techniques of benefit-cost analysis
are helpful in this regard, but many types of public sector activities defy
quantification. It is virtually impossible to measure the dollar value of the
benefits flowing from national defense expenditures, for example. About
the best that can be hoped for is that decision makers in the public
sector have an ability to discern without hard data whether or not a
proposed government activity will justify its cost.

Whether they will actually use such ability to make decisions that will
maximize social welfare involves condition 2. Most economists are
willing to take for granted that in general terms, firms in the private sector
act so as to maximize profits, thereby satisfying the first part of condition
2. As Armen Alchian has argued, the actions of entrepreneurs need not
be deliberate for this condition to hold, since in the long run only those
firms that maximize profits—even if by accident—will survive and grow.[3]
The second part of condition 2—that public decision makers attempt to
maximize the excess of benefits of government activity over its costs—is
problematic. Most standard textbooks in the principles of economics,
while giving due attention to potential failings of the private sector, seem
nonetheless to assume that public decision makers act to maximize
social welfare as they perceive it.[4] At a more advanced level, the 1960s
and 1970s have witnessed the development of the "public choice"

---

[3]A. Alchian, "Uncertainty, Evolution, and Economic Theory," *Journal of Political Economy,* vol. 58, June 1950, pp. 211–221.

[4]Two strong exceptions are J. Gwartney, *Economics: Private and Public Choice,*
Academic, New York, 1976; and R. McKenzie and G. Tullock, *Modern Political
Economy,* McGraw-Hill, New York, 1978.

approach. This approach to the analysis of public decision making does not employ the assumption that public officeholders act so as to maximize social welfare. Rather, it employs the less naive assumption that public officeholders maximize their own utility, as economists have assumed to be the case for everyone else in society. For the public officeholder, utility maximization largely means maximizing the likelihood of reelection. In the next section we point out the ways in which utility maximization by public officials contradicts welfare maximization.[5]

Condition 3 is in effect implied by condition 2. For the same reasons that the behavior of public officials may not result in welfare maximization, the maximization of reelection chances may not lead to the use of wage adjustments as a device for rationing excess demand for or supply of labor in the public sector.

Condition 4 is not a necessary condition for an efficient allocation of labor per se. It *is* a necessary condition for the efficient allocation of labor to correspond to equality of pay between the public and private sectors. If nonwage aspects of work (for example, working conditions) differ between the two sectors, then there should be an equalizing difference in wages. The size of that differential would be whatever wage difference would result in the absence of excess demand or supply in each sector. For example, job security may be greater in the public sector than in the private sector. If so, then pay rates should be less in the public sector so that net advantage will be equal in both sectors.

Because nonwage aspects of employment as between the public and private sectors are not comparable, we cannot determine precisely whether public employees are overpaid or underpaid simply by discovering whether they are paid more or less than private sector employees in comparable occupations. The question of whether or not public pay levels are efficient is further complicated by the fact that many public occupations, such as policemen and air traffic controllers, have no reasonable counterpart in the private sector. The absence of comparable occupations in the private sector would not pose a problem if workers regarded nonwage aspects to be identical between the best-paying jobs they could qualify for in both the public and the private sector, given their human capital endowments. In this case, the efficient allocation of labor would result in pay scales that provide equal rates of return on human capital between the two sectors. But given that workers will in fact regard nonwage aspects of jobs differently as between public and private employment, unequal rates of return on human capital would not necessarily reflect an inefficient allocation of labor between the two sectors.

---

[5] The pioneers of the public choice approach are J. Buchanan and G. Tullock. See their *Calculus of Consent,* University of Michigan Press, Ann Arbor, 1962.

Nonetheless, we should not expect to see greatly differing wage rates between the two sectors for jobs requiring comparable investments in human capital. We shall examine later in this chapter the actual public-private pay differentials, but first we must discuss the effect of the political process on the allocation of resources.

14.2

THE POLITICAL PROCESS

Having discussed the optimal allocation of labor between public and private employment, we now examine the manner in which the political process may thwart the attainment of the optimal allocation. If a politician's prime impulse is to act in such a manner as to maximize chances of election (or reelection), what is implied about the level of government spending that will result from the political process? To arrive at an answer, we should be mindful of two political postulates:

1. In general, the more spending programs that an elected official supports, the more votes he or she will receive.
2. In general, the higher the level of taxes that an elected official supports, the fewer votes he or she will receive.

Thus, a "politician's dilemma" is created: support of a program attracts votes, but the taxes necessary to pay for the program lose votes.

In a world where all voting citizens have perfect knowledge of the benefits and costs of all government programs, and where the taxes each individual pays are in proportion to the benefits received, then our two postulates would force politicians to support only those programs for which total benefits exceeded the total costs; they would support spending on such activities only up to the point where the marginal benefits equaled the marginal costs. In other words, the political process would result in the optimal allocation of labor between the public and private sectors. Unfortunately, the real world can be characterized by three additional postulates:

3. Society is made up of many interest groups, many of which have conflicting interests.
4. There is no necessary connection between the benefits that a group receives and the taxes its members pay. In fact, it is in the interest of every group to see to it that other people pay the taxes.
5. Knowledge about government program benefits and costs is highly imperfect. However, those most affected by a program will be more highly motivated to acquire information.

As a consequence of the latter three postulates, the politician's ideal strategy will not be consistent with the maximization of society's welfare.

Since the recipients of the benefits of government programs will be inclined to reward the incumbent politician with their votes, while the bearers of the corresponding tax burden might be more inclined to reward the incumbent's opponent, it is in the politician's interest to propose a *package* of programs or policies in which the benefits of each are highly visible and concentrated, whereas the costs of each are vague and widely dispersed. With a benefit for every interest, the officeholder may maximize his or her chances of election or reelection even though the costs of the proposals may in the aggregate greatly exceed the benefits. The politician's dilemma is thus resolved in principle.[6] The application of these principles comprise the chief challenge facing any professional politician.

One such program in a politician's package may be the payment of higher than necessary wages to public employees since public employees are a large and significant voter group. As long as the higher salaries are financed out of general revenues rather than user taxes, the criteria mentioned above will have been met: the benefits will be very clearly understood by the recipients. The salaries will be largely unknown to the rest of the public, most of whose members could not quote the pay of more than one or two public employees or elected officials. Even if those salaries were known, the impact on any one taxpayer would seem insignificant to her or him, and in any event the explicit cost is hidden by being buried among the other items that the individual's taxes pay for. There is also a secondary reason for expecting the political process to produce an overpayment of public employees. Public sector jobs are frequently dispensed as rewards for political campaign effort. Especially for non-civil service jobs, retention may or may not depend upon the assumption of continued campaign effort. Obviously no payoff takes place if the job pays no more than what the holder could obtain in the private sector.

The role of information costs is particularly significant. At the local level, voters have much more information about salaries (and whether an existing salary level would draw a waiting line of applicants) than they have for higher levels of government. Further, the impact on their taxes is more readily discernible. Consequently, local officials sometimes win or lose elections largely on issues directly or indirectly related to pay levels and the provision of public services. The same is much less frequently the case for state government officials, and occurs even less frequently for federal government officeholders. In fact, the possibility of financing deficit spending through inflation at the federal level makes excessive spending particularly attractive. The federal government can cover a

---

[6] The optimality of this strategy for the politician is developed in J. Gwartney and J. Silberman, "Distribution of Costs and Benefits and the Significance of Collective Decision Rules," *Social Science Quarterly,* vol. 54, December 1973, pp. 568–578.

deficit through increases in the money supply. The cost to taxpayers will be just as high as direct taxation, but will take the form of inflation rather than higher explicit tax rates. The resulting inflation is seldom viewed as a tax by the voting public whose members are more likely to regard the inflation as the result of the greed of monopolists and, even more so, of trade union officials and members. A member of Congress who supports deficit spending (on excessive public pay levels, among other things) and who also supports price controls of one form or another can acquire votes in two ways: Support of political goods, such as higher government wages, wins votes; if these are financed through inflation, this creates the demand for another political good, price controls, support for which will gain additional votes. Given the varying degrees of disincentive of state, local, and federal government officials to seek the lowest cost of labor, we should expect that overpayment, if it exists, will be least at the local level and highest at the federal level.[7]

14.3

COMPETITION FOR RENTS

The overpayment of public employees should be regarded as rent inasmuch as it is a pay level higher than that necessary to attract the requisite quantity and quality of labor to the public sector. As a consequence of the existence of such rent, there will be a surplus of persons seeking jobs in the public sector. There then must be a way of rationing the available jobs. In the private sector the real wage would fall over time in response to an excess supply of labor. If overpayment is to be a matter of political strategy, some other way of rationing jobs in the public sector must be devised. One frequently used device is the civil service exam. When a vacancy exists in a civil service job, the job goes to the individual with the highest exam score or to an individual who is among the top several scorers. An individual's ability to score well on the exam is largely determined by the amount of human capital that he or she has acquired. The skills necessary to score well on the exam might be largely unrelated to the skills necessary to perform the job. Consequently, civil service jobs may be filled by people who are overqualified, in terms of human capital, for the jobs they will perform. The excess supply to the public sector is fully rationed when the required test scores are high enough so that the human capital required to obtain the jobs could receive as high a return in the private sector. *At the margin,* then, rents on human capital will have been competed away. In other words, the workers who are able to obtain the jobs receive no higher return on

---

[7]It is also the case that the political process as described above will lead not only to overpayment of public employees but also to the employment of a larger than optimal number of persons in the public sector.

their human capital than they could in the private sector, at the same time that they are overpaid for the type of work that they will do in the public sector. Rents will be received only by public sector workers who obtained their jobs when the human capital requirements necessary to get those jobs were lower than at present.

14.3a
Empirical evidence on public-private wage differentials
Economists and other social scientists have been quite slow to examine the pay scales of public workers in comparison with private workers. Consequently the view that public employees are underpaid has until the mid-1970s gone unchallenged. The evolution of this generally held belief is an interesting sociological phenomenon in itself. It may be true that virtually no workers in any sector regard themselves as overpaid, but public employees, as a class, apparently have been able to cohesively vocalize their belief about the inadequacy of their pay scales quite successfully. Equal success has apparently not been achieved by private sector workers as a class. The reason may lie in the fact that public employees have been supported in their claims by their employers, who are other public employees or elected officials. This support has been forthcoming because it is in the political interest of the public employers that their employees be highly paid. Private employers, of course, have an interest in minimizing payroll costs and thus are unlikely to support arguments that their workers are underpaid.

A recent set of articles and a book, all written by economist Sharon Smith, have accumulated an overwhelming amount of empirical evidence on the degree of comparability of public and private wage levels.[8] As we have established earlier, it is hazardous to attempt public-private comparisons of wages inasmuch as (1) where the same ocupation exists in both sectors, the work done may be only superficially similar (e.g., police and uniformed security guards are not really engaged in the same line of work), and (2) for many public occupations, there exists no private counterpart (for example, air traffic controllers). For these reasons, Smith has avoided direct occupational comparisons and instead examined the return on human capital received by public employees as compared to private employees possessing the same amount of human capital. Combining and manipulating some of her results from the 1975 Current Population Survey we can infer ratios of public to private wage rates illustrated in Table 14.1. Specifically, the numbers illustrate the ratio of

---

[8] Two of the articles are "Government Wage Differentials by Sex," *Journal of Human Resources,* vol. 11, spring 1976, pp. 185–199; and "Pay Differentials between Federal Government and Private Sector Workers," *Industrial and Labor Relations Review,* vol. 29, January 1976, pp. 179–197. The book is *Equal Pay in the Public Sector: Fact or Fantasy?* Princeton University Press, Princeton, N.J., 1977.

Table 14.1
Public-private wage ratios, 1975

Sectoral comparison	Wage ratio
Federal government/private sector	1.200
State government/private sector	1.022
Local government/private sector	.995

SOURCE: Derived from data contained in Sharon Smith, *Equal Pay in the Public Sector: Fact or Fantasy?* Princeton University Press, Princeton, N. J., table 3.6 and appendix B.

average wages in each public sector to what wages those same public workers could obtain in the private sector, given their human capital endowments and the wage structure prevailing in the private sector in 1975. The figures in the table suggest that federal government workers receive wage rates 20 percent higher than those earned by comparable private sector workers. We would certainly seem justified in concluding that, as a class, federal government workers are overpaid, unless working conditions, fringe benefits, and job security are very much inferior in the federal government sector. Yet job security and fringe benefits seem to be features which *attract* workers to government employment, particularly to the federal government. As Smith points out, in 1972 fringe benefits in the federal government equaled 32.1 percent of base pay, but in the private sector only 28.7 percent. Had we included fringe benefits in our calculations (Smith does not), our federal/private wage ratio in Table 14.1 would have been 1.232. Thus, there appears to be strong evidence that federal employees, taken as a whole, are overpaid as compared to persons working in the private sector. Of course, no such statement can be made, on the basis of these figures alone, about whether any individual or any group within the federal government is overpaid.

Similar conclusions cannot be drawn for the state and local levels of government. Table 14.1 indicates that state employees are paid only about 2.2 percent more than comparable employees in the private sector. If we include fringe benefits, the difference becomes 6.2 percent. Again, if workers attach a monetary value to the job security typically associated with state government jobs, then the true differential would be more than 6.2 percent. While there is some evidence of excessive pay at the state level, the excess is not that great and the evidence of it not so strong as at the federal level.

At the local level there is no evidence of excessive returns on human capital. In fact, Table 14.1 indicates that local government workers earn about 0.5 percent less than similar workers in the private sector. Information on fringe benefits at the local governmental level is particularly poor, but on the basis of available information it appears that including fringe benefits would but marginally change the local government/private pay ratio to 1.011. Given the highly aggregate nature of this ratio, it is so close to 1.00 as to provide strong evidence against the hypothesis of systematic excess returns on human capital for local government employees.

To say that local government employees do not receive excessive returns on their human capital is not quite the same as to say that the pay attached to local government jobs is not excessive. Again, public employees may be willing to accept a wage in the public sector that is lower than that in the private sector in exchange for the job security enjoyed in the public sector. The ultimate test of whether local government employees are overpaid would require us to determine if there is a persistent queue of qualified applicants for local government jobs at existing wages. Similarly, a chronic shortage of applicants would signal underpayment. Unfortunately, such information is usually difficult to obtain on a uniform basis, but there seldom appear to be reports of shortages in local government occupations except for nurses and occasionally for police officers.[9] Further, the effect of competitive rent seeking as discussed earlier may bring about rough equality of returns on human capital between public and private sectors. Yet the distribution of labor between the private and public sectors will be inefficient. Because of initial rents, persons whose productivity in the private sector is high are attracted to jobs in the public sector for which they are overqualified. Hence their productivity cannot be as high as it would be in the private sector. If competitive rent seeking is substantial, then the ratios indicated in Table 14.1 understate the extent to which public sector employees are overpaid. Empirical estimation of the effects of competitive rent seeking is presently nonexistent, but the area is a promising one for future research.[10]

14.3b
Unionization and wages in the public sector

We have up to this point excluded any mention of public sector unions. In principle, unionization might affect relative wages differently in the public sector than in the private sector. On the one hand, there is some

---

[9] See R. Hurd, "Equilibrium Vacancies in a Labor Market Dominated by Non-Profit Firms: The 'Shortage' of Nurses," *Review of Economics and Statistics,* vol. 50, May 1973, pp. 234–240; and D. Lewin, "Wage Parity and the Supply of Police and Firemen," *Industrial Relations,* vol. 12, February 1973, pp. 77–85. The Lewin article provides evidence that a policy of equal pay between police and firefighters can result in a shortage of police and long queues of applicants for positions in fire departments.

[10] An interesting general article on competitive rent-seeking is A. Krueger, "The Political Economy of the Rent-Seeking Society," *American Economic Review,* vol. 64, June 1974, pp. 291–303. See also G. Tullock, "The Transitional Gains Trap," *The Bell Journal of Economics and Management Science,* vol. 6, autumn 1975, pp. 671–678.

evidence that the demand for labor is less elastic in the public sector than in the private sector.[11] This would suggest the potential of a greater union-nonunion wage differential in the public sector. On the other hand, union activities are far more restricted in the public than in the private sector. There have been a number of empirical studies on the effect of unionization on public sector relative wages, but the evidence is not entirely unambiguous. However, the stronger evidence suggests that unions raise the wages of their members about as much in the public sector as in the private sector.[12]

14.4

CONCLUDING REMARKS

We have argued that only if there are no differences between the public and private sectors in job security, fringe benefits, and nonpecuniary job aspects will an efficient allocation of labor dictate equality of wage rates between the private and public sectors. If, as seems to be the case, fringe benefits, job security, and other job aspects are superior in the public sector, then economic efficiency requires that public sector wage rates be less than those of the private sector. This inequality of wages will provide equality of net advantage between jobs in the public and private sectors. Yet the political system is likely to lead to overpayment of workers in the public sector. The empirical evidence supports this contention. As theory predicts, the extent of public sector overpayment is greatest at the federal level and least, if at all, at the local level.

We have chosen to present comparisons of the entire federal, state, and local public sectors with the private sector. To be sure, such highly aggregated data usually mask a considerable degree of variation. There are most assuredly some classes of public employees in some places who are underpaid. There must be shortages of such workers; otherwise, they are by definition *not* underpaid. Those interested in a more detailed analysis should refer to Smith's work, mentioned in footnote 8 above.

What are the consequences of overpayment in the public sector? For one thing, every dollar of excess payroll in the public sector comes at the expense of persons in the private sector. Given that one worker in five is a public employee, this can amount to a sizable redistribution of income. To the extent that there is competition for the rent created by the

---

[11]This evidence is presented in R. Ehrenberg, "The Demand for State and Local Government Employees," *American Economic Review,* vol. 63, June 1973, pp. 366–379.

[12] Two studies reaching this conclusion are D. Shapiro, "Relative Wage Effects of Unions in the Public and Private Sectors," *Industrial and Labor Relations Review,* vol. 31, January 1978, pp. 193–204; and D. Hamermesh, "The Effect of Government Ownership on Union Wages," in D. Hamermesh (ed.), *Labor in the Public and Nonprofit Sectors,* Princeton University Press, Princeton, N.J., 1975, pp. 227–255.

overpayment, human capital is wasted since competition for the rent results in a misallocation of human capital. The misallocation of labor imposes a welfare loss of unknown size on society, in very much the same way that the misallocation of labor associated with monopoly and unionization creates a welfare loss as shown in Chaps. 10 and 13.

Since both theory and evidence suggest that overpayment of public workers increases with higher levels of government, "federalization" of many state and local government functions seems less prudent than it otherwise might. If there are any efficiencies to be gained from centralization of government functions, they are certainly not in the area of average payroll costs. In any event, the public-private pay differential, especially at the federal level, seems to be at least as large as that associated with racial and sex discrimination. While there is some evidence of diminishing wage differentials by race and sex, the evidence presented by Smith suggests a widening public-private differential. As public employment continues to grow much more rapidly than private employment, public employees will grow in importance as a political force. As a consequence, there are strong reasons to expect the public-private pay differential to continue to grow over time. If it does, the redistribution of income from private employees to public employees may come to be regarded as a serious social problem.

QUESTIONS AND EXERCISES

1. A government agency may be the sole employer of a particular occupation and thus have a potential monopsony power. Why will the use of that monopsony power be incapable of reducing the rate of return on human capital in that occupation in the long run?

2. In general, public employment has been rising faster than private employment. This relative increase in public employment is usually explained by the contention that the income elasticity of public goods and services is high relative to that of private goods and services. Can the relative rise in public employment be explained any other way?

3. The Hatch Act prevents federal civil servants from engaging in political activities. How might the pay levels of federal civil servants be affected by repeal of the Hatch Act?

4. A few occupations such as lawyers earn less in the public sector than in the private sector. What explains their lower pay?

5. We explained how the demand for public goods is determined. What problems prevent that demand from being measured?

REFERENCES FOR FURTHER READING

Readers interested in a theoretical treatment of wage and employment determination in the public sector should consult M. Reder, "The

Theory of Employment and Wages in the Public Sector," in D. Hamermesh (ed.), *Labor in the Public and Nonprofit Sectors,* Princeton University Press, Princeton, N.J., 1975, pp. 1–48. The remaining articles in the book analyze particular issues concerning the employment of labor in the public sector. Also of interest is W. Fogel and D. Lewin, "Wage Determination in the Public Sector," *Industrial and Labor Relations Review,* vol. 27, April 1974, pp. 410–431.

For a detailed analysis of the comparability of pay between the public and private sectors, see the book by Sharon Smith cited in footnote 8 above.

Legislators are unique among public employees in that, in large measure, they determine their own wages. For an economic analysis of the legislative wage-setting process, see R. C. McCormick and R. D. Tollison, "Legislatures as Unions," *Journal of Political Economy,* vol. 86, February 1978, pp. 63–78.

PART IV

PART IV

MACROECONOMICS AND LABOR MARKETS

In the following chapters we explore the implications of the neoclassical analysis of the labor market for the aggregate economy. In particular, we explore the topics of unemployment, inflation, and the distribution of income. In our discussion of unemployment in Chap. 15, we relax the assumptions we made in our basic model developed in Chap. 3 so as to understand the frictional, structural, and demand deficiency unemployment that is characteristic of the United States economy. In Chap. 16 we present a contemporary neoclassical view of the Phillips relation and interpret the United States unemployment-inflation record during the 1960s and 1970s within this framework. We present in Chap. 17 an analysis of both the size and functional distributions of aggregate income. In our concluding Chap. 18, we recapitulate and reflect upon the main thrusts of the neoclassical analysis of the labor market.

UNEMPLOYMENT

Recall from Chap. 4 that the Bureau of Labor Statistics (BLS) defines an individual as unemployed if, during the survey week, the individual did no work, was available for work, and had engaged in some specific job-seeking activity during the prior 4 weeks. In the macroeconomic model we presented in Chap. 3, we reached the conclusion that no labor resources would be unemployed. This conclusion depended, however, on a number of simplifying assumptions we made there, namely:

1. That resources have perfect information and mobility, i.e., that the costs of information and mobility are zero.
2. That employers view all labor as perfect substitutes for each other.
3. That all product prices and wages are perfectly flexible.
4. That the level of aggregate demand is given.

In this chapter we relax this series of assumptions so as to understand the *frictional, structural,* and *demand deficiency unemployment* that results from doing so. The relations that exist in the labor market between wages and employment can be analyzed within either a static or a dynamic framework. Our framework here is essentially static. In the following chapter we explicitly consider the relation between wages and employment when both these and other market variables are changing over time.

We examine first the concepts of frictional and structural unemployment and develop the notion of a natural rate of unemployment. We then introduce changes in aggregate demand and see that demand deficiency unemployment is the consequence of disequilibrium in the markets for goods and services. Much of modern macroeconomics has been concerned with outlining the processes of adjustment necessary to eliminate demand deficiency unemployment. A key element in these discussions is the role and significance of prices and money wages which do not adjust instantly to clear markets. We present this literature and set the stage for our discussion of the dynamics of wages and employment which appears in the following chapter.

We conclude this chapter with a brief discussion of the incidence of unemployment, as well as an examination of the merits of using the economywide unemployment rate as a measure of economic performance.

15.1

UNEMPLOYMENT AND FULL EMPLOYMENT

We can distinguish conceptually among frictional, structural, and demand deficiency unemployment. Demand deficiency unemployment exists when, *at existing wage and price levels,* the level of aggregate demand is too low, with the result that the economywide effective quantity of labor demanded is less than the quantity of workers willing to supply their labor.

It is possible, nonetheless, for the level of aggregate demand to be sufficiently high to provide employment for the entire labor force, yet for substantial numbers of workers to be unemployed. These workers will be classified as either frictionally or structurally unemployed. When jobs exist within a given occupational-geographic category in sufficient numbers to employ all persons seeking to supply their labor to that market, we may find that workers engaged in search have not as yet found the employers who are willing to hire them. Or conversely, we could say that the employers who have vacancies and who are engaged in the search process have not yet found those workers. The unemployed workers are classified as frictionally unemployed. They are unemployed because information is imperfect and costly to obtain.

Structural unemployment is similar to frictional unemployment in the sense that in both cases there are a sufficient number of jobs to employ all workers. However, structural unemployment is said to exist when either the available vacancies require different skills than those possessed by the unemployed workers or the jobs are available in geographical areas other than those in which the unemployed workers are located. As with frictional unemployment, structural unemployment can be associated with imperfect and costly information. But more fundamentally, structural unemployment exists because the transfer of unemployed workers to fill existing vacancies would involve significant transfer costs in terms of either the costs of acquiring skills or the costs of moving to another geographical area, or both. We will now analyze in detail each of the three types of unemployment.

15.1a
Frictional unemployment

Let us maintain the assumptions that the aggregate demand for and supply of labor are given and that all workers are qualified to fill the existing job vacancies, but relax the assumption of zero costs of information. It will now be the case that the number of available vacancies as well as the wages associated with those vacancies are not perfectly known to workers. Workers will choose to devote time and other resources to job search, and as they do so, they acquire information about job characteristics and wages. Similarly, firms will search the labor market in order to acquire information about the skill characteristics of available workers. The unemployment that results from this search process can be defined as *frictional unemployment.*

Frictional unemployment arises because of changes in the composition of aggregate demand, and because of the entrance into the labor market of first-time job seekers for whom information is particularly imperfect and costly. Let us examine the former source of frictional unemployment. Consider an economy of two industries, A and B, illustrated in Fig. 15.1. Assume that both industries use the same labor inputs so that the equilibrium wage W_e is the same for both. Let the

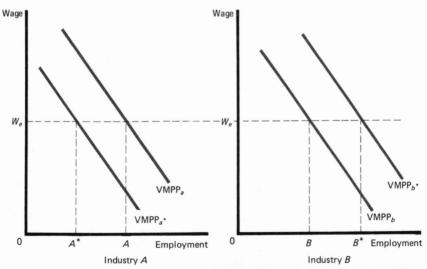

Figure 15.1. Changes in the composition of aggregate demand, holding constant the level of aggregate demand. In an economy of two industries A and B, a decline in labor demand in industry A reduces employment there to A*. An offsetting increase in labor demand (the level of aggregate demand is assumed constant) creates BB* vacancies in industry B. Workers who lose jobs in industry A are qualified to fill jobs in industry B and will do so. During the time that these workers are searching for the existing vacancies in industry B, however, they will be frictionally unemployed.

demand for labor in industry A decline because of, say, a change in consumer tastes for the product of industry A. At the same time let the demand for labor in industry B increase so that economywide labor demand remains constant. The decline in labor demand in industry A reduces employment there. But the unemployed workers are able to find employment in industry B at wage W_e because they have the skills for the jobs and the firms in the expanding industry B are attempting to fill BB^* vacancies. During the time workers search for these vacancies, however, they will be frictionally unemployed.

Workers have not had to adjust their asking wage to become reemployed in industry B. This is because we have assumed that the level of aggregate demand is sufficient to provide vacancies for workers looking for work at the existing real wage, and that workers are qualified to fill the existing vacancies. Frictional unemployment has developed because information and mobility are costly. As the pattern of labor demand changes because of changes in the composition of aggregate demand, it takes an investment by both workers and firms to acquire information. The frictional unemployment that accompanies job search is chosen by workers and firms and is necessary to ensure that labor resources move into their highest-valued uses. If, for any reason, the costs of information and mobility should decline, frictional unemployment will also decline.

15.1b
Structural unemployment
The reallocation of labor that constantly occurs because of changes in the composition of aggregate demand will be slowed if unemployed workers do not have the skills required for reemployment at existing real wage levels. Thus, as we relax the assumption that all workers are perfect substitutes for each other, structural unemployment can arise. The fact that workers are imperfect substitutes for each other means that shifts in the various demands for labor will change relative wages and will require that some unemployed workers adjust their wage demands downward in order to be reemployed. This will be the case even though job vacancies in the aggregate are sufficient to employ all unemployed workers. In terms of Fig. 15.1, the decline in labor demand in industry A results in unemployed workers there who are now not able to find identical jobs in industry B, the reason being that the two industries employ different types of labor. Displaced workers can become employed in industry B if they acquire the skills necessary for employment there, or can become employed again in industry A if, given their existing skills, they accept lower wages. Workers do not instantly lower their asking (or reservation) wage. For reasons that will be discussed in Sec. 15.2d, firms are not initially inclined to offer employment at lower wages. As workers engage in job search, however, it becomes increasingly clear to them that vacancies are available to workers with their skills (the demand for which has declined) only at lower wages.

Consequently, the asking wage of unemployed workers typically declines as their duration of unemployment increases.[1]

Structural unemployment, then, arises because workers are not perfect substitutes for each other. Changes in the composition of aggregate demand reallocate labor among the various sectors of the economy, and many times reemployment of labor can occur only at lower wages. Workers are reluctant to lower their asking wage, and search longer in hopes of not having to do so.

The duration of structural unemployment is longer the more costly the investment necessary to relocate labor in response to changes in the composition of aggregate demand. If industries A and B are located in the same geographic labor market, unemployed workers in industry, A may be reemployed with perhaps a relatively minor investment in new skills. If the two industries are located in separate geographic regions, workers must invest in migration as well. These considerations emphasize that the process of adjustment necessary to eliminate structural unemployment may be quite lengthy. This process can be aided by various manpower programs which lower the costs of acquiring new skills, but is hampered by any factors such as minimum wage laws which prevent downward wage adjustments.[2]

15.1c
The natural rate of unemployment

Changes in the *composition* of aggregate demand are an ever-present characteristic of a dynamic economy. Further, there are always new participants entering the labor force. Hence there will always be some frictional and structural unemployment in such an economy, even if the *level* of aggregate demand were sufficiently high to employ the entire labor force. Economists have labeled the sum of frictional and structural unemployment as the natural rate of unemployment. In principle, the natural rate could be measured as the amount of unemployment equal to the number of job vacancies in the economy. Although the concept of the natural rate is relatively straightforward, reaching a consensus about its size is particularly difficult. One reason is that in the United States there are no estimates of job vacancies.[3] This means that whereas we have in the monthly unemployment estimates by BLS detailed figures on the number and characteristics of people looking for work, the fact that there

---

[1]See H. Kasper, "The Asking Price of Labor and the Duration of Unemployment," *Review of Economics and Statistics,* vol. 49, May 1967, pp. 165–172; and W. Barnes, "Job Search Models, the Duration of Unemployment and the Asking Wage: Some Empirical Evidence," *Journal of Human Resources,* vol. 10, spring 1975, pp. 230–240.

[2]Political promises can also affect structural unemployment. See J. H. Yeager, Jr., "Budgetary Cutbacks, Political Promises, and the Unemployment Problem," *Public Choice,* vol. 23, fall 1975, pp. 115–120.

[3]From 1969 to 1973 the BLS did publish estimates of job vacancies in manufacturing, but this program has been discontinued.

are no corresponding estimates of job vacancies makes it impossible to make even rough comparisons of the overall balance between the number unemployed and the number of job vacancies. The size of the natural rate of unemployment, then, is difficult to measure, and its size tends to change over time. Variations in the rate of technological change, in the rate at which new participants enter the labor force, in the costs of acquiring new skills and information, and in the incentives to invest in search will change the amount of structural unemployment. In short, all dynamic forces which result in the reallocation of labor will have an effect on the natural rate of unemployment.

One could choose to define *full employment* as that aggregate unemployment rate consistent with the natural rate of unemployment. (There are a variety of other definitions of full employment that are proposed by economists.) Both the concept of full employment and the natural rate of unemployment acknowledge that even with sufficient job vacancies there will never be a zero unemployment rate. However, in our view the concept of the natural rate of unemployment is preferred, for it compels us to focus on dynamic adjustments in an economy and on the forces which either speed or dampen the processes of adjustment. By contrast, the common concept of full employment tends to become associated with a specific unemployment rate, say 4 percent, and lends itself to political sloganeering. As we shall see in the following chapter, given a situation where the natural rate of unemployment exceeds the common conception of full employment, policies which attempt to reduce aggregate unemployment below its natural rate will have no permanent effect on employment but instead will only cause the price level to rise.

15.2
CHANGES IN AGGREGATE DEMAND

In our discussion to this point we have allowed the composition of aggregate demand to change but have held its level constant. In a changing economy both the composition and the level of aggregate demand vary continuously. Disequilibrium will be characteristic of many markets as aggregate demand changes. A fall in aggregate demand, for example, results in declines in the demands for labor which are widespread. Thus, the wage, price, and employment adjustments which are necessary to restore equilibrium are not concentrated in a few labor markets but are characteristic of most labor markets, and can be of such magnitude and duration that aggregate unemployment rises well above its frictional and structural level. The consequence in the labor market of declines in aggregate demand is demand deficiency unemployment.

Before we turn to demand deficiency unemployment, we examine briefly how increases in aggregate demand can reduce both frictional and structural unemployment.

15.2a
Increases in aggregate demand

Increases in aggregate demand and the resulting increases in the demands for labor can reduce both frictional and structural unemployment if the increased demand reduces the costs of information and mobility and results in firms' relaxing hiring standards. We know from the procyclical movement of help-wanted advertising that firms do advertise their vacancies more in periods of rising demand for labor. They may also offer more generous relocation allowances to attract additional workers. To the extent that these policies reduce the costs of information and mobility to workers, frictional unemployment will tend to fall.

Firms also adjust hiring standards during periods of rising demand for labor. Any firm's hiring standards are to some degree flexible. For example, the requirement of a high school diploma for an assembly line job may not be the result of a careful study of actual job requirements, but may be simply a practical method for rationing a limited number of such jobs among numerous applicants. Such a procedure reduces the firm's costs of screening and processing workers; it also results in numerous workers being unemployed because of their not having the skills, work experience, or education "necessary" for employment. Clearly, when demand for the firm's product increases and the firm attempts to fill new vacancies, this flexibility in hiring standards works in favor of the unemployed. Individual workers may have the same characteristics as before, but become employed as the firm adjusts its hiring standards so as to fill new vacancies.

In a period of very strong demand for labor such as existed in 1968 in the United States, the aggregate unemployment rate fell to the range of 3 to 4 percent. This was by almost everyone's definition that amount of unemployment consistent at that time with minimum amounts of frictional and structural unemployment.

15.2b
Decreases in aggregate demand: Demand deficiency unemployment[4]

An understanding of demand deficiency unemployment requires us to focus simultaneously on both the aggregate commodities market and the aggregate labor market. In Fig. 15.2 we illustrate demand and supply conditions in both markets. In the commodities market, aggregate demand is represented by the curve $E_0 = C_0 + I_0 + G_0$. This is aggregate demand in real (not nominal) terms, and is the sum of its component parts: real expenditures on consumption, C_0; real expendi-

---

[4]Our discussion is based on the work of D. Patinkin, *Money, Interest and Prices,* 2d ed., Harper & Row, New York, 1965; R. J. Barro and H. I. Grossman, "A General Disequilibrium Model of Income and Employment," *American Economic Review,* vol. 61, March 1971, pp. 82–93; and *Money, Employment and Inflation,* Cambridge University Press, Cambridge, 1976; and C. W. Baird, *Macroeconomics,* Science Research, Chicago, 1973.

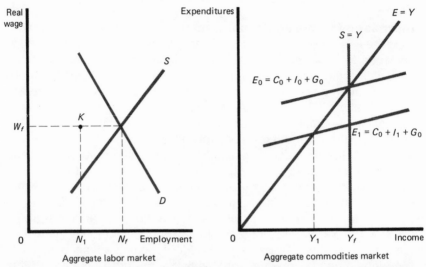

Figure 15.2. The aggregate labor market and the aggregate commodities market. In the aggregate commodities market, initial real aggregate demand is $E_0 = C_0 + I_0 + G_0$; real aggregate supply is the vertical line $S = Y$ (at the natural rate of unemployment). Real aggregate demand in conjunction with real aggregate supply results in an equilibrium level of income Y_f. In the aggregate labor market, the aggregate demand for and supply of labor result in an equilibrium real wage W_f and full employment N_f. If aggregate demand falls to $E_1 = C_0 + I_1 + G_0$ due to a fall in aggregate investment, the level of current income falls to Y_1. The disequilibrium in the aggregate commodities market leads to disequilibrium in the aggregate labor market, resulting in employers being "off of" their demand curves at point K. The excess supply of labor, $N_f - N_1$, represents involuntary unemployment of labor at real wage W_f.

tures on investment, I_0; and real expenditures by government, G_0. The vertical line $S = Y$ at Y_f is real aggregate supply at the natural rate of unemployment (which we assume here is identical to full employment). In the labor market, the demand for labor and the supply of labor result in an equilibrium real wage W_f. The real wage is defined as the ratio of the nominal or money wage MW to the price level as measured by an appropriate price index P, such as the consumer price index. Thus, $W = MW/P$.

Both the labor market and the commodities market are in equilibrium. In the labor market, the real wage W_f results in the full employment of labor, N_f, consistent with minimum amounts of both frictional and structural unemployment. Workers are supplying the labor services they choose to supply at the real wage W_f; firms are able to employ the quantity of labor they choose to employ at the same real wage. Similarly, the commodities market is also in equilibrium. Real aggregate demand in conjunction with real aggregate supply has resulted in an equilibrium level of income Y_f. Firms are selling the output that they are currently producing so that there is no unintended accumulation or decumulation of inventories.

Our interest is in explaining how a decline in aggregate demand in the commodities market leads to demand deficiency unemployment. Thus, let us introduce disequilibrium into the commodities market by assuming that real investment falls to I_1. *Ceteris paribus,* this leads to a decline in real aggregate demand to $E_1 = C_0 + I_1 + G_0$. Because product prices do not immediately adjust downward (we discuss why they do not in some detail in the following section), the commodities market is in disequilibrium. At existing prices and wages, firms would like to produce and sell the same quantities as before. But at these same prices and wages, firms cannot sell all that they would like to produce and supply. It is in this sense that producers are out of equilibrium. Because they cannot sell what they want to produce at present prices and because their initial response will not be to lower prices, they will reduce the rate of current production. Thus, current real income falls to Y_1.

The disequilibrium that has appeared in the commodities market creates disequilibrium in the labor market. Firms would like to continue employing N_f workers, as this would still be the profit-maximizing employment of labor at existing wages and prices, if only the firms could sell all that would be produced by N_f units of labor. Because they cannot sell that much output, they are "off of" their demand curves at point K. Their *effective* demand for labor in this disequilibrium situation is N_1. Note that workers are also in disequilibrium at point K since they would like to supply N_f units of labor at the going real wage; however, a sufficient number of jobs is not available, and some workers are thus involuntarily unemployed.

The excess supply of labor, $N_f - N_1$, that has developed could be eliminated if *both* money wages and prices fell, thereby pushing the sales constraint outward. Notice that the labor market could be restored to equilibrium via declines in nominal wages and prices without any change in the real wage. In fact, one of the important contributions of J. M. Keynes to our understanding of unemployment was his recognition that unemployment is not of necessity caused by a real wage that is too high for equilibrium, as pre-Keynesian economists thought. An even more important contribution which we have incorporated into our discussion is Keynes's recognition that when firms are faced with a decline in product demand, their initial reaction will be a quantity adjustment rather than a price adjustment.[5]

We have described a classic example of demand deficiency unem-

[5]J. M. Keynes, *The General Theory of Employment, Interest and Money,* Harcourt, Brace & World, New York, 1936. The consistency of Keynes's view on quantity adjustments with profit-maximizing behavior has been demonstrated in A. Alchian, "Information Costs, Pricing, and Resource Unemployment," *Western Economic Journal,* vol. 7, June 1969, pp. 109–127. The interpretation of Keynes is itself a subject of much debate. On this point see A. Leijonhufvud, *On Keynesian Economics and the Economics of Keynes,* Oxford University Press, New York, 1968.

ployment. The decline in aggregate real product demand combined with initial inflexibility in prices and nominal wages created disequilibrium in both the commodity and labor markets. Much of modern macroeconomics has been concerned with outlining the adjustment processes by which full employment can be restored. While a full discussion of these processes is beyond the scope of this book, we should point out that there are two paths by which a full employment equilibrium can be restored. One involves the realization that, however inflexible prices and nominal wages may be, given the passage of enough time, nominal wages and prices will adjust to provide equilibrium. However, that required period of time may be painfully long and very costly in terms of unemployment and lost output. The other path to full employment involves compensating for a decline in aggregate demand by using monetary and fiscal policies to increase aggregate demand. If the level of aggregate demand is too low for equilibrium at existing prices and nominal wages, and if prices and nominal wages won't fall to equilibrium levels (or won't fall fast enough), then increases in aggregate demand through monetary and fiscal policy can make the *existing* prices and wages equilibrium prices and wages. In principle, then, monetary and fiscal policy can be used to restore the unemployment rate to its natural level.

Problems can arise, though, from this use of monetary and fiscal policy. As we pointed out earlier in this chapter, it is difficult to determine what the natural rate of unemployment actually is. If monetary and fiscal policy are used to attempt to drive the unemployment rate below its natural level, serious inflationary problems arise. However, these problems are of a dynamic nature and are thus the subject matter of the next chapter.

Clearly, then, the inflexibility of prices and nominal wages is central to an explanation of demand deficiency unemployment. We now turn to a discussion of why product prices and nominal wages fall so slowly—if at all—and thus impede the process of regaining equilibrium.

15.2c
Product price adjustments

What does an automobile dealer do when actual current sales fall below expected current sales? Probably nothing for the first few weeks or months because he has little knowledge of why his current sales have fallen. Is this simply a random event which is unique to this firm and will quickly correct itself? Are the reduced sales due to some forces which are confined to the local market, such as the closing of a military base in the area? Are new car sales falling industrywide? Or, worst of all, are declining new car sales part of a larger pattern of falling sales in many industries economywide? The firm obviously has no way of knowing immediately, but it begins trying to find out. In short, it begins to invest in information.

Let us assume that it becomes increasingly obvious not only to this firm but to all automobile dealers who are similarly investing in information that declining auto sales are not unique to each of them, but are common to the industry; further, the auto industry is only one of many industries that is experiencing declining sales. In other words, let us assume that the level of aggregate demand has fallen. Auto dealers will want to stop the flow of new cars which they are unable to sell. Orders for new cars are either cancelled or not entered. As current orders decline, new auto production is slowed, and unemployment arises in the automobile industry. Reduced production of new autos makes itself felt in reduced current demand for the output of the steel, textile, glass, and other industries so that unemployment arises in these industries as well. Because a decline in aggregate demand affects final demand not only in the auto industry but in many (if not most) sectors of the economy, demand deficiency unemployment becomes widespread.

In this scenario the firm does not immediately reduce the selling price of automobiles. Only when it becomes convinced that the sales decline is permanent will it do so in order to reduce its unintended accumulation of new cars. Further, unintended accumulation of inventories has become characteristic of many industries, and prices begin to adjust downward throughout the economy. Only when inventories have fallen to the level that firms consider optimal will firms begin to enter new orders, and then only for the quantity that they expect to sell. Auto producers then begin to reemploy labor which they had earlier laid off, and the recovery begins.

How long does this period of adjustment last? It depends on several factors, such as the initial magnitude and duration of the fall in aggregate demand, the magnitude and duration of its subsequent rise, and the adjustments that firms make in the interim. The fall in aggregate demand which began in 1929 in the United States was mammoth; not until 1941 did the gross national product regain its 1929 level. The fall in aggregate demand which led to the recession in 1974 was less severe, but was still substantial enough to cause a 30 percent fall in industrial production, a 5 percent decline in employment, and a rise in the aggregate unemployment rate from 5.5 to 9 percent.

What of the price adjustments that firms make during a fall in aggregate demand? We have seen that firms do not reduce prices instantly because of lack of information about the present and future course of events, and that this lagged response delays recovery. But do prices fall in recessions and rise in recoveries so that their movement is procyclical, or do they rise in recoveries but never fall? In short, are they responsive to changes in aggregate demand? The "administered-price" hypothesis developed by Gardiner C. Means in the late 1930s and accepted by many economists argued that prices were unresponsive to declines in aggregate demand. In his words, an administered-price "is a price which is set by administrative action and held constant for a period of time. We have an administered-price when a company maintains a posted price at which it will make sales or simply has its own prices at which buyers may purchase or not as they wish."[6] It is, of course, true in a trivial sense that someone does decide what a product price will be, even in perfect competition. But does the actual selling price change in response to changes in aggregate demand?

Administered-prices were argued to be the rule (not the exception) in concentrated industries. If this were the case, demand deficiency unemployment, although initially brought about by, say, inappropriate monetary and fiscal policies which caused aggregate demand to fall for an extended period, could nonetheless be sustained and accentuated by unresponsive product prices in monopolistic (or concentrated) sectors of the economy so that the adjustment process returning the economy to full employment could be long and drawn-out.

In a study published in 1970, George J. Stigler and James J. Kindahl found no evidence which suggested that administered-prices are a significant phenomenon.[7] They examined prices paid by buyers (not prices asked by sellers) for a variety of 70 industrial commodities. Their sample of commodities was heavily weighted with commodities whose prices were argued to be administered. Stigler and Kindahl found a predominant tendency for this index of prices to move procyclically over the course of four business cycles encompassed by their study, 1957 to 1966. During these four business cycles, prices moved in the same direction as general business conditions 56 percent of the time, remained constant 17 percent of the time, and moved in the opposite direction as general business 27 percent of the time.[8] In short, the degree of price inflexibility that existed did not seem to be the result of concentration in the product market.

If prices decline during recessions, then money wages must also fall if real wages are to remain unchanged. By contrast, if money wages remain rigid during downturns in the level of economic activity but prices fall, then real wages rise. Rising real wages clearly impede the process of recovery.

15.2d
Money wage adjustments

Workers resist cuts in money wages; this has been a commonplace observation for centuries. It is easy to understand why unionized firms do not lower wages when faced with a decline in demand. Collective bargaining agreements are legally binding contracts, and firms cannot

---

[6]G. C. Means, *Industrial Prices and Their Relative Inflexibility,* U.S. Senate Document 13, 74th Cong., 1st Sess., 1935, p. 1.

[7]G. J. Stigler and J. K. Kindahl, *The Behavior of Industrial Prices,* National Bureau of Economic Research, New York, 1970.

[8]Ibid., p. 9. We recommend to students the debate which publication of this book prompted. See G. C. Means, "The Administered-Price Thesis Reconfirmed," *American Economic Review,* vol. 62, June 1972, pp. 292–306; and G. J. Stigler and J. K. Kindahl, "Industrial Prices, as Administered by Dr. Means," *American Economic Review,* vol. 63, September 1973, pp. 717–721.

pay a wage below the wage provided for in the contract. What has not been generally understood until recently is that nonunionized firms do not offer lower money wages to their workers because there exist implicit contracts between workers and employers not to do so.[9] Instead, employers lay off some workers and retain other workers at unchanged money wages. The contract is an implicit contract (or a quasi contract) because the legal system makes it impossible to rent or sell labor services under enforceable contracts for long periods of time. Nonetheless, it is a tacit agreement between a worker and an employer that "under reasonable and more or less understood conditions, employees have a certain security with respect to both wages and employment."[10]

A system of implicit contracts has arisen because of differences in attitudes toward risk as between workers and employers. Workers face the risk of an interrupted labor income stream due to layoffs; employers face the risk of interrupted revenues and profits due to declines in product demand. Employers can reduce at least part of the risk faced by workers by entering into implicit contracts with them. Thus, at least part of the risk "is transferred from wages to profits and, via the capital market, to the income streams of the firm's owners and creditors."[11] As Baily points out clearly, a firm must pay higher wages to attract any given work force the higher the expected unemployment. Thus, because risk-sharing policies enable the firm to attract any given work force at lower wages, it is profitable for the firm to engage in these policies.

Thus, a distinction has developed in the labor market which closely resembles the distinction in capital markets between stocks and bonds. Some employees will have little employment and income security; others will be as secure as possible against arbitrary fluctuations in demand. The fact that employers will, in making such assurances to workers, discriminate in favor of those employees in whom they have made (or plan to make) substantial investments in on-the-job training, a system of implicit contracts has clear implications for the incidence of unemployment given fluctuations in aggregate demand.

15.3

THE INCIDENCE OF UNEMPLOYMENT

It is clear from inspection of Table 15.1 that unemployment is not a random event to which all age, race, sex, and occupational groups in the

[9]Discussions of implicit contracts appear in C. Azariadis, "Implicit Contracts and Underemployment Equilibria," *Journal of Political Economy,* vol. 83, December 1975, pp. 1183–1202; M. N. Baily, "Wages and Employment under Uncertain Demand," *Review of Economic Studies,* vol. 41, January 1974, pp. 37–50; D. F. Gordon, "A Neo-Classical Theory of Keynesian Unemployment," *Economic Inquiry,* vol. 12, December 1974, pp. 431–459; and R. E. Hall, "The Rigidity of Wages and the Persistence of Unemployment," *Brookings Papers on Economic Activity,* vol. 2, 1975, pp. 301–335.

[10]Gordon, op. cit., p. 442.

[11]Azardiadis, op. cit., p. 1184.

economy are equally vulnerable. *Ceteris paribus,* unemployment rates are higher for women than for men, for teenagers than for prime-age workers, for blacks than for whites, and for blue-collar workers than for white-collar workers.

Part of the explanation of differential unemployment rates concerns the investment that firms have made in on-the-job training of workers. Recall from Chap. 7 that once such an investment has been made in a worker, the investment becomes a sunk cost. The firm will be reluctant to lay off immediately a worker in whom a great investment has been made, even if the worker's current marginal product is less than his current wage. Thus, in a period of declining demand for the firm's product—particularly when the firm is uncertain whether reduced demand is temporary or permanent—the firm will want to reduce current production. It achieves this by laying off first those workers in whom it has made the least investment. Thus, there will be differential shifts in the demands for various types of labor employed by the firm: the demand for workers in whom the firm has made little if any investments in training may decline precipitously; the demand for trained workers may decline little if at all.[12]

The literature on implicit contracts suggests that not all workers will have equal access to the employment security provisions of implicit contracts. Firms may, for example, choose to allocate such on-the-job training as is available to male rather than female workers if they view male workers as more permanent employees. If a female has shown by her work experience a less regular attachment to the labor force, the firm's decision is rational in that such a worker may not return a stream of benefits comparable to the costs of providing the training. Thus, female workers may not receive the same employment security provisions as males; consequently the incidence of unemployment would be higher among female members of the labor force. Further, among those females who do experience an intermittent participation in the labor force, frictional unemployment will be higher because reentry into the labor force typically involves some period of search, regardless of how efficient this search is.

Unemployment rates for teenagers are extremely high; further, they have been getting higher over time. A major reason for these unusually high rates is no doubt the rapid turnover of teenagers in low-skilled jobs. However, many economists point to the existence of minimum wage laws which aggravate the situation by setting wages above their equilibrium values. Teenagers will have little or no work experience as they search for entry-level jobs in the various sectors of the economy, and employers will be reluctant to hire them at wages which they regard as too high.

---

[12]See G. S. Becker, *Human Capital,* 2d ed., National Bureau of Economic Research, New York, 1975; and W. Oi, "Labor as a Quasi-Fixed Factor," *Journal of Political Economy,* vol. 70, December 1962, pp. 538–555.

Table 15.1
Average annual unemployment rates, 1974, by sex, race, age, and occupational categories

Category	Rate
All civilian workers	5.6
Men, 20 years and over	3.8
Women, 20 years and over	5.5
Both sexes, 16 to 19 years	16.0
White	5.0
Negro and other races	9.9
White-collar workers	3.3
Professional and technical	2.3
Managers and administrators	1.8
Sales workers	4.2
Clerical workers	4.6
Blue-collar workers	6.7
Craft and kindred	4.4
Operatives	7.5
Nonfarm laborers	10.1

SOURCE: *Handbook of Labor Statistics, 1975— Reference Edition,* U.S. Department of Labor, Bureau of Labor Statistics, Bulletin 1865, 1975, tables 59 and 65.

Black unemployment rates exceed those of whites, *ceteris paribus,* because blacks in the past have typically had lower levels of educational attainment than whites, and employers have to some degree rationed specific training opportunities to those employees with greater amounts of general training. Discrimination in hiring has also been a major factor leading to higher average unemployment rates for blacks, although we have seen in Chap. 11 that the manifestations of discrimination against blacks have virtually disappeared among recent college-educated additions to the labor force. As this progress continues, black-white differences in unemployment rates should narrow.

The higher average unemployment rates for blue-collar workers reflect in part changes in consumer expenditures given a fall in aggregate demand. Consumers can postpone purchases of durable goods such as new cars, television sets, and so forth, even though their purchases of nondurable goods such as food remain largely unchanged. To the extent that this is true, employment will fall to a greater extent in durable goods industries and in those industries such as steel, rubber, and glass which are major suppliers to them; these industries are characterized by a heavy concentration of blue-collar workers.

15.4

EMPLOYMENT AND UNEMPLOYMENT AS INDICATORS OF ECONOMIC PERFORMANCE

The United States economy provides jobs to a higher percentage of its age-eligible population than does almost any other western industrialized country. Yet at the same time, the unemployment rate in the United States is unusually high when compared to unemployment rates in these same countries. This seeming paradox has provoked discussion among labor market analysts about the relative merits of employment and unemployment statistics as indicators of economic performance.[13]

Figure 15.3 illustrates this paradox very vividly. In the lower portion of Fig. 15.3 we trace the movement of the employment-to-population

[13]See, for example, J. Shiskin, "Employment and Unemployment: The Doughnut or the Hole?" *Monthly Labor Review,* vol. 99, February 1976, pp. 3–10.

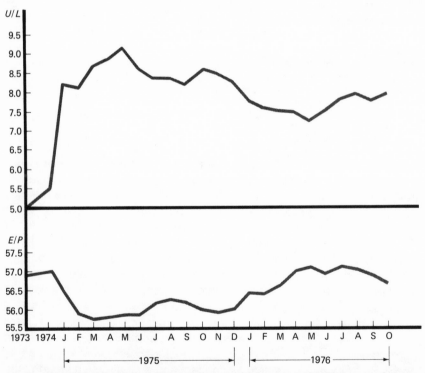

Figure 15.3. Movements in the unemployment rate and the employment-to-population ratio, 1973 to October 1976. Both the unemployment rate and the employment-to-population ratio reflect changes in the level of economic activity. The unemployment rate rose sharply in the recession in 1975, and stayed above 7 percent for the remainder of the period. The employment-to-population ratio fell in the recession, but began a rise in March 1975, reaching record highs in mid-1976.

ratio, E/P. We present annual averages of this ratio for 1973 and 1974, and monthly values from January 1975 to October 1976. The numerator of E/P is total civilian employment; the denominator is the noninstitutionalized population 16 years of age or older. In periods of economic expansion the number employed grows as job vacancies are created in the various sectors of the economy; the ratio E/P rises if the growth in employment exceeds the growth in the age-eligible population. The annual average of E/P in 1974 was 57.0 percent, the highest value for this ratio since 1947. During the early months of the recession in 1975, E/P fell, reaching a low in March 1975. After that date, the trend in E/P was upward. Indeed, E/P reached record highs in mid-1976.

By contrast, the picture painted by movements in the unemployment rate in Fig. 15.3 was quite different. The ratio U/L rose dramatically, of course, in the early months of the recession, reaching 9.2 percent in May 1975. After that date, the trend in U/L was downward as economic recovery from the recession proceeded. Yet the unemployment rate fell very slowly and remained above 7 percent for the remainder of the period shown.

The existence of generous unemployment compensation payments has been an important factor contributing to high unemployment rates. First, because it lowers the cost of job search, unemployed workers search longer for new jobs. Thus, the duration of unemployment increases, and the additional duration of unemployment expands the unemployment rate. S. T. Marston has estimated that insured workers remain unemployed 16 to 31 percent longer because of unemployment compensation payments.[14] Martin Feldstein has shown that the current unemployment compensation system entails very strong adverse incentives. In the more generous states, an unemployed male can replace through unemployment compensation over 80 percent of his lost net income; an unemployed female can replace over 100 percent of her lost income.[15] Reflecting these generous benefits, some collective bargaining agreements now contain "inverse seniority" provisions that specify that the most senior employees be laid off first and rehired last.

Feldstein has also argued that the rationale of providing unemployment compensation insurance to enable an unemployed worker to search longer in hopes of finding a suitable new job is largely irrelevant because the typical adult unemployed worker is rehired by his former employer.[16] Because unemployment compensation payments are not

[14]S. T. Marston, "The Impact of Unemployment Insurance on Job Search," *Brookings Papers on Economic Activity,* vol. 1, 1975, pp. 13–48. See also A. Holen and S. A. Horowitz, "The Effect of Unemployment Insurance and Eligibility Enforcement on Unemployment," *Journal of Law and Economics,* vol. 17, October 1974, pp. 403–431.

[15]M. Feldstein, ."Unemployment Compensation: Adverse Incentives and Distributional Anomalies," *National Tax Journal,* vol. 27, June 1974, pp. 231–244.

[16]M. Feldstein, "Temporary Layoffs in the Theory of Unemployment," *Journal of Political Economy,* vol. 84, October 1976, pp. 937–957.

subject to tax, they constitute a subsidy to workers and cause unemployment rates to be higher than they otherwise would be.

None of these remarks should be interpreted necessarily as criticisms against either the form or the spirit of unemployment compensation. The United States is a wealthy country, and handsome unemployment compensation benefits are one of many features of such a society. But if these payments clearly cause the aggregate unemployment rate to be higher than it would be in their absence, it is a serious mistake then to call for a lowering of the unemployment rate through expanded growth in aggregate demand.

QUESTIONS AND EXERCISES

1. All unemployed workers have one characteristic in common: They are unsuccessful in finding employment. Why, then, is it necessary or helpful to distinguish among types of unemployment as we have done in this chapter?

2. What is "natural" about the natural rate of unemployment?

3. There seems to be widespread support for retraining structurally unemployed workers at governmental expense. If you favor such a proposal, would you also favor a policy of refurbishing unsold homes at governmental expense? Why or why not?

4. What advantages and disadvantages are associated with using the employment-to-population ratio as a measure of performance of the aggregate economy?

5. How might declines in aggregate demand increase the amount of frictional and structural unemployment?

REFERENCES FOR FURTHER READING

Portions of three intermediate texts in macroeconomics provide material which supplements much of our discussion. See C. W. Baird, *Macroeconomics,* Science Research, Chicago, 1973, chap. 4; W. R. Hosek, *Macroeconomic Theory,* Irwin, Homewood, Ill., 1975, Chap. 17; R. L. Crouch, *Macroeconomics,* Harcourt Brace Jovanovich, New York, 1972, chap. 16.

A good discussion of types of unemployment and their incidence is in E. Kalachek, *Labor Markets and Unemployment,* Wadsworth, Belmont, Cal., 1973, chaps. 4–6.

WAGES, EMPLOYMENT, AND INFLATION

In a dynamic economy the forces which determine both the demand for labor and the supply of labor are constantly changing. Consequently, the equilibrium real wage and the equilibrium level of employment are also changing. In the absence of any movement in the price level, money wage changes are identical to real wage changes, and both workers and employers adjust their behavior as real wages change. However, in a dynamic economy the price level also changes, and it changes in ways which are not fully anticipated by either workers or employers. Thus, the introduction of price level changes which are not fully anticipated into the analysis of wages and employment blurs the distinction between nominal and real wage changes and, as we shall see, generates changes in employment and unemployment which are not permanent but temporary.

The relation between the rate of inflation and the level of unemployment is known as the *Phillips relation.*[1] Our first task is to outline a contemporary neoclassical explanation of this relation. Our focus is on

---

[1]A. W. Phillips, "The Relation between Unemployment and the Rate of Change of Money Wage Rates in the United Kingdom, 1861–1957," *Economica,* vol. 25, November 1958, pp. 283–299. Phillips's study established the statistical relation between unemployment and the rate of change of money wages. For the price-level modification transforming this relation into one between the unemployment rate and the rate of change of the price level, see P. A. Samuelson and R. M. Solow, "Analytical Aspects of Anti-Inflation Policy," *American Economic Review,* vol. 50, May 1960, pp. 177–194.

individual workers and employers as they adjust to changes in prices and wages in a world characterized by costly information. We see that it is only in the short run that any relation exists between the rate of unemployment and the inflation rate. In the long run, the inflation rate and the natural rate of unemployment are seen not as twin aspects of one problem, but as separate problems requiring separate solutions. We examine the actual relation that has existed between these two variables in the United States from 1961 to 1976, and interpret this evidence within the framework of the Phillips relation in the long run. In our concluding section, we outline the political problems which have prevented the United States economy from arriving at the long-run goals of price stability, high levels of employment, and correspondingly low levels of unemployment.

16.1

THE PHILLIPS RELATION IN THE SHORT RUN[2]

To begin our analysis in the simplest way, consider an economy in which the *actual* rate of inflation is zero. Further, assume that both workers and employers *anticipate* a continued zero rate of inflation so that there is no discrepancy between the actual and the anticipated rate of inflation. At the existing real wage, the equilibrium level of employment is that consistent with the natural rate of unemployment.

Now assume that monetary authorities increase the rate of growth of nominal aggregate demand by increasing the rate of growth of the money supply so that the price level begins to rise unexpectedly at a rate of 3 percent. Because employers anticipate a stable price level, each employer who experiences rising sales will interpret them at least partially as due to an unexpected increase in relative demand for his product, and will anticipate higher future sales and a higher future product price. Because, for each employer, the real wage relevant to him is the nominal wage in terms of the price of his product, real wages will have fallen from the perspective of each of these employers, and each will seek to hire additional workers, *ceteris paribus,* at the lower real wage. If the employer must raise nominal wages somewhat in order to attract additional workers (which is likely given that we begin our analysis from a position of equilibrium in the labor market), the higher nominal wage will still result in a lower real wage so long as nominal wage changes lag behind product price changes.

To workers, the same course of events is interpreted somewhat differently. The real wage relevant to them is the nominal wage in terms

---

[2]Our presentation of a neoclassical model of the Phillips relation is based on the following works: M. Friedman, "The Role of Monetary Policy," *American Economic Review,* vol. 58, March 1968, pp. 1–17; "Wage Determination and Unemployment," in *Price Theory,* Aldine, Chicago, 1976, pp. 213–237; "Nobel Lecture: Inflation and Unemployment," *Journal of Political Economy,* vol. 85, June 1977, pp. 451–472.

of the prices of goods and services in general. Because workers are not likely to perceive immediately the upward movement of prices in general, they will interpret a higher nominal wage as a higher real wage, and the higher real wage will cause the quantity of labor supplied to increase from two sources—more hours from those currently employed, and new entrants into the labor force.

Thus, the unanticipated 3 percent rate of inflation has resulted in an increase in employment and a reduction in unemployment illustrated by the movement from combination A to combination B in Fig. 16.1. The short-run Phillips curve $SRPC_0$ contains all those possible combinations of unemployment rates and actual rates of inflation *given that both employers and workers anticipate a zero rate of inflation.* We say "possible" combinations because, contrary to the example we chose, the monetary authorities could have decreased the rate of growth of nominal aggregate demand so that the price level began to fall unexpectedly at a rate of 2 percent. In this case employment would have declined and unemployment would have risen, as illustrated by, say, combination C in Fig. 16.1. The movement from combination A to C has resulted from the unexpected rate of deflation of 2 percent. Employers will likely interpret a reduced rate of sales as due at least partially to a decline in relative demand for their product. Anticipating lower future

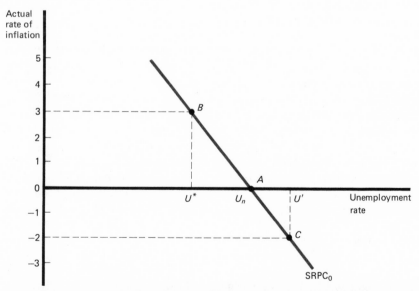

Figure 16.1. The Phillips relation in the short run. Beginning from an initial equilibrium at point A at the natural rate of unemployment and a zero rate of inflation, an unanticipated increase in the inflation rate to 3 percent reduces the unemployment rate to U*. Similarly, an unanticipated rate of deflation of 2 percent increases the unemployment rate to U'. The short-run Phillips relation SRPC₀ contains all those possible combinations of actual inflation rates and unemployment rates, given that both employers and workers anticipate a zero rate of inflation.

sales, a lower future product price but no reduction in money wages, employers will perceive that *real* wages have risen and will reduce employment. Workers will not perceive immediately that the price level has fallen, and will continue searching unsuccessfully for jobs at real wages which are now higher. Thus, the unanticipated deflation of 2 percent has reduced employment and increased unemployment.

But inflation has an effect on employment only if it is unanticipated, as in the two cases illustrated here. Once market participants adapt their expectations of inflation to the actual rate of inflation, the effects on employment and unemployment prove to be temporary, not permanent. We turn now to a neoclassical model of the Phillips relation in the long run, that period of time necessary for both employers and workers to adapt their expectations of inflation to the actual rate of inflation.

16.2
THE PHILLIPS RELATION IN THE LONG RUN

Following our previous discussion, assume that the rate of inflation has increased unexpectedly to 3 percent, and that consequently employment has increased and the unemployment rate has declined—combination B in Fig. 16.1. Assume further that the 3 percent rate of inflation is now maintained at that rate. Market participants will cease anticipating a zero rate of inflation and will come to anticipate the actual rate, 3 percent. Employees will come to realize that their higher nominal wages do not represent higher real wages, and will incorporate higher nominal wage demands in future wage contracts. As nominal wages begin to rise, real wage levels which existed earlier are reestablished, and employers reestablish employment levels which existed earlier, *ceteris paribus,* at the earlier real wage level. Thus, the short-run Phillips curve $SRPC_0$ shifts outward to $SRPC_3$ in Fig. 16.2. The new equilibrium in the labor market is at the natural rate of unemployment U_n and a 3 percent rate of inflation—combination D in Fig. 16.2. By contrast, the Phillips relation would shift to the left if, as in our previous example, the unexpected deflation of 2 percent had been maintained. In this case, the reduction in employment and the increase in unemployment represented by combination C would have been temporary. As market participants came to anticipate a rate of deflation of 2 percent, future wage contracts would include smaller rises in money wages, and real wage levels which had existed earlier would be reestablished. After real wages had fallen to their earlier, lower level, equilibrium levels of employment would be reestablished at the natural rate of unemployment. In terms of Fig. 16.2, the short-run Phillips curve would shift left to $SRPC_{-2}$, and equilibrium in the labor market would be at the natural rate of unemployment and a 2 percent rate of deflation—combination E in Fig. 16.2.

There are two important conclusions in the neoclassical analysis of the Phillips relation. First, equilibrium in the labor market at the natural

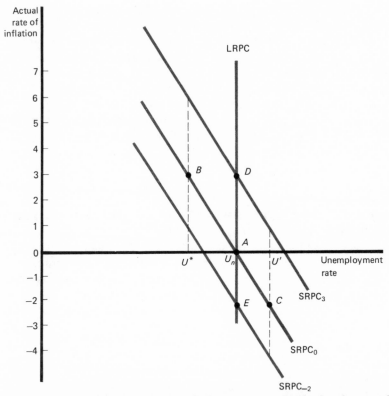

Figure 16.2. The Phillips relation in the long run. Beginning from an initial equilibrium at point A on SRPC₀, an unanticipated inflation rate of 3 percent reduces the unemployment rate to U* (combination B); similarly, an unanticipated deflation of 2 percent increases the unemployment rate to U′ (combination C). Once market participants adapt their expectations of inflation to the actual rate, the short-run Phillips curve shifts. In the first case SRPC₀ shifts outward to SRPC₃; in the second case SRPC₀ shifts left to SRPC₋₂. Thus, the long-run Phillips relation LRPC illustrates that equilibrium in the labor market at the natural rate of unemployment is possible at any actual rate of inflation once that rate of inflation becomes anticipated.

rate of unemployment is possible at any actual rate of inflation so long as that rate of inflation is anticipated. Second, a reduction in the unemployment rate below its natural rate will be possible only so long as the actual inflation rate is greater than market participants anticipate.[3] Once the higher actual inflation rate comes to be anticipated, the unemployment rate returns to its natural rate. Pursuing this point further, if

---

[3]For a study which tests for the United States the hypothesis that only the unanticipated part of money expansion influences unemployment, see R. J. Barro, "Unanticipated Money Growth and Unemployment in the United States," *American Economic Review,* vol. 67, March 1977, pp. 101–115. See also Barro's extension of this argument, "Unanticipated Money, Output, and the Price Level in the United States," *Journal of Political Economy,* vol. 86, August 1978, pp. 549–580.

monetary authorities attempt to keep the unemployment rate below its natural rate for an extended period, such attempts will require accelerating rates of inflation. This is because market participants will come to expect continuously higher rates of inflation and adapt more speedily to the higher actual rates.

In the neoclassical view, then, the Phillips relation in the long run is the vertical line LRPC at the natural rate of unemployment. This vertical line signifies that equilibrium in the labor market is possible at the natural rate of unemployment and any rate of inflation, so long as that rate is anticipated.

16.3

A NEOCLASSICAL INTERPRETATION OF UNITED STATES EXPERIENCE, 1961 THROUGH 1976

In Fig. 16.3 we illustrate the actual annual rates of inflation and average annual unemployment rates that existed in the United States during the 16-year period 1961 through 1976. Our purpose in this section is to interpret these movements within a neoclassical framework.

The combinations of inflation rates and unemployment rates for the years 1961 through 1969 appear to lie on a nonlinear Phillips curve

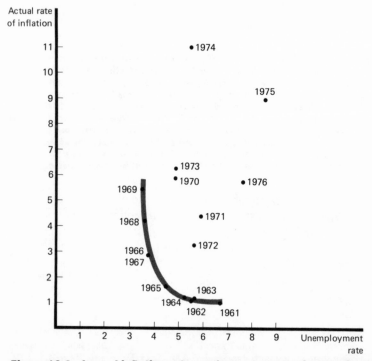

Figure 16.3. Annual inflation rates and average annual unemployment rates in the United States, 1961 to 1976. Combinations for 1961 to 1969 appear to lie on a nonlinear short-run Phillips relation. Combinations after 1969 lie to the right of this relation, suggesting a rightward shift in the Phillips relation as higher inflation rates became anticipated.

along which anticipated rates of inflation were low. Indeed, actual inflation rates for the first 7 years of this period were low—below 3 percent—and government policies to expand aggregate demand were successful in lowering the unemployment rate from 6.7 percent to 3.8 percent with a minimal impact on the rate of inflation. There was substantial agreement at the time that an unemployment rate in the neighborhood of 3.8 percent corresponded to full employment. The late 1960s, however, were a time of increasing United States involvement in the Vietnam war, and political authorities chose to finance increasing military expenditures by selling government bonds rather than by raising taxes. (Raising taxes is, of course, unpopular. Raising taxes to pursue a war about which many United States citizens were becoming increasingly concerned was doubly unpopular.)[4] The rapid increase in the sale of government bonds led predictably to a rise in the rate of growth in the money supply and, given that the United States economy was at a position of full employment in 1967, to a rise in the rate of inflation. Notice that the actual rates of inflation increased substantially in 1968 and 1969 with a minimal further impact on the aggregate unemployment rate. As the higher rates of inflation experienced in 1968 and 1969 became anticipated, the short-run Phillips relation shifted to the right, reflecting these higher anticipated rates.

The combinations of unemployment rates and inflation rates which occurred in 1970 and 1971 are particularly instructive because they represent the adjustments made by market participants to the higher actual rates of inflation. In 1970 both the inflation rate and the unemployment rate were higher than in 1969. In 1971 the unemployment rate continued to rise although the actual rate of inflation slowed as compared to 1970. The rising unemployment rate *and* inflation rate which existed in 1970 would be labeled today as "stagflation." But in the neoclassical analysis stagflation is not an anomaly requiring a special theory of labor markets. It is entirely consistent with the lagged adjustments by both employers and workers that we discussed earlier in this chapter, and corresponds to a shift to the right in the short-run Phillips curve.

There are two features of the adjustment which require special notice. First, the adjustment process in 1970 and 1971 traces out a clockwise pattern of unemployment rate and inflation rate combinations. Second, the expansion which begins again in 1972 begins from a higher actual rate of inflation.[5] We point out these characteristics now because

---

[4]An interesting question is whether there might be fewer wars if there were a requirement that they be financed on a pay-as-you-go basis.

[5]We speak somewhat loosely here because our data are annual averages. Decisions to pursue expansionary policies begin with decisions to increase the rate of growth of nominal aggregate demand. These policies affect nominal income and employment after a lag of approximately two quarters. The actual *months* of peaks and troughs in the level of economic activity are established by the National Bureau of Economic Research and are published in U.S. Department of Commerce, *Survey of Current Business,* monthly.

they preview the adjustments made after 1972 as well. The expansion resulted in some reduction in the unemployment rate in 1972. However, the rate of growth of aggregate demand was again substantial, and the actual rate of inflation rose in 1973 to 6.2 percent and in 1974 to 11 percent, the highest rate of inflation experienced in the United States since the post-World War II inflation of the late 1940s. If one argues that the combinations of inflation rates and unemployment rates for 1972 and 1973 lie on a short-run Phillips curve—however temporary and unstable—along which the anticipated rate of inflation was in the neighborhood of 4 to 5 percent, such anticipations were quickly dispelled by the inflation in 1974. The rising unemployment rate *and* higher inflation rate in 1974, followed in 1975 by the highest unemployment rate experienced in the United States since the Depression (but with a lower rate of inflation), were again adjustments to higher actual inflation rates of 1974, and parallel the clockwise adjustments described above for 1970 and 1971. The notable difference for the last years, however, is that the expansion in the growth of nominal aggregate demand in 1975 began from an even higher aggregate unemployment rate and inflation rate.

16.4
POLICY IMPLICATIONS OF NEOCLASSICAL ANALYSIS

If the same policies are pursued in the future which have produced in the 1970s both the highest inflation rate since the late 1940s and the highest unemployment rate since the Depression, then both the inflation rate and the unemployment rate will be higher in the future. In terms of Fig. 16.3, the clockwise adjustment traced out by the combinations of inflation rates and unemployment rates for the early 1970s will be replicated by similar clockwise adjustments in the late 1970s at higher inflation rates and higher unemployment rates.[6] But the same policies need not be pursued. The major thrust of the neoclassical analysis of the Phillips relation is that the natural rate of unemployment and the inflation rate are related in the short run in a known way and for known reasons, but are independent of each other in the long run, that period of time necessary for market participants to adapt their expectations of inflation to the actual rate. If this analysis is correct, then inflation and unemployment are not twin parts of the same problem in the long run, but are different problems requiring different solutions. But, as we shall see, the fact that unemployment and unanticipated inflation are related in the short run makes it difficult to arrive at long-run solutions to these two problems.

---

[6]In Friedman's Nobel lecture cited in footnote 2, he discusses the possibility of a positive relation between inflation and unemployment.

16.4a
Price stability

Let us consider the inflation problem first. What should the inflation rate be in the United States? Most economists and laymen alike would probably favor a stable price level; certainly they would favor lower rates of inflation than prevailed in the 1970s in the United States. Some economists—notably Friedman—favor a mildly declining price level for reasons that go far beyond the scope of this discussion.[7] There is a widespread consensus in the economics profession that this is accomplished by slowing the rate of growth of nominal aggregate demand. There are some divisions within the profession about how best this can be accomplished, however. Monetarists argue that nominal aggregate demand can best be controlled through monetary policy—in particular, through controlling the rate of growth of the money supply. Fiscalists argue that nominal aggregate demand is best controlled through fiscal policy—the taxing and expenditure policies of the federal government. But the divisions separating monetarists and fiscalists are not what they once were, and both would argue that a slowing in the rate of growth of nominal aggregate demand, however achieved, is necessary to achieve lower rates of inflation.

But, as the neoclassical analysis makes clear, there are short-run costs associated with slowing the rate of growth of nominal aggregate demand so that actual inflation rates are less than anticipated. In particular, the unemployment rate rises, and interest rates tend to rise as well. These effects in the short run combined with a 2-year political time horizon for most members of Congress set into motion predictable demands to "do something" about rising unemployment rates and interest rates the instant these adjustments begin occurring, and the demands have proved irresistible in the past. "Doing something" has usually meant reversing the appropriate long-run policy—in particular, increasing government spending to "create jobs" and/or putting pressures of one type or another on the Federal Reserve to achieve lower short-term interest rates through increases in the rate of growth of the money supply. Of course, the ultimate effect of increases in the rate of growth of the money supply is to increase the rate of growth of nominal aggregate demand, producing a higher unanticipated rate of inflation (and higher interest rates as higher inflation rates become anticipated) and a short-run reduction in the unemployment rate—a movement along a short-run Phillips curve which will eventually shift outward as higher inflation rates become anticipated. In brief, the short-run costs of attaining price stability are in the present, while the benefit—price stability itself—lies down the road a few years.

---

[7]M. Friedman, "The Optimum Quantity of Money," in *The Optimum Quantity of Money and Other Essays,* Aldine, Chicago, 1969, pp. 1–50.

It is important to appreciate the conclusion that inflationary policies have a lasting impact only on the rate of inflation, not on the unemployment rate. As we have seen, the impact on employment and unemployment is only temporary, exists because workers and employers do not anticipate the actual inflation rate, and is dissipated once they do adjust to the higher inflation rate. (As we have stressed repeatedly throughout the book, adjustments do not occur immediately because of costly information.) This understanding, we would guess, is some number of years away. The economics profession itself has only recently come to a widespread (but by no means universal) acceptance of the neoclassical interpretation of the Phillips relation in the short and the long run, and several more years will be necessary to disseminate this interpretation to a wider audience.

Bound up in the neoclassical interpretation of the Phillips relation is the larger question of macroeconomic policy itself. Since the Keynesian revolution, the dominant macroeconomic view has been one which tends to perceive the aggregate economy as inherently unstable, requiring constant attention. This is analogous to a doctor who views all patients as inherently ill, requiring constant treatment. In this view, active monetary and fiscal policies must be pursued in order to control a host of destabilizing forces which otherwise might prevent the attainment of the desired goals of price stability and full employment. Thus, monetary policy must "lean against the wind," and fiscal policy must be "counter-cyclical."

By contrast, a contemporary neoclassical view is that the aggregate economy is inherently stable. This is analogous to a doctor who views all patients as normally healthy. Aggregate demand policies are best described in this view as a "game against rational economic agents," not as a "game against nature."[8]

16.4b
The natural rate of unemployment

The analysis of the Phillips relation in the short run argues that the unemployment rate can be reduced *below its natural rate* only by unanticipated inflation. But what determines the natural rate of unemployment? Another way to ask this question is: What unemployment rate would result in the long run in a society in which there were no divergence between the actual and the anticipated rate of inflation? Clearly there would be frictional and structural unemployment, as we explained in some detail in the previous chapter. There are real factors in the labor market—such factors as the degree of competition in both

---

[8] This distinction is from F. E. Kydland and E. C. Prescott, "Rules Rather than Discretion: The Inconsistency of Optimal Plans," *Journal of Political Economy,* vol. 85, June 1977, p. 473.

product and labor markets, the rate of technological change, the degree of unionization, and many other real factors—which assure a positive amount of unemployment. But has the natural rate of unemployment risen in the recent past? Friedman argues that it has risen for two important reasons.[9] There may be other reasons as well. First, women, teenagers, and other secondary workers now constitute a larger percentage of the labor force, and these groups have higher than average unemployment rates. Second, unemployment compensation benefits are often attractive enough to induce individuals to search longer for the "right" job, raising both the magnitude and duration of the unemployment rate. Philip Cagan estimated the natural rate of unemployment in the United States in 1977 to be 6 percent, possibly higher.[10] If indeed the natural rate of unemployment has been rising for these and/or other reasons, there clearly exists a difference between full employment properly defined and full employment defined by past experience.

QUESTIONS AND EXERCISES

1. If Cagan's estimate is valid that the natural rate of unemployment in the United States is in the neighborhood of 6 percent, what are the likely consequences of attempting to lower the aggregate unemployment rate to 4 percent, as some have urged?

2. The combinations of inflation rates and unemployment rates in Fig. 16.3 trace out a clockwise pattern of loops when values for successive years are connected. What might explain this pattern?

3. If the natural rate of unemployment can be achieved in the long run with any rate of inflation, what inflation rate would you choose? Why? What short run adjustments are predictable as the economy moves toward your target rate of inflation?

4. How do individual workers and employers form expectations about anticipated rates of inflation?

REFERENCES FOR FURTHER READING

Friedman's Nobel lecture cited in footnote 2 is accessible to students who have read and understood what we have said here. Also, the same is true for parts of H. Frisch, "Inflation Theory 1963–1975: A 'Second Generation' Survey," *Journal of Economic Literature,* vol. 15, December 1977, pp. 1289–1317.

A discussion of the role of information costs in the Phillips relation is

---

[9]Friedman, "Nobel Lecture: Inflation and Unemployment," op. cit.

[10]P. Cagan, "The Reduction of Inflation and the Magnitude of Unemployment," in W. Fellner (ed.), *Contemporary Economic Problems, 1977,* American Enterprise Institute, Washington, D.C., 1977.

given in C. Baird, *Macroeconomics,* Science Research, Chicago, 1973, pp. 295–299.

For an appreciation of the developments in Phillips curve analysis since 1958, see Phillips's seminal article cited in footnote 1.

For an analysis of the relation between inflation and unemployment that antedates Phillips, see I. Fisher, "A Statistical Relation between Unemployment and Price Changes," *International Labour Review,* vol. 13, June 1926, pp. 785–792, reprinted as "I Discovered the Phillips Curve," *Journal of Political Economy,* vol. 81, March/April 1973, pp. 496–502.

LABOR MARKETS
AND THE
DISTRIBUTION OF INCOME

All the previous chapters of this book have focused on the allocation of labor and the determination of wages. The resulting wage rates and allocation of labor across firms, industries, occupations, and regions are seen by and large as the result of human choices made subject to constraints. The choices and constraints in turn affect the distribution of income among the members of society. In fact, the question of the process by which the distribution of income is determined was the motivating factor leading to J. B. Clark's development of marginal productivity theory. Interest in the distribution of income seemed to have declined continuously after the Marginalist Revolution. However, interest in the topic has been revitalized during the 1960s, and continues increasingly to attract the efforts of economists. We will present in this chapter an overview of the fundamentals of income distribution analysis.

17.1

THE FUNCTIONAL DISTRIBUTION OF INCOME
The distribution of income deals with the relative shares of total income received by various groups. The income distribution can be viewed from any of a number of perspectives, but economists have concentrated on two: the "functional" distribution and the "size" distribution of income. The functional distribution, the topic of this section, concerns the division of income as between labor and the owners of capital.

17.1a
Demand, supply, and the functional distribution of income

The functional distribution of income can be examined within the marginal productivity framework. Figure 17.1 illustrates long-run demand and supply curves for labor in the aggregate. Under purely competitive conditions, labor's wage will equal the value of its marginal physical product. The total value of output produced (i.e., GNP) is the area under the VMPP curve up to the equilibrium quantity of labor employed. The hatched area—the so-called "wage bill"—is the total income of labor. The solid area is the return to capital, which we will hereafter call profits although it includes both profit and all other property incomes. It is simply the total product (the area under the VMPP curve) minus the wage bill.

We know from Chap. 6 that increases in the supply of labor, *ceteris paribus,* will decrease wage rates and that increases in capital, *ceteris paribus,* will tend to increase wage rates. What we do not know is whether or how these changes alter labor's relative share of income—the wage bill as a percent of GNP. Whether labor's share will be increased or decreased depends on the elasticities of both the demand for labor and the demand for capital. Because there are a number of conceptual problems in dealing with the aggregate demand for labor, we will not analyze the issue here. It should be pointed out here, though, that Paul Douglas in his pioneering work on aggregate production functions found relevant elasticities to be such that changes in the quantities of labor and/or capital leave the relative shares of labor and capital about the

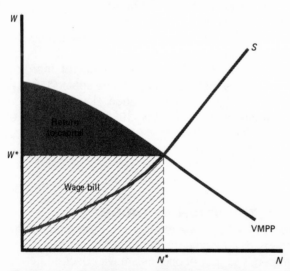

Figure 17.1. The division of GNP between labor and capital. The area under the aggregate VMPP curve of the economy, up to N* units of labor, is GNP. Given the equilibrium wage of W*, total labor income is W* · N*. The remainder of GNP goes to property owners.

same. In fact, he found that over quite a long period of time, labor's share has been about 75 percent of income.[1] This is about the relative share that Douglas expected to find on the basis of predictions made from his well-known Cobb-Douglas production function, assuming perfect competition. The fact that empirically, labor's relative share tends to be about what is predicted thus indicates that the distribution of income as between labor and capital in the aggregate is about what would result under perfect competition. This is not to say that the United States economy *is* perfectly competitive. What we can say is that such imperfections in competition as do exist have not affected the *aggregate* distribution of income between labor and capital. It should be recognized that market imperfections do affect the distribution of income, but the greatest effect of these imperfections has been to redistribute income *within* the labor sector rather than between labor and the owners of capital. As explained in Chap. 13, unionization has redistributed income from nonunion to union labor. Racial discrimination has redistributed income from black to white labor. Since the notion is so widely held that unions have increased labor's share of income, a careful consideration of the effect of unionization is in order here.

17.1b
Unionization and the distribution of income

We established earlier that growth in aggregate productivity causes growth in wages. Yet a significant portion of the American public is of the belief that such growth in real wages as has occurred is the result of unionization. Most assuredly, the public does not view the effect of unionization as working through increases in productivity. Rather, the gains of labor are thought of as coming at the expense of profits, i.e., through a union-caused redistribution of income from owners of capital to labor. A poll reported in the *Wall Street Journal* indicates that nearly half of United States adults believe that were it not for the existence of unions, living standards among workers would be no higher than in underdeveloped countries.[2] This is a rather remarkable belief, given that per capita income in the so-called less developed countries is typically less than a fourth of what it is in the United States. The same poll also reveals that a large majority of the public believes unions to be the principal cause of inflation. This belief is even held by a majority of union members.

Obviously, unions can raise labor's share only if they can raise the

---

[1] C. W. Cobb and P. H. Douglas, "A Theory of Production," *American Economic Review,* vol. 8, March 1928, pp. 139–165; and P. H. Douglas, "The Cobb-Douglas Production Function Once Again: Its History, Its Testing, and Some Empirical Values," *Journal of Political Economy,* vol. 84, October 1976, pp. 903–915.

[2] "Labor Letter," *Wall Street Journal,* vol. 190, Oct. 25, 1977, p. 1.

average wage of all labor above the competitive level. Yet the ability of unions to raise wages in the unionized sector is offset by the spillover effects of unionization in the nonunion sector. If unionization results in a higher wage in the unionized sector and a lower wage in the nonunion sector, the average wage of the two sectors combined may not be raised at all, or at least not significantly. Hence there may not be any significant effect of unionization on the distribution of income between labor and capital. Empirical support for this line of reasoning is contained in the work of E. H. Phelps Brown and Margaret H. Browne.[3] Examining wage and productivity changes from 1860 to 1960 for France, Germany, Sweden, the United Kingdom, and the United States, Brown and Browne found that in all five countries, rises in the real wage were attributable almost entirely to rises in productivity. Very little rise in wages was left to be explained by unionization or, indeed, anything else. The historical pattern of relative shares in the United States casts further doubt on the belief of the public that unions have raised labor's relative share. Total employee compensation as a percent of gross national product was about 0.75 for the 1930–1934 period, as it was for the 1970–1974 period, by one estimate,[4] providing more recent justification for Douglas's treatment of labor's share as relatively constant. Not all economists who have studied labor's share have concluded that it has not changed over time. The reason for the dissimilarity is that various researchers have disagreed about fine details in the definition of labor's share. A study by Simon Kuznets shows labor's share in the United States growing by 6 percent from the 1899–1908 period to the 1954–1960 period.[5] Even if we accept this highest estimate of the increase in labor's share, it represents an average increase of approximately one-tenth of one percent per year. Even if unions are responsible for all of the 6 percent change in labor's relative share, the magnitude of that change has been trivial. Productivity growth has caused the real wage to increase at an average annual rate of about 2.5 percent during this century. The total change in labor's share over a half century thus has been roughly equivalent to the effect of less than 2 $^1/_2$ years of productivity growth.

While unionization may have little impact on the level of real wages and hence little effect on the functional distribution of income, it is theoretically possible for unionization in a sense to affect the level of money wages. Certainly the results of the poll cited in footnote 2 concerning the public's belief about unions and inflation suggest the desirability of an explanation. As we indicated in Chap. 13, the initial effect of the attainment of a higher than competitive wage in the

[3]E. H. Phelps Brown and M. H. Browne, *A Century of Pay,* St. Martin's, New York, 1968.
[4]J. Gwartney, *Microeconomics: Private and Public Choice,* Academic, New York, 1977.
[5]S. Kuznets, *Modern Economic Growth,* Yale University Press, New Haven, 1966.

unionized sector is to reduce employment in the unionized sector. If the government does not respond by attempting to stimulate aggregate demand, there is a spillover of unemployed workers into the nonunion sector. As illustrated in Fig. 13.1, the spillover of workers depresses wages in the nonunion sector. This case was described in Chap. 13 where we implicitly assumed no response on the part of the government to the initial unemployment in the unionized sector. Let us now examine the case where the Federal Reserve System reacts to the existence of unemployment.

In Fig. 17.2, we begin by assuming no initial union-nonunion wage differential. We also express the demand for labor in terms of the real wage. Assume that the original real wage in both sectors is W_0/P_0. Now suppose that through collective bargaining the nominal wage in the union sector becomes W_1 and as a consequence the real wage becomes W_1/P_0. The quantity demanded of labor falls from N^u_0 to N^u_1, leaving $N^u_0 - N^u_1$ workers unemployed. In the absence of any response by the Federal Reserve, the unemployed workers would eventually spill over into the nonunion sector. But suppose that the Federal Reserve does respond to the unemployment that is initiated in the unionized sector. Specifically, let us assume that the Federal Reserve engages in an increase in the money supply. Neglecting the short-run consequences of

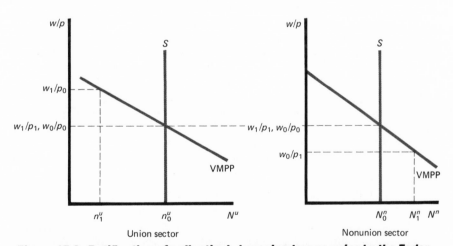

Figure 17.2. Ratification of collectively bargained wage gains by the Federal Reserve. Assume the initial real wage to be W_0/P_0 in both the union and nonunion sectors. If unions achieve a rise in the nominal wage to W_1, the real wage rises to W_1/P_0, creating unemployment in the union sector. If the Federal Reserve responds by increasing the money supply, the unemployment can be eliminated by causing the price level to rise to P_1, which returns the real wage to its original level. The rising price level lowers the real wage in the nonunion sector ot W_0/P_1, creating an excess demand for labor in that sector, in turn causing the nominal wage in that sector to rise to W_1, thereby restoring the original real wage.

the increased money supply, we can expect that in the longer run, the effect of the increased money supply will be to raise the price level.[6] The unemployment can be eliminated if the price level rises to P_1, thereby returning the real wage to its original level. The nonunion sector is also affected. When the price level rises to P_1, the real wage in the nonunion sector falls to W_0/P_1. The quantity of labor demanded in the nonunion sector increases from N^n_0 to N^n_1. An excess demand for labor is thus created, which causes an upward pressure on the wage level in the nonunion sector. The final result of the Federal Reserve's action would be to prevent the establishment of a permanent union-nonunion differential and to raise the price level. If unions continually try to establish a union-nonunion differential and the Federal Reserve continually negates the union's attempts, then inflation will result. The rate of inflation will be affected by the degree of success of unions in obtaining through collective bargaining increases in nominal wages above the competitive level. The Federal Reserve's process of increasing the money supply in response to collectively bargained pay raises is labeled by economists as "ratification" of union pay raises.

If the Federal Reserve passively ratifies any collectively bargained increase in wages, then some economists will view unions as in a sense being responsible for inflation. But it is the Federal Reserve's willingness to engage in the process of ratification that is the key. If the Federal Reserve did not increase the money supply in response to transitory unemployment generated in the union sector, the inflation would not result. It should be pointed out that in an era of inflationary expectations, if the Federal Reserve were to reverse itself and cease ratification of union wage gains, the immediate result would be an increase in unemployment, as the analysis of Chap. 16 suggests. In the long run, however, if the Federal Reserve would refuse to engage in ratification, there is reason to believe that unions would not be inclined to press for wage gains that would significantly reduce employment among their memberships, as we pointed out in Chap. 13.

The above model of collective bargaining–monetary policy interaction is somewhat inexact, and several qualifications should be kept in mind. First, the governors of the Federal Reserve may not and need not be consciously aware of their own involvement in the ratification process. They need only respond to unemployment by pursuing an expansionary monetary policy. Whether they regard collectively bargained wage agreements as the source of that unemployment is

---

[6]If our analysis begins at the natural rate of unemployment, the initial effects of the increased money supply will be to increase employment and output as well as to raise prices. This was discussed in the previous chapter. But as workers and employers adjust their expectations, the longer-run effect of the monetary expansion can for our purposes be regarded as causing only prices to rise.

immaterial. Second, fiscal policy as well as monetary policy may be used to ratify collectively bargained wage gains. Whether one expects the same result as with ratification by the Federal Reserve depends on one's views about the potency of pure fiscal policy. If we begin from a situation where the economy is at its natural rate of unemployment preceding the increase in the union wage level, then the result should be the same as with Federal Reserve ratification, except that government spending may tend to "crowd out" or displace a portion of private spending. However, the analysis of crowding out is beyond the scope of this text and tangential to our argument.[7] Third, the use of ratification to eliminate any union-nonunion differential is never complete. If it were, economists would not be able to observe the magnitudes of the union-nonunion differential that were reported in Chap. 13. The important conclusion to be reached from this discussion is this: To the extent that the Federal Reserve ratifies collectively bargained wage gains, the real wage of both union and nonunion labor will be unaffected. Hence, collectively bargained nominal wage increases do not increase labor's share. To the extent that the Federal Reserve does *not* ratify collectively bargained wage gains, income is redistributed from nonunion to union labor, but not from owners of capital to labor.

17.1c
The functional distribution of income in the short run

The neoclassical or marginal productivity theory of distribution has been criticized since the 1930s as not being a general theory of distribution, but rather a theory of income distribution under conditions of full employment equilibrium. Models which purportedly remedy this lack of generality by taking into account fluctuations in aggregate demand have been developed by members of the "Cambridge school" of economists. Important contributors to this school include Nicholas Kaldor, Joan Robinson, and Luigi Pasinetti.[8] Their criticism is essentially correct—the marginal productivity theory of distribution is basically an explanation of the functional distribution of income over the long run. As Charles Ferguson has pointed out, however, this is the function of neoclassical distribution theory, and it is a valuable function.[9] Nonetheless, we should be aware that there is a cyclical pattern to the distribution of income.

---

[7]For a discussion of crowding out, as well as the issue of collective bargaining and inflation, see C. Baird, *Macroeconomics,* Science Research, Chicago, 1973.

[8]N. Kaldor, "Alternative Theories of Distribution," *Review of Economic Studies,* vol. 23, 1955, pp. 94–100; J. Robinson, *The Accumulation of Capital,* Macmillan, London, 1956; L. Pasinetti, "Rate of Profit and Income Distribution in Relation to the Rate of Economic Growth," *Review of Economic Studies,* vol. 29, 1962, pp. 267–279.

[9]C. E. Ferguson, *The Neoclassical Theory of Production and Distribution,* Cambridge University Press, London, 1969. This volume is the most comprehensive treatment of neoclassical production and distribution theory in existence.

During a recession, labor's share tends to rise, and during the recovery phase, it tends to fall. There are perhaps two reasons for a rising labor share during a recession. The first is that during a recession, the downward inflexibility of wages is greater than that of prices. Hence profits will fall more quickly than wages, if wages fall at all. Second, profit margins are generally reduced during a recession for another reason, namely the contraction of output which forces the firm to operate at a less efficient scale at which output per man decreases.

The countercyclical movement of labor's share serves to remind us of the weakness of labor's share as a measure of labor's wellbeing. Labor's share of total income has never been greater than it was during the depths of the Depression of the 1930s. Yet few would argue that labor's wellbeing was at its peak during this period. Because of this paradoxical relation, few economists regard labor's share as an indicator of labor's wellbeing. The major exception to this rule are the Marxists, for whom any labor share less than 100 percent indicates "exploitation" of labor. In fact, most of the recent concern of economists over income distribution has been with regard to the size distribution, a subject to which we now turn our attention.

17.2
THE SIZE DISTRIBUTION OF INCOME

The size distribution of income is a concept concerned with the dispersion of income across persons or households in the society. Stated otherwise, the size distribution of income concerns the degree of inequality in the distribution of income. Most current concern over the distribution of income has to do with the size distribution. One frequently hears remarks to the effect that the degree of income inequality in our society is "too great," but one may never hear remarks that it is "too little." Yet such remarks are meaningless without some notion, however vague, of what would constitute an "ideal" distribution of income. There is also a more fundamental problem involved in any discussion of the inequality of income, and that is: How can we *measure* the degree of inequality?

17.2a
The Lorenz curve and the Gini coefficient

Income inequality can be measured graphically and numerically. The graphical method usually employed is the Lorenz curve. This curve shows the cumulative percent of income received, plotted against the cumulative percent of the society's households who receive that income. Figure 17.3 is a Lorenz curve for 1970. The curve illustrates the fact that the lowest 20 percent of households received 5.5 percent of total income, the lowest 40 percent received 17.5 percent of total income, and so forth for other percentiles. The straight line shows what the Lorenz

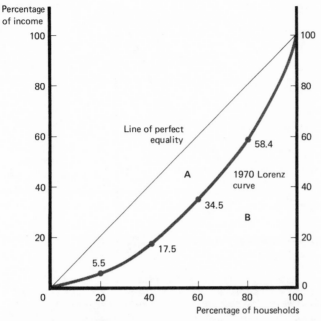

Figure 17.3. Lorenz curve for the United States population in 1970. The Lorenz curve shows the cumulative percent of income received by the cumulative percent of households, where households are ranked from poorest to wealthiest. A Gini coefficient is calculated as the ratio of area A to the total area A + B. SOURCE: U. S. Bureau of the Census, Current Population Reports, ser. P-60, no. 80, Income in 1970 of Families and Persons in the United States, 1970.

curve would be if income were distributed perfectly equally across households. The opposite extreme, perfect inequality, would exist if all income were received by one household. In this case, the Lorenz curve would follow the horizontal axis and the right-side vertical axis, forming a right angle. Obviously, then, the closer the Lorenz curve is to the line of perfect equality, the more equally incomes are distributed.

The information graphically conveyed by the Lorenz curve can also be numerically illustrated by means of the Gini coefficient. This coefficient is the ratio of the area between the Lorenz curve and the line of perfect equality (area A in Fig. 17.3) to the total area under the line of perfect equality (the sum of areas A and B in Fig. 17.3). The Gini coefficient would have a value of zero if incomes were divided perfectly equally, and a value of 1.00 under perfect inequality. Figure 17.4 shows the Gini coefficients for the United States in 1947 and 1972.[10] During the 25 years separating the two dates, the degree of income inequality had

---

[10]M. Paglin, "The Measurement and Trend of Inequality: A Basic Revision," *American Economic Review,* vol. 65, September 1975, pp. 598–609.

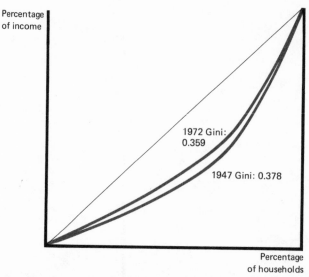

Figure 17.4. Lorenz curves for the United States in 1947 and 1972. The Lorenz curves and their associated Gini coefficients for the two years illustrate a small decline in the degree of income inequality between 1947 and 1972.

apparently changed very little. Since so many are prone to view the apparently stable distribution of income in the United States as "too unequal," we should ask what causes the distribution to be less than perfectly equal.

17.2b
The sources of inequality

It is popularly believed that inequality of property income is a basic source of overall income inequality, yet this belief is a gross misconception. Lowell Gallaway has calculated Gini coefficients for 1972 for the United States using total income as well as total income less property income. Using total income, the Gini coefficient is .342. Using all income other than property income, the Gini coefficient becomes .338.[11] The near identity of the two coefficients demonstrates rather convincingly that inequality in the distribution of property income is not a major source of overall income inequality. On the contrary, inequality of labor income is the major source.

Why, then, are labor incomes unequal? Our earlier chapter on

---

[11]L. Gallaway, "The Folklore of Unemployment and Poverty," in S. Pejovich (ed.), *Government Controls and the Free Market,* Texas A&M University Press, College Station, Tex., 1976. The difference between Paglin's and Gallaway's calculations of Gini coefficients is due to a difference in the inclusion of income-receiving units. Paglin's measure includes only family units; Gallaway's measure also includes single individuals.

occupational wage differences explained some of the reasons. For instance, people differ in their internal rates of time preferences. This difference leads to differences in the acquisition of human capital, which in turn leads to differences in earnings. People also differ considerably in their native abilities, which must affect their earnings. People also differ substantially in their tastes and preferences. This difference affects earnings in several ways. First, some people are less materialistic than others, and willingly enter professions where pay is less than in others, but nonpecuniary job aspects are better than in others. Second, people differ with respect to their willingness to substitute work (or income) for leisure. Consequently, people differ in the amount of work that they are willing to do, and this affects earnings. People differ vastly in terms of motivation, which can affect both the amount and the quality of work undertaken.

All the above variables are systematically related to earnings and will cause inequality of income. Besides these variables the element of luck or chance affects the distribution of income, although the importance of chance should not be overstated. As J. Mincer has pointed out, human capital models of the size distribution of income (which incorporate the variables mentioned above) are quite consistent with observed distributions of income, whereas chance models are unable to explain many features of the observed distribution.[12] In short, the human capital approach can readily explain the shape of the existing distribution of income. If the existing distribution is to be considered "bad," it should at least not be considered surprising.

If the existing distribution is to be considered "bad," we should ask: Compared to what? The Gini coefficient and the Lorenz curve both take the line of perfect equality as the norm against which the existing distribution is compared. But, given the differences that exist in tastes, ability, investment in human capital, hours of work, and the other variables mentioned above, perfect equality of income becomes a meaningless standard. Perhaps those who consider the existing degree of inequality to be "bad" use the distribution of income in other countries as the standard of comparison. If the distribution of income were less equal in the United States than in a welfare state such as Sweden or a totalitarian state such as the U.S.S.R., there are undoubtedly some who would then infer the United States distribution to be inferior. But such an inference is baseless unless there is a rationale for considering the Swedish or Soviet distributions "ideal," or at least closer to some specific ideal. Perhaps the identification of these distributions as "ideal" is a purely normative or philosophical matter, not subject to economic

---

[12]For a discussion of these features, see J. Mincer, "The Distribution of Labor Incomes: A Survey with Special Reference to the Human Capital Approach," *Journal of Economic Literature,* vol. 8, March 1970, pp. 1–26.

analysis. Even if one or the other distribution is accepted as "ideal," the United States distribution cannot be inferior unless it deviates substantially from the "ideal" distribution. Gallaway, in the article previously cited in footnote 11, has calculated Gini coefficients for the United States, Sweden, and the U.S.S.R. on income after all taxes and transfer payments. He has found the 1971 coefficients to be .27 for Sweden, .29 for the U.S.S.R., and .32 for the United States. Can we consider these differences to be substantial? Gallaway points out that the Gini coefficient for the United States fell by about .03 between 1947 and 1968, but most critics of the United States distribution have considered this change to be negligible. It should then follow that the difference of .03 between the United States and the U.S.S.R. Gini coefficients must similarly be regarded as negligible. By the same token, the .05 difference between the United States and Swedish coefficients can hardly be labeled as dramatic. Apparently, the degree of income equality popularly perceived to exist in Sweden is largely mythical.

Even the conclusion that the degree of income inequality in the United States has changed only negligibly in the last 25 years may be erroneous. It is quite true that the degree of inequality *as measured by the Gini coefficient* has fallen only slightly, as in Fig. 17.4. But we have also argued that the line of perfect equality, the norm against which inequality is calculated in the Gini coefficient, is inappropriate. In particular, we know that over the life cycle, an individual's income will be low in his or her youth, continually grow through middle age, and fall in old age. Further, the more schooling the individual has, the steeper will be the rise in income over the life cycle. In effect, individuals who choose to invest in a college degree accept lower income than high school graduates in their earlier years in order to have a higher income than high school graduates in their later years.[13] But even if every individual had the same level of schooling and the same lifetime pattern of income, the Gini coefficient would show some inequality of income since people of different ages will be at different stages of their life cycles of earnings. It then becomes desirable to construct some measure of income inequality which abstracts from variation in an individual's earnings over the life cycle. Morton Paglin, in the article previously cited in this chapter, has constructed such a measure. We shall label it the "Paglin coefficient." As with the Gini coefficient, the Paglin coefficient can range between zero and one. A Paglin coefficient of zero indicates perfect equality of *lifetime* earnings. While for 1947 the Gini coefficient was .378, the Paglin coefficient for the same year was .303. The difference between the two coefficients measures the effect of variation in income over individual life cycles. More importantly, by 1972

---

[13] This idea is elaborated in L. A. Lillard, "Inequality: Earnings vs. Human Wealth," *American Economic Review,* vol. 67, March 1977, pp. 42–53.

the Gini coefficient had declined to .359, whereas the Paglin coefficient had declined further to .239. In other words, the relative decline in the Paglin coefficient was more than 21 percent, but in the Gini coefficient was only 5 percent. Recall that much concern has been expressed about the "negligible" drop in the Gini coefficient. But as Paglin has demonstrated, a more appropriate measure indicates a considerable lessening over time in the degree of income inequality. One possible reason why the Gini coefficient failed to capture the decline in income inequality is the increase in educational attainment that has occurred over time. The increase in educational attainment has produced steeper life cycle income profiles. *Ceteris paribus,* the increase in educational attainment would have raised the Gini coefficient, though no increase in lifetime income inequality had taken place. As it was, the effect on the Gini coefficient of the increase in educational attainment nearly offset the decrease in inequality of lifetime earnings that took place between 1947 and 1972. Edgar Browning has shown evidence of a decline in the degree of income inequality completely apart from the life cycle effect measured by Paglin. All the previously discussed measures of inequality exclude so-called in-kind transfers. These transfers include such items as food stamps, Medicaid, public housing, and a variety of other items. Browning has recalculated the percent of total income going to the poorest one-fifth of the population, defining total income to include in-kind transfers. He finds the poorest one-fifth of families in the United States to have received 12.5 percent of total income in 1972. Without the inclusion of in-kind transfers, the share of the poorest one-fifth was 5.4 percent. More importantly, the share of total income including in-kind transfers received by the poorest 20 percent of the population increased by 62 percent between 1952 and 1972.[14] Thus, economists who have been dismayed by the apparent stability of the size distribution of income have based their despair on a faulty statistic.

17.3

JUSTICE AND THE DISTRIBUTION OF INCOME

The question of what constitutes a "just" distribution of income has not been answered by economists, nor can it be answered by economists. So far as the neoclassical analysis of the functional distribution is concerned, it is an analysis of what the distribution is, and not what it ought to be. Economists may be able to demonstrate that the functional

---

[14]E. K. Browning, "The Trend toward Equality in the Distribution of Net Income," *Southern Economic Journal,* vol. 43, July 1976, pp. 912–923. For a study of the income distributions in two experimental economies in which many of the alleged sources of unequal incomes were greatly reduced and in some cases entirely eliminated, see R. C. Battalio, J. H. Kagel, and M. O. Reynolds, "Income Distributions in Two Experimental Economies," *Journal of Political Economy,* vol. 85, December 1977, pp. 1259–1271.

distribution of income predicted by neoclassical theory is the most efficient distribution, but there is no ethical content to such a demonstration, whether or not it is valid, unless one is willing to *define* justice as efficiency. While some are willing to do so, there is no basis in economic science for such a definition. In fact, the science of economics provides no known rationale for *any* definition of justice. To be sure, economists as citizens have opinions as to what constitutes justice, but their opinions are no more than just that, having no more or less ethical validity than the opinions of noneconomists.

Much the same remarks can be made about the size distribution. Although the connection between efficiency and the income distribution is less clear in the case of the size distribution than in the case of the functional distribution, the connection does exist. For instance, most economists would agree that it is possible for a distribution to be so unequal that economic mobility is virtually impossible. For the great bulk of the population, income levels will always be low in such a society where incentives for self-improvement are lacking. On the other hand, redistributive schemes can produce such a small degree of inequality as to dampen individual initiative and thereby limit the growth of national wealth. Unfortunately, economists as yet have not been successful in determining just how much equality or inequality is efficient. Nonetheless, economists do have a degree of expertise in analyzing the efficiency effects of any distribution or redistribution. This type of analysis is quite within the bounds of economic science. But when economists express a moral concern about the degree of income inequality, they are again stating an ethical opinion, just as any individual can state his or her ethical views. Economists as citizens should not hesitate to state their opinions concerning justice. However, the citizen or policy maker who listens to what economists have to say should be aware of the difference between personal values and economic analysis. And the economist should not try to disguise one as the other.[15]

QUESTIONS AND EXERCISES

1. How could a program of in-kind transfers financed by a progressive income tax actually increase a Gini coefficient that does not take in-kind transfers into account?

2. How would a Lorenz curve of family incomes be affected by (*a*) the trend toward lower marriage rates and (*b*) the trend toward the increasing age at which people marry?

---

[15]For a discussion of what economists can contribute to the analysis of the size distribution of income, see A. Rivlin, "Income Distribution—Can Economists Help?" *American Economic Review,* vol. 65, May 1975, pp. 1–15.

3. The minimum wage has often been argued to be an antipoverty device, yet some researchers have found that increases in the real minimum wage would have a negligible effect on the percentage of families that are below the poverty level. How can this result be explained?

4. We have concluded that unions have had little impact on the functional distribution. Does this imply that unions have had no impact on the size distribution of income? Why or why not?

5. The Social Security system redistributes income. Some economists view the system as progressive in its effect on the distribution of income, while others view it as regressive. Assuming that both groups of economists are assessing the same "facts," how do you account for the difference of opinion?

REFERENCES FOR FURTHER READING

On both the functional and size distribution of income and the relation between the two, see M. Friedman, *Price Theory,* Aldine, Chicago, 1976, chaps. 9, 10, 14, and 15.

For the Marxist view on the distribution of income, see D. Gordon, *Theories of Poverty and Unemployment,* Heath, Lexington, Mass., 1972, chaps. 5 and 7. For another view see L. C. Thurow and R. E. B. Lucas, "The American Distribution of Income: A Structural Problem," in H. Wolozin and R. Torto (eds.), *Domestic Economic Problems,* Holbrook Press, Boston, 1974.

For a series of discussions of various topics involving the redistribution of income, see C. D. Campbell (ed.), *Income Redistribution,* American Enterprise Institute, Washington, D.C., 1977.

SOME FINAL THOUGHTS

We have attempted in this book to demonstrate that the neoclassical model provides a framework for understanding human behavior in the markets for labor services. In the neoclassical model, individuals with their unique tastes and preferences attempt to make themselves better off in a world characterized by scarcity. This is necessarily an imprecise process due to limitations of knowledge about conditions in the environment as well as other constraints that we have mentioned at various points. Nonetheless, by developing the implications which flow from this conception, we have seen that labor markets are characterized by order, not chaos.

The power of this conception combined with the energy and intelligence of generations of economists has resulted in a highly developed social science. Indeed, numerous economists have in recent years come to the view that the neoclassical approach is even more powerful than commonly realized, and have succeeded in showing that many human activities normally thought of as lying beyond the scope of economic analysis can be understood using a neoclassical framework.[1] Our discussion of fertility in Chap. 5 is one such cogent instance of this broader application of neoclassical analysis.

---

[1]Perhaps the most outstanding exemplar of this view is G. S. Becker. See, for example, his work, *The Economic Approach to Human Behavior,* The University of Chicago Press, Chicago and London, 1976.

For reasons best left to historians of economic thought to uncover, there has been in the past a certain reluctance to apply neoclassical analysis to human activities in the labor market. As a result, labor economics until relatively recently has remained an underdeveloped area as compared with other subsystems within economics, such as international economics and the theory of consumer behavior, for example. That this no longer is the case is a conclusion we argue is warranted by developments which have taken place in labor economics in the last few decades.

We discussed in Chap. 1 the role of facts in scientific thought and saw there that facts alone do not overturn theories. Facts either support or do not support theoretical arguments. The facts that we have presented in the form of empirical tests of various theoretical arguments developed in our chapters are presented in this spirit. In the main, they are cited because they *do* provide empirical support for neoclassical arguments. But it would be contrary to our intentions for anyone to conclude on the basis of the evidence we have chosen to cite that neoclassical arguments are unchallenged. On the contrary, it is quite regularly the case that each new extension of the neoclassical approach provokes lively debates in the economic journals. This is, however, part of the constant process of discovery and reassessment so necessary for the healthy growth of any scientific endeavor. We make these statements so as to dispel any notion that all problem areas in labor economics have been successfully resolved by the use of the neoclassical approach. That is simply not the case. Neoclassical economists do argue, however, that many problem areas thought to be anomalies in the domain of labor economics have been made comprehensible by the use of the neoclassical approach, and they are led by their work to be hopeful of resolving successfully in the future problems which at present appear to be intractable.

Having said this, we wish to direct students to other views as well. There is a growing number of labor economists who analyze labor markets not within the neoclassical framework, but from an explicitly nonneoclassical view—either a dual labor market perspective or a radical (or Marxist) perspective. These views are not very well developed at this time, but complete development of a systematic view normally takes many years of effort. Students who would like to investigate these alternative perspectives might examine first the works of dual labor market theorists and radical theorists themselves,[2] as well as some critiques of their views which we present at the end of this chapter.

We do not think it appropriate at this point to reiterate any of the

---

[2]P. B. Doeringer and M. J. Piore, *Internal Labor Markets and Manpower Analysis,* Heath, Lexington, Mass., 1971; D. M. Gordon, *Theories of Poverty and Underemployment,* Heath, Lexington, Mass., 1972.

particular propositions we have developed in the preceding 17 chapters. Rather, we wish to highlight the most general conclusion which flows from neoclassical labor economics. Based on the particular analyses developed in detail in all our previous 17 chapters, what broad generalization emerges from the use of the neoclassical model in labor markets? We think the answer is very clearly and simply that labor markets work in the way hypothesized by the neoclassical model. This conclusion was supported in our examination of labor supply when we saw that individuals do adjust their hours of work and participation in the labor force on the basis of changes in income, wages, and other constraints. When we examined the firm, we discovered that the firm chooses to alter its employment of labor on the basis of changes in relative prices and other constraints. In the acquisition of human capital, the decisions regarding schooling and career choices were seen to depend on changes in constraints facing the individual. In these and other instances, utility maximizing individuals were seen to behave in the manner predicted by neoclassical economics so as to allocate their labor in an ordered fashion across occupations, industries, and regions. Not all individuals adjust to changed circumstances in as rapid a manner as they could, given more information, or would choose to, given the information that they do have. Indeed, there is clearly a return to the ability to perceive, interpret correctly, and act upon changed circumstances.[3] Nonetheless, the adjustments predicted by neoclassical economics are the adjustments observed in actual labor markets. We cannot stress too strongly the importance of this generalization. The discovery of a spontaneous order in the myriad labor markets in which people spend a large portion of their lives strengthens and reinforces the analytical power of the neoclassical approach, further brightening the prospects of extending this approach into areas of human behavior which up to now have been regarded as impenetrable.

REFERENCES FOR FURTHER READING

Critiques of dual labor market and radical theories are found in G. G. Cain, "The Challenge of Segmented Labor Market Theories to Orthodox Theory: A Survey," *Journal of Economic Literature,* vol. 14, December 1976, pp. 1215–1257; M. C. Wachter, "Primary and Secondary Labor Markets: A Critique of the Dual Approach," *Brookings Papers on Economic Activity,* no. 3, 1974, pp. 637–680; M. Bronfenbrenner, "Radical Economics in America, 1970," *Journal of Economic Literature,* vol. 8, September 1970, pp. 747–766.

---

[3] T. W. Schultz, "The Value of the Ability to Deal with Disequilibrium," *Journal of Economic Literature,* vol. 13, September 1975, pp. 827–846.

INDEXES

NAME INDEX

SUBJECT INDEX